PEARL
by the
RIVER

Sudipta Mitra is the author of *Gir Forest and the Saga of Asiatic Lion* and *History and Heritage of Indian Game Hunting*. He is an aficionado of colonial Calcutta and a freelance columnist focussing on history and nature. A doctor by profession, he is also associated with several NGOs. He has more than fifty essays on colonial India, environmental science and wildlife history to his credit, both in English and vernacular publications.

PEARL
by the
RIVER

NAWAB WAJID ALI SHAH'S
KINGDOM IN EXILE

SUDIPTA MITRA

RUPA

Published by
Rupa Publications India Pvt. Ltd 2017
7/16, Ansari Road, Daryaganj
New Delhi 110002
Sales Centres:

Allahabad Bengaluru Chennai
Hyderabad Jaipur Kathmandu
Kolkata Mumbai

Copyright © Sudipta Mitra 2017

The views and opinions expressed in this book are the author's own
and the facts are as reported by him/her which have been verified to
the extent possible, and the publishers are not in
any way liable for the same.

All rights reserved.
No part of this publication may be reproduced, transmitted,
or stored in a retrieval system, in any form or by any means,
electronic, mechanical, photocopying, recording or otherwise,
without the prior permission of the publisher.

ISBN: 978-81-291-4488-1

First impression 2017

10 9 8 7 6 5 4 3 2 1

The moral right of the author has been asserted.

This book is sold subject to the condition that it shall not,
by way of trade or otherwise, be lent, resold, hired out, or otherwise
circulated, without the publisher's prior consent, in any form of binding or
cover other than that in which it is published.

A tribute to all the great souls resting in eternal peace underneath the marble floor of Sibtanabad Imambara, Metiyaburj.

Contents

Foreword	ix
Prologue	xiii
Preface	xvii

1.	Boarding the Caravan to Calcutta	1
2.	The English Drama and the Deposition	13
3.	The Oudh Commission and the British Empire	35
4.	The First War of Independence	53
5.	Wajid Ali's Gloomy Days in Fort William	68
6.	Wajid Ali Shah Establishes 'Chota Lucknow' in Calcutta	87
7.	The Private Life of the Banished King	106
8.	Wajid Ali Shah: A Theatrical Genius	113
9.	An Exponent of Kathak	120
10.	A Prelude to Thumri in Calcutta	129
11.	Wajid Ali Shah and the Dulcet Symphony of Metiyaburj	141
12.	'Nawabi-yana' in Metiyaburj	153
13.	His Majesty's Incredible Menagerie	171
14.	The Epitaph	182

Notes	196
Royal Family Tree of Awadh	226
Bibliography	228

Foreword

It seems extraordinary that a character as colourful as Wajid Ali Shah of Awadh would vanish completely from Bengali consciousness. Yet this is what has happened. Very few people, unless they are descendants of the deposed king, are aware that he lived the last thirty years of his life on the outskirts of Calcutta, the then seat of British Government. Even if they are aware of this fact, none can say how the King's extravagant court at Metiyaburj may have influenced the cultural and social life of the then capital.

It is to Dr Sudipta Mitra's credit that he is determined to put the record straight, and to reinstate the King as a serious patron of musicians, dancers, poets, courtesans, and even cooks, who either followed him from their Lucknow home, or arrived in Metiyaburj from other parts of India. Using mainly published sources, both in English and Bengali, and backed by interviews with his descendants, Dr Mitra has painted a convincing portrait of how the 'King in exile' spent his time creating a 'Chota Lucknow' on the banks of the Hooghly.

It is always difficult to conjure up the ephemeral world of musical performances before recordings of singers existed, and before dancers could be captured on film. Certainly the King had sufficient funds to patronize the very best artists, some of whom lived in Metiyaburj on a royal pension. How much of this rich cultural life spread from the court and permeated the Bengali society? This is the theme of the book. How much interaction was there between 'Little Lucknow' and the forbidding, British-created 'City of Palaces'? Some, if not all, of the answers, are to be found here. And it was not only high culture that was translated into late nineteenth-century Bengal, but delicious Awadhi cuisine too, in particular, the rice-based biryani.

One of the most interesting chapters in this book is about the King's menagerie, and Dr Mitra is particularly well-qualified to explore this facet, because he has already published a comprehensive and beautifully illustrated book on Indian wildlife and game-hunting.* The fact that Wajid Ali Shah had to buy back, in Calcutta, some of his own animals that had been auctioned off in Lucknow after the annexation, is particularly poignant. Over the years, the King was able to build up his Metiyaburj menagerie, although he was charged ridiculously extravagant prices for animals and birds.

Extravagance is one of the main themes that run through the King's life and one of the supposed reasons given by the British for taking away his kingdom in February 1856. Dalhousie is said to have been annoyed with Awadh standing as a buffer between the British Presidency of Bengal and the old seat of Mughal rule in Delhi. The dynamics of power had shifted dramatically during the first half of the nineteenth century, particularly given the 'Forward Policy' that saw kingdom after kingdom fall into British hands. Pensioned off, with an annual income of twelve lakh rupees per annum, even this great sum did not seem enough to fulfil all the King's desires, but it certainly paid for a lot of talented artists.

The sad story of the annexation itself is touched upon, together with the visit of the King's mother and other relatives

---

* Sudipta Mitra, *History and Heritage of Indian Game Hunting*, Rupa & Co, 2010.

to England, in a fruitless attempt to win back the throne of Awadh. At the same time, Wajid Ali Shah was imprisoned in Fort William, either because Governor-General Lord Canning saw him as a genuine rallying point for the freedom fighters in the First War of Independence, or, as seems more likely, to keep him out of harm's way, should the rebellious sepoys try to make him a figurehead in their struggle, as had happened to the old emperor, Bahadur Shah Zafar, a reluctant and tremulous hero.

There is much here for discussion and debate. Dr Mitra has thrown a challenge to Bengalis, and indeed to readers elsewhere, positing that Wajid Ali Shah's exile had a beneficial and substantial influence on his new home. This is an enjoyable book that extends our knowledge of the King of 'Chota Lucknow' after he moved to Calcutta.

Dr Rosie Llewellyn-Jones, London
Member of the Most Excellent Order of the British Empire,
January 2015
Council Member of The Royal Asiatic Society

Prologue
A Pearl or a Teardrop?

Even though a century and a half has elapsed since Wajid Ali Shah, the unfortunate poet-king of Awadh, set foot on the soil of Bengal, his name still conjures up images of his times, bringing forward tales and travails of his life and his ultimate destination to adopt this alien land and culture as his second home. His interaction with the local 'Bhadrolok' gentry was very limited primarily because of the alien language and the in-bred refinement and aloofness he brought with him with that famed culture of Lucknow.

Wajid Ali Shah's forefather Asaf-ud-Daula had transformed a non-descript town 'Lakhna' into the historic city of Lucknow, which now dwells as a great centre of oriental arts and learning in history. This munificence and love for culture contributed immensely to reintegrate the remnants of Mughal glory ebbing from the country at that time. In this transformation, the city got dotted with numerous imambaras, buildings, mosques and the towering Rumi Darwaza, which is the face of today's Lucknow. These architectural masterpieces stood as a mute testimony to Lucknow emerging as the new centre of culture against the backdrop of Delhi, slowly fading away with the decline of the Mughal Empire.

With these memories deeply embedded in his childhood, the deeply rooted Wajid Ali Shah decided to recreate a miniature replica of his beloved Lucknow in the new surrounding that he found himself entrenched in. With no power, wealth or resources that were once the indulgences befitting a king, he could only make the best use of whatever was given to him from the unauthorized auction of family heirlooms, artefacts, marbles, horses, elephants and other animals from the royal stables by the firangis.

The First War of Independence in 1857 brought with it a brand of bloodshed that Awadh had never witnessed before, and pillage that seemed to sound the death knell of the aggressors. In retaliation, the Awadh restoration mission failed miserably and its two leading members, the Queen Mother and her second son, while returning from Karbala, found a resting place in Paris. Their palace in Awadh was annihilated beyond recognition, as were other similar homes. This was largely due to fighters like Hazrat Mahal, the militant wife of Wajid Ali Shah, and their teenage son Birjis Qadr taking up arms against the injustice of annexing their kingdom without a just cause.

Anticipating such a catastrophic situation, Wajid Ali Shah was lodged in Fort William. Within these walls he received cold water to drink, home-cooked delicacies for daily meals, khus-drenched air to relax in and well-wishers for domestic chores and conversation. This house arrest was in contrast to the dungeon within the same precincts where Asaf-ud-Daula's only son and immediate successor, Wazir Ali Khan, was placed. It was there that Wazir Ali Khan breathed his last, eighteen years later.

While the seclusion initially shocked Wajid Ali Shah, the isolation proved to be a blessing in disguise as it kept him blissfully unaware of many distracting domestic and political news. It enabled him to revive his innate interest in composing poetry or revising his previous works. He compiled these works into one *Kulliyat-e-Akhtari*. *Huzn-e-Akhtari* gave a chronological detailed account of his stay in Fort William. *Qamar Mazmoon*, the original fourth Diwan, comprised personal anecdotes. *Sheo-e-Faiz* was the unique Diwan of ghazals (or sonnets) alphabetically arranged to give the real or pet names, titles, personal traits and characteristics of his numerous wives. While gleaning through the ten volumes of love letters compiled by Wajid Ali Shah during his exile, one can see him emerging from the psychological setback and its depressing load of over two years.

Bidding adieu to Fort William, Wajid Ali Shah's chief concern was to revive the royal press Mutba-e-Sultani, and secure homes and jobs for his scores of loyal followers who had lost employment because of the unforeseen upheavals. A cross section of people from Lucknow were waiting for his signal to migrate to Calcutta. Without distinction of caste, creed, colour or vocation, Wajid Ali Shah welcomed hordes of men and women to join him in order to give his new township its own identity.

Sultan Khana, Shah Manzil, Rahas Manzil, Qasr ul Baiza, Baitun Nijat, Noor Manzil, Sibtainabad and various other tenements all along the bank of the Hooghly, beautifying its coastline, are precursors to everything that is being planned today to beautify the city.

Dr Sudipta Mitra has painstakingly tried to glean through the scant first-hand material available to him to describe the miniature Lucknow, which Wajid Ali Shah had created in a remote corner of Calcutta on the south-eastern bank of the Hooghly. He has excelled in recreating in the reader's mind the enormity of the tragedy a man suffered, and how he chose to sculpt his choked passion into a concrete beauty. It is truly a tragedy that the grandeur of Metiyaburj is now reduced to a massive slum, just as the beauty of old Lucknow is getting lost in the modernity of today and the tomorrow that awaits us.

Dr Meerza Kaukub,
Great-grandson of Wajid Ali Shah and
Hazrat Mahal,
21 January 2013, Kolkata

Preface

Wajid Ali Shah reached the banks of the Hooghly on 26 May 1856, following a long and weary journey of two months in the scorching summer, from Lucknow to Calcutta. Destiny was not kind to him and soon he was arrested and placed in Fort William by the British Government under the pretext of safeguarding him from the tumult of the Sepoy Mutiny of 1857. After twenty-five months, the former king was finally set free. A twist of fate had changed his path and taken him from luxury to austerity. Finally, the wrath of mutineers was over and the King had a conciliatory settlement with the British. Harmony and tranquillity prevailed yet again. Wajid Ali Shah purchased a large riverside estate in the southeastern fringe of Calcutta. The memories of Lucknow were fading fast. The ripple of Hooghly had entwined the Badshah's heart with deep and enduring bonds.

During this time, the banished king tended to paint subtle impressions of life in the style he had nurtured all through his life. So, the archetypal mannerisms of the renowned Lucknow slowly seeped into the hearts of the Bengali intelligentsia making an indelible impression on all who came in contact with the culture. This culture began impacting the dance, drama, poetry, cuisine, etiquette, music and melody of the time and can be seen deeply entrenched even in the current culture of Calcutta. The chronicles of pathos and romance emanating from the Badshah's mausoleum can fill endless volumes.

Today, Wajid Ali Shah's Metiyaburj is lost and forgotten.

It is difficult to decipher the real man from all that has been told about him. Even the people from his native town remain ignorant of the fact that he spent his concluding days in this colonial capital.

As my quest went on for years, there were many, who in one way or another, contributed to this research. The trail of indebtedness is enormous and the people too many to name. Still, it would be ungrateful of me to not mention the names of Prince Niyyar Kadar, chairman, Sibtainabad Imambara Trust; Burhan Ali Meerza, trustee, Sibtainabad Imambara; and other direct descendents of Wajid Ali Shah. My sincerest gratitude to Dr Rosie Llewellyn-Jones for her academic guidance, Prof. Rila Mukherjee, sitar maestro Prof. Subroto Roy Chowdhury, Ustad Irfan Mohammad Khan of the Lucknow-Shahjahanpur sarod gharana, Prof. Abhijit Roy of Rabindra Bharati University and many others. My special thanks to the authorities of Indian Museum, Calcutta; Victoria Memorial Hall; The British Library, London; The British Museum, London; Victor and Albert Museum, London; and The Royal Collection of Her Majesty Queen Elizabeth II for their valuable contributions. And last, but not the least, I am deeply indebted to my research guide, Prof. Meerza Kaukub of Aligarh Muslim University, grandson of Meerza Birjis Qadr, whose sincere guidance, help, suggestions and enthusiasm from the outset helped me tremendously to complete my research work.

My special thanks to all the team members of Rupa Publications without whom this book would not have seen the light of day.

Sudipta Mitra
Sherwood Estate
November 2012, Calcutta

one

Boarding the Caravan to Calcutta

There are times when history tends to emerge in retrospect. Events become significant only when one looks at the past. Perhaps no one would have thought that the exile of Wajid Ali, the King of Awadh from the city of Lucknow, would eventually lead to a cultural and aesthetic reawakening in far-off Calcutta. The seeds of an artistic and intellectual enrichment were sown the day Wajid Ali Shah stepped into his caravan for what was to become the last ride of his life, leading him to Calcutta, the colonial capital of India.

It was a long and mournful march for the deposed King. This was to be a journey that would take him to his new home. Wajid Ali Shah sat in silence, immersed in the weary and grievous thoughts of a banished king. Being too optimistic, he had misjudged the deception of the colonial rulers, just like his predecessors. Nothing caused him more anguish than being forced to leave his beloved Lucknow forever.

A line from his favourite thumri echoed in his broken heart:

Babul mora naihar chchooto jaay
Chaar kahaar mil, mori doliya uthaye
Mora apna begaana chchooto jaay

Meaning—

> O Father, My Father! I'm leaving home
> The four pall-bearers lift my palanquin
> I'm leaving those who were known and my own
> And leaving those who were unknown

The caravan left Lucknow with the King seated in a bedecked carriage drawn by a pair of his favourite horses. A thousand followers, displaced from the city, trailed behind the royal carriage.[1] The farewell was heartbreaking and Lucknow was plunged in grief. People bewailed their beloved king and burst into tears.

On 13 March 1856, Wajid Ali stepped out of his favourite Zurd Kothee Palace for the last time. The caravan left at eight in the evening taking the route of Hazaratgunj road for Kanpur from where the ex-king would then go to Calcutta. Wajid Ali's intention to appeal before the Governor-General for reinstatement did not go down well with the Resident, James Outram. He was promoted to the Chief Commissioner of Awadh[2] a week before the annexation and was doing his best to persuade His Majesty to sign a new treaty.

Nothing could be better than to have that treaty signed and to expose to the world the King's failure to rule Awadh. Lord Dalhousie too was uncertain. If this were to happen then he could justify his (mis) deed before the world. Outram, who was 'acclaimed' in the East India Company as being 'foxy' and cunning, had something to prove before his mentor. He impressed upon the Prime Minister Ali Naqi Khan and even the Queen Mother, urging them to prevail upon the King to ink the deal. Ali Naqi Khan was lured with a jagir yielding an annual income of one lakh rupees, just as the Queen Mother was offered an annual stipend of an equal amount. Eventually Outram was able to influence Ali Naqi to affix the royal seal on the papers, which in those days, was virtually the same as endorsing the signature. Ali Naqi Khan, a confidant of Wajid Ali and also his father-in-law, was an alleged accomplice since he was the only confidential custodian of the royal seal. Notwithstanding Outram's threats and allurements, and the Prime Minister's efforts, Wajid Ali Shah stood firm and declined to sign.

Wajid Ali Shah's petition to arrange for his journey to Calcutta fell on Outram's deaf ears. The former king aspired to plead for his destiny before the Governor-General, and subsequently to the Queen in England in case the Governor did not give him a hearing or was not supportive of his cause. The Chief Commissioner did not want Wajid Ali Shah to reach London and appeal for justice in front of the British public. Outram adopted dilatory tactics, and stipulated that the ex-king would require sanction from the government for security arrangements wherever he planned to halt on his proposed route to Calcutta. Outram used all his ploys to prevent the ex-king from leaving Lucknow, and to frustrate him to such an extent that he would sign the treaty and stay back. The Chief Commissioner went one step further by restraining Ali Naqi Khan, Maharaja Balkrishna and other confidants of distinguished ranks from joining the ex-king and put them under surveillance and interrogation. Wajid Ali's appeal to release Ali Naqi and allow him to accompany the ex-king to Calcutta fell on deaf ears. All records, public acts, official documents and other valuable papers of the ex-king were seized and destroyed so that they could not be exhibited before the British Parliament. Babu Pooran Chand, the custodian of the government records, was also detained. Even the horses of the royal carriage were confiscated so that there was no way that the ex-king could leave.

The approval for Wajid Ali's shift to Calcutta came more than a month after his appeal. However, there was a caveat: he had to restrict the number of his companions to five hundred who would accompany him as 'arrangements' en-route to Calcutta.[3] The Chief Commissioner was scared of the King's popularity and his long march, which could put to the test the atrocious image of Wajid Ali Shah that had been portrayed to the British people. Though Outram made an appeal saying, 'The King is in a hurry for his journey to London for lodging his complaint, but we have to, *somehow*, put it off. Now orders are awaited', it was vetoed by a reply from Governor-General Lord Canning from Calcutta, 'The King has not shown any disobedience to the government orders, he should not be stopped.'[4]

Wajid Ali Shah was accompanied by the Queen Mother Malka Kishwar, three of his wives, Khas Mahal, Akhtar Mahal and Maashuq Mahal, his brother Prince Mirza Sikandar Hasmat, his eldest son and heir apparent Mirza Hamid Ali, Raza Yusuf Ali Khan, Munshi Mir Baqar Ali, Hakim Mir Muhammad Ali, Mr Brandon, an English merchant of Kanpur and Major R.W. Bird, and a host of his followers. Ali Naqi Khan's wife wanted to join the group but was given a cold shoulder by the ex-king. He could not accept his father-in-law's move to side with the British. Only Mr John Rose Brandon sat with Wajid Ali Shah in the Coach Box.[5]

Why him?

Patronizing Europeans in the court of Awadh was a practice followed since the days of Nawab Suja-ud-Daulla. Tilly Kettle, the first English painter to work in India, was patronized by Suja-ud-Daulla in 1772 in Faizabad. His son Asaf-ud-Daula supported the renowned German painter Johann Zoffany. King Ghazi-ud-din Haidar sponsored a Roman painter Robert Home. Likewise, Major General Claude Martin came to Lucknow in 1776, almost at the same time when Nawab Asaf-ud-Daula moved his capital to the city. His close association with the Nawab brought him a fortune worth forty lakh rupees and a colossal palace called Constantia.

Wajid Ali had forty-eight trusted European associates till 1849 in his court[6] and Mr John Rose Brandon was one. Presumably, Brandon advised the banished king to seek justice in Calcutta and also to call on Queen Victoria in case justice was denied. He was forthcoming to facilitate the ex-king's mission to England for his reinstatement if the situation so demanded.

Brandon was an English merchant who came to Lucknow to make a fortune. The British Resident censured his friendship with the King and eventually coerced Brandon to leave the city. By now Brandon had developed his mercantile base in Kanpur, although his loyalty and sincerity to the King remained unscathed. He also started an English newspaper from Kanpur called *Central Star*.[7] Brandon was also the son-in-law of George Harris Derusett, the famous barber of King Nasir-ud-din Haidar who became one of the most influential persons behind the curtains of Awadh in the mid 1830s.[8]

The retinue tailed off as the bewailing citizens on foot slowly gave up. When Wajid Ali Shah reached the Karbala of Mir Khuda Baksh on that gloomy night, a team of musicians were singing to their heart's content. In the most poignant moment, the broken-hearted King sang a line from one of his favourite couplets—

Daro deewar par hazrat se nazar karte hain,
Khush raho ahl-e-watan,
Hum tau safar karte hai

Meaning—

I cast my eyes longingly at the doors and the walls,
Goodbye countrymen,
I proceed for my journey[9]

Thus, the caravan went on its journey. The entourage breathed a sigh of relief when Ali Naqi Khan managed to free himself after a great effort and joined the party.[10] However, a different literary source reveals that Ali Naqi Khan was released from Lucknow in the month of July and started his journey towards Calcutta on 15 July 1856. Khan's caravan reached Allahabad from where he boarded a steamer and finally reached Calcutta on 29 July 1856. But the latter may not be true as according to some other sources, when the ex-king arrived in Calcutta the British Government gave him four houses, one of which was allotted to Ali Naqi Khan.[11]

Wajid Ali Shah reached the riverbank of Ganga at Unnao in the wee hours of the morning and sat for namaz. His men formed a bridge by joining the boats across the Ganga and finally at five in the morning of 13 March 1856, Wajid Ali Shah walked into Kanpur. The lamenting crowd, consisting of the hundreds of citizens who had followed their king, was gently persuaded to go back to Lucknow. Rented houses had been prearranged for the retinue to stay, but the ex-king preferred Mr Brandon's house to rest.[12] Wajid Ali spent the whole month of Rajab in Kanpur where he convened with his followers and some of the British agents as well. But Wajid Ali refused to meet Sir John Lawrence, the chief commissioner of Punjab on the plea of his ill health.[13]

Lawrence was a silent spectator of Dalhousie's countless misdeeds and the annexation of Punjab was one such event. On his way to Punjab, he stayed for six days in Kanpur where the royal retinue was resting. Though the deposed king was in no mood to meet his British admirer, Sir Lawrence had an opportunity to observe the people from close quarters and to try to read their minds. The British agent could sense the warning signs of a mutiny brewing up amongst the King's followers in Kanpur and Wajid Ali Shah's sojourn had further encouraged the sepoys[14] for an upheaval. The platform for a rebellion had already been built since the days when forty thousand sepoys out of a total strength of eighty thousand, were enrolled from Awadh into the Bengal Army. The sepoys were overtly sympathetic to the ex-king and spoke against the British misdeed.[15]

On 7 April 1856, after sighting the 'Moon of Shaaban', Wajid Ali Shah left Kanpur and started his journey for Benaras. He cruised down the Ganges in a private steamer where he rested in a mansion called Panchghar for eight days in Allahabad. Allahabad had previously been a part of the realm of Awadh. From Allahabad, he reached Benaras by a horse-driven carriage on 16 April 1856.[16]

Wajid Ali Shah received a reverential salutation from the Maharaja of Benaras Ishwari Prasad Narayan Singh. The Kashi-Raj was courteous enough to offer his best palace at Ramgarh to the banished king and his begums. The grateful ex-king decided to take a short break from the exhaustive journey. The monarch of Kashi gifted him a nazrana of five thousand rupees to recognize his supremacy. The ex-king conferred a Khilat in return. The Maharaja responded with one thousand and one ashrafis to honour his master.[17] Notwithstanding his allegiance to the ex-king of Awadh, Ishwari Prasad was a confidant of the British Government and remained so when the mutiny broke out. As a reward of his faithfulness, he was given the rank of Maharaja Bahadur in 1859.

From Benares the royal retinue divided itself into two groups. Wajid Ali Shah, accompanied by his begums, mother, son, Ali Naqi Khan and other confidants, embarked on a ship named *General Mcleod* on Friday, 25 April 1856.[18] His followers boarded large bazras[19] to sail down the Ganges, while some of them travelled by road. The dreary journey continued. The ex-king cruised continuously for eighteen days in the incessant summer heat and reached Calcutta on 13 May 1856 at Bhootghat, near Metiyaburj.[20] By the time the gruesome journey ended he was almost burnt out by the scorching heat and worn out by attacks of dysentery and scabies.[21] Although the ex-king had been promised safety by the government en-route and assured of 'proper arrangements for the supply of provisions',[22] there was no sign of any British agent to receive the royal retinue at any place on his way to Calcutta. The reception was utterly unceremonious in the British capital as well, with the government merely sending an officer to receive the banished king of Awadh as he disembarked on the banks of the Hooghly.

Wajid Ali Shah's entourage in the streets of Calcutta was eye-catching. With musicians in the front, there followed a train of carts carrying cages of a variety of birds, monkeys, leopards, camels, elephants and giraffes on foot. The ex-king was seated in his gold-plated palanquin. Following him were his begums and zenanas in separate boxes, hidden from the public gaze by curtains that were drawn on both the sides. His khansamas, chefs, housekeepers, clerks, animal-keepers and domestic help were trailing behind. Throngs of curious eyes gawked at the unusual spectacle. His plight nonetheless evoked pity and not sympathy amongst the onlookers.

Wajid Ali Shah rented a palatial house in Garden Reach paying five hundred rupees per month for it. The house was a riverside resort of the Maharaja of Burdwan. However, the English records state that the government was conducive to finding a decent abode for the ex-king and his retinue. Therefore, a palatial riverside resort that belonged to Sir Lawrence Peel,[23] the former chief justice of the Supreme Court in Calcutta, at Garden Reach was rented out to him. Wajid Ali's own book *Sheo-e-Faiz* indicates that after his arrival in Calcutta Wajid Ali stayed in the house of Burdwan's Maharaja, which was rented at five hundred rupees per month. Wajid Ali Shah's writing testifies that

Raja Bardhawan ki kothi panch saye ki kiraet per raisa.

Meaning—

Burdwan's Maharaja's kothi was rented at five hundred rupees per month.

Therefore, the information that Sir Laurence Peel's house was arranged by the British is not true. But Wajid Ali Shah was arrested from the Maharaja's house. After he was released from Fort William, he settled once again in the same house and bought the surrounding area to build several palaces, including Sultan Khana. The Maharaja's house was assimilated and later demolished to construct a new palace.[24]

The palace, located in the immediate neighbourhood of Calcutta and close to Fort William, was at a strategic place for the colonial government to keep a watchful eye on the deposed king. On the other hand, Wajid Ali Shah, a man of extraordinary literary taste, was charmed by the rippling river amidst the sprawling nature.[25] This was the means by which the British gave a healing touch to console the despondent ex-king of Awadh. When Wajid Ali Shah stepped into his new home, he could hardly ascertain that his destiny had already been decided and that he would spend thirty-two long years on these banks of the Hooghly.

The British etiquette to lend a hand in the ex-king's search for a new abode is not convincing. A letter from the Commissioner clearly states the same:

On his [Wajid Ali Shah's] arrival at Calcutta, he should make his own arrangement for his own accommodation, for he will be looked upon as uninvited guest. In fact he is going to undertake this journey against the wishes of Government.[26]

Historians believe that the ex-king sent Moulavi Masih-ud-Deen to arrange for accommodation in Calcutta, which he did by renting the riverside abode of the Maharaja of Burdwan. There was a rumour too that Wajid Ali Shah had to wait in a steamer for a couple of days while his people hunted for a house for him. Abdul Halim Sharar, the commentator of the banished king talked about a series of houses on the banks of the Hooghly stretching about two-and-a-half miles along the riverbank, which were arranged and handed over to him by the British Government.

When Wajid Ali Shah disembarked on the eastern bank of river Hooghly, Garden Reach was an opulent niche of beautiful riverside resorts belonging to the great civilians of Calcutta.[27] The eastern riverbank was known locally as Metiyaburj, meaning 'earthen dome'. Sharar further edifies in his book that three of the houses were given to the ex-king for his personal use, while one was handed over to Ali Naqi Khan and the others were arranged for his retinue. Sharar's father was a courtier of Wajid Ali Shah who came to live in Metiyaburj in 1862. Sharar joined his father in 1869 when he was only nine. In all probability Sharar failed to mention Wajid Ali's initial days in Calcutta and his hardship in finding a residence. By the time he came to Calcutta the mutiny was over and the ex-king had made a peaceful settlement with the British.

Despite all his power and splendour being blotted out, the banished king was still a threat to the government. The colonial power was more apprehensive of the presence of European advisors who could transform the ex-king from a nobody to a somebody. An intelligence report thus cautions,

> *Calcutta is now, or is about to be, the headquarters of intrigue—such intrigue as miserable Europeans, destitute of principle as they are greedy of money, desire to create for their own profit.*[28]

Although it was uncertain if Wajid Ali Shah would sail across the oceans in ailing health, the colonial power was sceptic of him meddling with European acquaintances who could pilot his mission to England. While Brandon was their first suspect, the British intelligence had an eye on one Mr Menzies, a merchant of Mirzapore who had reportedly been engaged on a high salary by the ex-king to accompany him on his mission to England.[29]

Major Robert Wilberforce Bird, an 'abettor' in the ex-king's caravan was another suspect. He was an English Captain of the 4th Regiment Native Infantry and the nephew of William Wilberforce Bird who was the acting Governor-General for an interim term in 1844.[30] Major Bird resigned from his position of Assistant Resident under Colonel Sleeman and joined hands with the ex-king.[31] There were rumours that Colonel Sleeman had dismissed Major Bird for instigating Wajid Ali Shah and his ministers to dishonour the Company's edicts.

Nitpickers could see that Major Bird was extorting a large sum of money from the ex-king to represent him before the British Crown. Colonial newspapers such as *The Friend of India* and *The Bengal Hurkaru* took Bird's loyalty towards the deposed king with a pinch of salt.[32]

Two

The English Drama and the Deposition

Wajid Ali Shah ascended the throne of Awadh at a critical time when his father had died and the East India Company was desperate to seize the most coveted throne of 'the garden, the granary, and the queen-province of India'.[1] Wajid Ali's destiny was decided when his father, Amjad Ali Shah, chose him as the heir-apparent and ousted Wajid's overtly ambitious elder brother Prince Mustafa, who was conniving with the British to overthrow his father. There were four claimants to the throne of Awadh to succeed Amjad Ali Shah. Wajid Ali Shah was never the first choice, nor did he want to be so. From adulthood he was inclined towards performing arts and would have lived well with his poetry and learning. Wajid Ali, though the second child of his father, was the son of his principal wife. Although the British interference in selection of the heir-apparent was quite uncalled for, the colonial authority finally endorsed his nomination, albeit hesitatingly.

The first reform Wajid Ali initiated after ascending the throne was to restructure his army. He took personal interest in attending the morning parade and arm-drills. Under him, not only was the army's strength enhanced, the local landlords were impelled to ensure collection of revenue, and both the cavalry and infantry were reorganized.[2] The King's interest in augmenting his army did not find favour with the Governor-General Henry Hardinge, and it was he who first hatched the idea of overthrowing the King so that he could take full control of the state. Hardinge's letter to the Court of Directors of the East India Company dated 28 July 1847 is probably the first obvious display of no-confidence expressed by the Company. This letter was written only five-and-a-half months after Wajid Ali ascended the throne.[3]

A relentless threat from the British Residency under Colonel Richmond and later on from Colonel Sleeman pushed the King to the brink.

Wajid Ali Shah confessed:

Considering that even if I reorganized a small body of troops, the English Government would be displeased, and suspicion might arise, and relying upon the friendship of the Honourable East Indian Company, on whom rested the entire responsibility for preserving the kingdom for domestic and foreign foes, I at once abandoned this project, and devoted my attention to public affairs.[4]

Wajid Ali took keen interest in the administration of justice and in introducing reforms. He was generous, kind and compassionate to his subjects, and could have succeeded as the most felicitous ruler of his age for his qualities of a cogent administrator. However, he sank into a life of pleasures surrounded by courtesans, singers and dancers. The constant threat from the meddling Residency at the behest of the Governor-General was agonizing enough. The Resident had shot out a number of letters to the Governor-General, in which he highlighted complete anarchism and misrule but did not make any mention of the reforms being initiated by the King.

Thus, with deft deception Hardinge applauded the King at a banquet during his visit to Lucknow in November 1847, and recognized Wajid Ali as the 'undisputed master of the country'[5] while garlanding him with a priceless pearl necklace. Behind this façade, several mendacious activities were going on in the British camp. When Hardinge met Wajid Ali hardly eight months after the King's accession, annexing Awadh was already on the cards. In a letter to the Court of Directors he revealed his reasons for wanting to oust the King of Awadh. The letter (dispatch no. 33) dated 2 December 1847 was awash with caustic words to spell the 'misrule' and 'wickedness' of Wajid Ali Shah, which Hardinge supposedly 'witnessed' first-hand during his visit to Lucknow. Hardinge was resolute in his efforts to defame Wajid Ali from the very first day of his succession and thwarted the King's attempts to implement his welfare reforms. At that point of time, Lucknow was brimming with paid spies and with British agents who were actually employed as the King's bureaucrats.

Hardinge passed on his baton to Dalhousie on 12 January 1848. This only worsened the situation for the ill-fated king. Dalhousie's manic need for annexations had made him dream of Awadh as 'a cherry, which will drop into our mouths some day. It has long been ripening.' However, he was not sure if 'the court would approve of my [Dalhousie's] shaking the tree to help it down.'[6] Many such 'cherries' fell into his mouth with his Doctrine of Lapse policy and added four million pounds sterling to the Company's annual income. The only cherry left was Awadh, 'his Waterloo—the crowing victory of annexation.'[7]

Dalhousie's successful annexation of twelve princely states from Satara to Tanjore had made him obsessed with power. The East India Company, which was no longer an autonomous corporation but principally under the control of the British

Crown, rapidly spread its roots and became the predominant power in India. Interestingly, Dalhousie's annexation of Awadh, his thirteenth 'cherry', entailed grave political danger. Major General John Low, who was the Resident of Lucknow from 1831 to 1842, did not make the mistake of postulating the 'misrule' campaign against the rulers of Awadh. Low's assessment is a testimony to his unbiased view, which ascertained the character and conduct of the rulers of Awadh. It also exposed how the facts had been distorted and published in the newspaper articles while there was no one to write in their defence. 'The Kings of Oude have been spoken of in the English society as merciless tyrants over their own subjects,' regretted Low[8]. On the other hand, in a personal letter to his friend Sir George Couper on 18 September 1848, Dalhousie aspired to take over the administration of Awadh, rather than to assimilate it.

'Meantime I have got two other kingdoms on hand to dispose of—Oude and Hyderabad. Both are on the high road to be taken under our management—not into our possession; and before two years are over I have no doubt they will be managed by us.'[9]

Wajid Ali Shah proactively reviewed his reforms and prepared a fresh set based on the English model prescribed by Hardinge. The King wanted his reforms to be introduced experimentally in some of his divisions. Colonel Richmond succeeded Major General Low and supported the King's reforms. Richmond engaged the Assistant Resident Major Bird to get the reforms ratified by Mr Thomason, the Lieutenant-Governor of North-Western Provinces. The final draft, when placed before Dalhousie, was immediately shelved.[10] Thomason was also not true to his word. The King's proposal of disarming the local landlords was rejected by Thomason on the plea that they needed to protect themselves against dacoits. This was a deliberate act to goad 'misrule' and 'oppression' in the state so that he could have a pretext to justify British interference in the future.[11]

Misfortune was still stalking Wajid Ali. In 1849, he suffered a massive heart attack, which confined him to his palace for a whole year. During that period William Sleeman came to Lucknow and took over as the Resident.[12] On leaving India, Hardinge had suggested to Dalhousie that no time should be wasted in engaging a reliable British servant to traverse the country and gather accurate information about the present state of affairs. Dalhousie settled on Colonel William Henry Sleeman, who had already distinguished himself by cleansing Jabalpur of dacoits. Colonel Sleeman was appointed to prepare an inquiry report in the way Hardinge had advised, but the intent of the report was made clear to him even before he entered Awadh. As Assistant Resident Major Bird, succinctly put it, 'He professed to examine, but he was under orders to sentence; he pretended to try, but he was instructed simply to condemn.'[13] The enormous reserves of ninety-two lakh rupees and one hundred and twenty-four thousand gold mohurs in the King's treasury, and a government security worth twenty-four lakh rupees,[14] were coveted by the Governor-General. Dalhousie's order 'with special reference to the great changes which, in all probability, will take place'[15] gave Sleeman to understand that the Governor-General had set a thief to catch a thief in order to carry out a historic dacoity!

By now Lieutenant-Colonel Sleeman had earned the nickname 'Thuggee Sleeman' (slaying fourteen hundred thugs). He was quick to grab the coveted post of the Lucknow Residency. Allured by an annual offer of sixty-six thousand rupees, the thuggee-hunter promised to do his best 'to carry out your Lordship's views in the new change.'[16]

On 6 January 1849, while Wajid Ali Shah was still fighting for his life, Lieutenant-Colonel Sleeman assumed his new duties. The King had refused to be examined or treated by a European doctor, and used to rely totally on indigenous medicines. The new Resident was uncertain about the King's recovery and was toying with the idea of enthroning the heir-apparent immediately after the King's death.[17] Sleeman, indeed, was thinking of using this opportune time to enforce a new treaty, by taking the King's discontented elder brother Prince Mustafa and the Queen Mother into confidence and bringing them over to his side.[18] The heir-apparent, Mirza Hamid Ali, was a minor and Sleeman saw an opportunity to play out a crooked game plan. He was planning to engage a regent to guide the heir-apparent. The regent would be facilitated by a council of members who would be the Company's nominee. Sleeman had been an accomplice in imposing one such regency in Gwalior during his Residency in 1843, when the minor king—Jayajirao Scindia ascended the throne. The British held full control over the crown, although the trail was spattered with blood. A similar treaty was enforced in Lahore and the colonial rulers abrogated the power by assuming guardianship of King Duleep Singh when he was a minor.

The situation was rather favourable in Lucknow. Sleeman was aspiring to play the role of a virtual ruler analogous to the model prescribed in Gwalior or Lahore. There would be hardly any skirmish or bloodshed as Sleeman had already won over the King's discontented brother and the Queen Mother. The King's army was practically incapacitated after the Treaty of 1801.[19] This together with the 'misrule' encumbering Awadh for years would certainly pave the way for Sleeman. The change was inevitable, awaiting only the Governor-General's final nod.

Meanwhile, the King's long confinement to bed encouraged his adversaries to start a rumour about his failing mental health. This was a deliberate and calculated canard so that the kingdom could be annexed on the flimsiest of grounds. The air was rife with gossip that the King could not concentrate on public affairs because of his over-indulgence in sex and mental sickness and that he was on the brink of insanity.

Wajid Ali Shah's heart attack is again controversial. Probably he was suffering from some venereal disease; he had given a hint of this in his book *Tareekh-e-Parikhana (Isshqnama)*. The King mentioned that he was suffering from such an unspeakable disease that even his wives were scared to touch him physically.[20]

The King purposely avoided European physicians, as he feared being poisoned by unknown doctors. His predecessor Nasir-ud-din Haidar was a victim of unknown poison, while his father's death was still a mystery.[21] Wajid Ali Shah was in constant dread of being poisoned by his chief wife, or his uncle or even by the courtesans. This fact was not unknown to Sleeman.[22] The British Resident's proposal that he be examined by European doctors came to light when the Residency Physician Dr Bell took over from Dr Leekie. Both the physicians went for a courtesy call and met His Majesty, as required by tradition. Sleeman was baffled when the English physicians, who had a long conversation with His Majesty in the presence of Captain Bird, announced that the King was in a sound state of health and mind and showed no signs of confusion!

Sleeman was frustrated. He was enraged with Captain Bird and Dr Bell for their diagnosis that rebuffed his plans, and shot out a letter to Lord Dalhousie, charging the officers of being intriguers 'to convey wrong impression to the Durbar'.[23]

In his letter addressed to Sir Elliot, Sleeman favoured forming a board (instead of his original plan of a regency) with the King's nominees and to interpose his authority where nobody would dare question him. If the King was defiant, he would be compelled to abdicate in favour of his minor son. In an exhaustive letter to the Governor-General in August 1849, Sleeman tried to impress on his new model, and emphasized on the huge outstanding revenue, which the King avoided collecting even though he was in sound health. Before he started his journey across the kingdom of Awadh, Colonel Sleeman sent off a communiqué to His Lordship. In the most acrid words, he described Wajid Ali's follies and his apathy in running the administration. Further, he accused the King of spending most of his time with women and claimed that he was more dependent on his singers than on his ministers. Sleeman strongly recommended constituting a governing board or a council of regency, but did not try to impress upon His Lordship the idea of annexation.

Sleeman's several attempts to tarnish the King's image and to portray him as an 'imbecile' or 'helpless as that of an infant'[24] to His Lordship, failed to cut any ice. Dalhousie was aware of Sleeman's knack of building mountains out of molehills for his personal interest. Sleeman was casting aspersions upon the King's private life; and proving him 'imbecile' could only end up in replacing the King by one of his sons or brother. But that would not craft a judicial platform for Dalhousie to usurp the kingdom. The Governor-General was plotting a chaotic condition in Awadh, which would provide enough justification for annexation on the ground of misgovernment and oppression on the people. Thus, Dalhousie turned a deaf ear to Sleeman's proposal.

Eleven months after assuming his office, William Sleeman set out on an extensive tour of the kingdom of Awadh. Sleeman's political journey began on 2 December 1849 and ended on 28 February 1850. Fluent in Hindi, Urdu and Bengali and well versed in Indian culture and customs, Sleeman was possibly the first British officer to set foot in Awadh with a better understanding of the people's needs than any of his predecessors. His observations, which were inscribed in roughly forty-one letters written to the authorities, did not give any suggestions to support Dalhousie's rationale of annexation. Rather, the British Resident who had to do the spadework defied the reverie of annexation by saying 'our good name in India would inevitably suffer; and that good name is more valuable to us than a dozen of Oudes'.[25] In his bid to oust the King, Sleeman had spent a massive amount of three lakh rupees on his tours from the King's treasury. However, he failed in his mission. Reiterating his strong opinion against annexation he cautioned His Lordship 'the annexation of Oude would cost the British power more than the value of ten such kingdoms, and would inevitably lead to a mutiny of the sepoys.'[26] This was further corroborated by his private correspondence in 1854–55 as the Resident of Lucknow, which was later published in the *Times*.

> *The system of annexation, pursued by a party in this country, and favoured by Lord Dalhousie and his Council, has, in my opinion, a downward tendency—a tendency to crush all the higher and middle classes connected with the land... In fact, the aggressive and absorbing policy, which has done so much mischief of late in India, is beginning to create feelings of alarm in the native mind; and it is when the popular mind becomes agitated by such alarms that fanatics will always be*

> *found ready to step into... I shall have nothing new to do at Lucknow. Lord Dalhousie and I have different views, I fear. If he wishes anything done that I do not think right and honest, I resign, and leave it to be done by others. We have no right to annex or confiscate Oude; but we have a right, under the treaty of 1837, to take the management of it, but not to appropriate its revenues to ourselves. To confiscate would be dishonest and dishonourable. To annex would be to give the people a government almost as bad as their own, if we put our screw upon them.*[27]

Even as the Resident portrayed the King's imbecility and, therefore, his incapability to rule, he was not able to give any allegation that confirmed a state of anarchy in the kingdom. Sleeman admitted that Wajid Ali was 'neither tyrannical nor cruel, but altogether incapable of devoting any of his time or attention to business of any kind, but spends the whole of his time with women, eunuchs, fiddlers, and other parasites.'[28] 'The King, by over-indulgence, has reduced his intellect below the standard of that of a boy of five years of age.'[29] Apart from his follies, Sleeman rather praised the King in his narratives, saying:

There never was on the throne, I believe, a man more inoffensive at heart than he [Wajid Ali Shah] and he is quite sensible of my anxious desire to advise him rightly, and see justice done in all cases.[30]

Dalhousie was doubtful of the King's mental ill-health as portrayed by Sleeman; instead, he was impressed by the report furnished by the Residency physicians, Dr Leekie and Dr Bell, which ran contrary to the Resident's observation. Sleeman confessed to His Lordship that 'though everybody knows that the King has become crazy and imbecile, it would be difficult to get judicial proof that he is so.'[31] Sleeman's advice was clear and unmistakable: 'Assume the administration but do not grasp the revenues of the country.'[32]

Sir William Sleeman, the most distinguished yet controversial servant of British India, and whose service was recognized for more than forty years by three Governor-Generals of India, virtually failed to deliver his task, which was vested upon him by Lord Dalhousie. At the fag end of his career and when his health was failing, Sleeman had no reason to flatter his masters. The annexation of Awadh did take place but not as a consequence to his report. Post-annexation results proved beyond doubt that Sleeman had judged the minds of the people of Awadh better than Dalhousie had. This versatile character in the history of British rule in India left Lucknow on 5 October 1854, never to return again.

In a letter addressed to Dalhousie, William Sleeman endorsed James Outram of Bombay Army as his successor.[33] Outram, a confidant of Lord Dalhousie, took the charge of Awadh on 5 December 1854 with his mind intent on fulfilling a certain purpose. A popular Bombay saying describes Outram as 'a fox is a fool and a lion a coward by the side of Sir James Outram.'[34]

The reception was warm and perhaps more demonstrative than his predecessor's. As he set his foot in Lucknow, Outram was accompanied by the heir-apparent in a vibrant procession of state officials, citizens, elephants, camels, dancers, and festoons. A lavish banquet was laid out at the Moti Mahal Palace followed by an animal show, which was in keeping with the Awadhi tradition. Perhaps the King breathed a sigh of relief to see the last of Major General Sleeman. Now he could see the silver lining in the arrival of James Outram.

Sir Outram took less than four months to establish his loyalty to his mentor and submitted an exhaustive report to Dalhousie on 15 March 1855 in which he recommended the annexation of a dynasty, which had shown allegiance to the British crown for over a century. To conclude the incomplete work of Sleeman, James Outram poured over the Residency records and reports that had been furnished by his predecessors. In preparing his report Outram was largely aided by Dr Joseph Fayrer,[35] the Residency doctor-cum-political assistant. Dr Fayrer was well versed in Urdu and kept daily records on various proceedings in the King's harem and court. Fayrer's mention of incredible animal fights in the court, the luxury of kite flying, the King's recitation of his poem *Love of the Bulbuls* to his wife, or his reward of a costly shawl and two thousand rupees to the keeper of his pigeons for exhibiting a pigeon with one black and one white wing[36] added nuances to Outram's report instead of substance to prove misrule.

Unlike Sleeman, Outram confined himself within the four walls of the Residency except to stroll at the break of dawn on the terrace of his quarters. Dalhousie, however, was in a hurry. It was probably his failing health and impending retirement that made him impatient. Dalhousie's health remained far from good despite close monitoring by Dr Fayrer. Excessive smoking and a wasting disease took a toll and when he returned to Calcutta from Nilgiris in October 1855, he was almost a cripple. However, his physical incapacitation could not prevent him from his last task of annexing Awadh. The report prepared by Outram, even though it had no sum or substance, bolstered Dalhousie to prove Wajid Ali's reckless deceit and his worthless reforms before the Court of Directors. In his personal letter to Sir George Couper on 2 May 1855 from Ootacamund, the Marquis wrote:

General Outram, in pursuance of instructions with which he was furnished, has sent up a report on the condition of Oude. It seems impossible that the home authorities can any longer hesitate to overthrow this fortress of corruption and infamous misgovernment.[37]

While stationed in the Nilgiris to recoup, Dalhousie wasted no time and immediately got down to prepare the minutes. He started by annulling the Treaties of 1837[38] and then of 1801 and demanding the complete handover of the civil and military controls of Awadh over to the British.[39] His notes were fundamentally based on the observations of Sleeman and Outram. Dalhousie signed the minutes on 18 June 1855 and finally despatched it to London on 23 June for approval.[40]

The long delay was becoming unbearable for Dalhousie and was becoming a test of his endurance. His health was giving up and the Marquis was almost at a point where he had to cling onto crutches. The incessant strain took a heavy toll on his health. Lady Dalhousie too could not stand the enervating climate of India and breathed her last on her voyage back to England on 6 May 1853 when the ship was within sight of the English shore. Dalhousie was only forty-one years old at this time and facing the supreme trial of his life. Moreover, his doctors strongly advised him to cut short his tenure in India and return to England. When his masters asked him to extend his stay in office he could not bring himself to refuse. He did not allow his personal misfortunes to come in the way of his professional tasks. It was in the same year that the first railway track was laid down in India and the first telegraph was wired.[41] Nevertheless, Dalhousie lived with his desire to gulp his 'cherry' someday. In a letter, he accounted for his aspiration:

> *I count it internally a symptom of improving health in myself that the desire to upset that court before I go has revived within me. It would make a good windup; and if they will let me, I think I could engage to have the country at our feet—every fort dismantled, and every man disarmed in three months[sic].*[42]

Dalhousie's seventy-five paragraph minutes covering one hundred and forty-four pages appeared to be overstated but, after meticulously weighing the merits of the minutes, the Court of Directors and Her Majesty's Ministry gave him the go-ahead. The despatch, signed on 21 November 1855, reached the hands of the Governor-General in Calcutta at midnight on 2 January 1856.[43]

In his significant minutes, Dalhousie offered three options to assimilate Awadh. The first option entailed that the King surrender the province of Awadh to the British Government for a limited period of time. The second option allowed him to retain his title and his throne while the administration would be vested in the hands of the British forever. The final option called for Awadh to be fully and permanently annexed to the British domain. The despatch had given a *carte blanche* to Dalhousie and a free hand to do what he felt was in the best interests of the Company. Dalhousie favoured the second option, since the directors intended to show some tenderness towards a family that may have committed some offences, but had not been unfaithful to the British Crown.[44]

Dalhousie's long wait ended after six-and-a-half months. The annexation of Awadh was inevitable. Dalhousie was confident of getting a nod from his directors. It was only a matter of time. He started to make preparations for this take over. He did not want to waste precious time as his health was fast deteriorating. The role of the Resident was formulated, a new treaty was framed, the proclamation to be issued to the people was drafted, the Company's machinery was mobilized and the master-role of the new government was chalked out. Vital documents were kept safely in the custody of the Foreign Secretary. He took only a day to call on the Council and three days to mobilize the troops.[45] Dalhousie was confident of his ability to overwhelm Wajid Ali in handing over the baton of administration in lieu of preserving his title. 'The King won't offend or quarrel with us, and will take any amount of kicking without being rebellious,'[46] he was confident. However, he prepared an alternative proclamation lest the transaction recoiled. 'We shall offer him a treaty, and if he refuses it, swallow him,'[47] Dalhousie mused, 'either the King must give up administration or we shall take it. I think he will give; if not, we certainly shall take.'[48]

Outram reached Lucknow from Calcutta on 30 January 1856 with the Governor-General's decree and his alternative proclamations in hands. Regardless of his master's explicit approbation, Outram was doubtful, rather apprehensive if the British would succeed in confiscating Awadh without taking recourse to arms. Outram had known the King closely for a full year, and had reason to believe that the King would not enter into any such arrangement to give up his government in lieu of his crown. Outram's apprehensions kept Dalhousie in a state of perpetual unease even though he had unquestionable authority and confidence to win the situation. Dalhousie could not understand the hesitancy of his most trusted General, on whom he had set the fulcrum of his dream plan. Thus, he was sarcastic in his remarks:

> *This surprised me, until I recollected that heroes have indigestions like other people; and I hope that when he (Outram) comes out of the doctor's hands, in which he now is, he will take a more cheerful view of our prospects.*[49]

The news was out in the open because the British troops in Kanpur were in a state of readiness to act. It was a gathering of sixteen hundred soldiers under Colonel Wheeler as the Brigadier.[50] Speculations had been rife in Indian newspapers of the exact amount of revenue that would go to the Company from the state of Awadh. Articles appeared in print speculating upon the annexation of the country. Rumours reached inside the King's palace and conjectures were all around. It was unimaginable for Wajid Ali Shah that the East India Company could stoop so low as to instigate a breach of reliance and violate the Treaty of 1801. The King rebuffed the rumours and reprimanded the tattlers. However, the rumours would not die down and forced the King to send his emissary to the Resident to enquire of the facts. Outram had no other way but to take refuge in a flagrant lie. He fibbed that the concentration of troops in Kanpur were part of pre-emptive steps to quell a rebellion on the Nepal frontier. The King was relieved.

The relief was not for long because the rumours rang true. Outram on his arrival on 30 January 1856, met the Prime Minister Ali Naqi Khan and explained what the British Government had in mind and the new treaty, which His Lordship would like to enforce. The task, which Outram was given to perform, was difficult as well as delicate. Outram's apprehension was correct and as anticipated, Ali Naqi Khan refuted the charges concocted against the King and remonstrated the concentration of British troops at Kanpur. The Prime Minister made all possible efforts to impress the Resident citing the reforms the King had brought about following Hardinge's visit, the amelioration of law and order of the state, the Treaty of 1801, and the century-old faithfulness that the dynasty had affirmed to the British crown. All was in vain. The Resident's hands were tied and he was bound by his duties. He had nothing to add further nor did he deny the arguments adduced by Ali Naqi Khan. Even so, Outram could not defy the great task entrusted on him.

A second meeting was arranged on the following day at the Lucknow Residency, where Ali Naqi Khan was shown a copy of the new treaty. The Prime Minister also read Lord Dalhousie's letter addressed to the King, explaining the government's resolution and the terms of the treaty, which he would be requested to sign. The discussion was brief and Ali Naqi Khan questioned if the King could be allowed to seek an appointment with the Governor-General and, if required, with the Queen of England as well, for a more favourable resolution. Outram was focused on signing the treaty, for which he gave the King only three days to think about and decide following the official handing-over of the document. Thereafter, the Company would have no other option but to assume the government of Awadh and the King would be responsible for the consequences. On the other hand if the King acceded to sign the document, the Company would agree to a pension of one lakh rupees per month for the King and would allow him to retain his title.

The next day on 1 February 1856, the British Resident received a letter from the King which bore an acquiescent tone. As anticipated, he refuted the charges framed against him by the Governor-General but submitted to adopt any other reforms that the British Government felt would be in the interest of his people. The King enumerated the reforms he had undertaken since the visit of Lord Hardinge and once again expressed his fidelity to the British Crown, but declined to endorse the contents of the treaty. The Resident acknowledged the receipt of the letter on the same day, but his reply was sharp. It said that the resolution passed by the British Government was irrevocable and the Governor-General would not accept any more communication in this regard; rather the Resident regretted that he could not extend the period for more than three days and no further delay would be contemplated.

Within the palace walls the air was thick with rumours. Tattlers fanned out gossip that the King's obsession with dancing and singing had frustrated the British lords, and sooner or later, Awadh would be annexed. On 1 February, the Queen Mother received a sealed envelope from the Prime Minister. She was in the midst of getting dressed after a wash. Leaving everything aside, she tore open the letter and was baffled by the contents. Without caring to cover her head or her feet, she rushed into her son's quarters, with the letter in her hands. 'The Kingdom is destroyed,' she wailed.[51] The King was sitting alone in a corner, his face covered in his hands. He sobbed at the sight of his mother but could not utter a word.

At four in the evening, General Outram stepped inside Zurd Kothee Palace on the invitation of the Queen Mother. A futile attempt at reconciliation began. Aulea Begum's efforts to defend her son and to prove his fidelity to the British Crown did not cut ice with the Resident. He accused the King of misgovernment and said that the government's decision to assume the state in order to restore peace was irrevocable. Outram hoped that the Queen Mother would be able to convince her son so that the British command could avoid the unpleasant task of dethroning him. He trusted that the Begum, being a sensible woman, would influence the King to accede to the terms. However, the Resident had no answers to several questions fielded by the Begum regarding governance. The meeting concluded without a resolution.

Dalhousie was desperate to get the treaty signed. He would not hesitate to increase the King's stipend to eighteen lakh rupees per annum. Outram, in his meeting with the Queen Mother earlier had assured to compensate the King with a sum of one lakh rupees per mensem which would be guaranteed to his heirs forever. In addition, a sum of three lakh rupees per annum would be spent for His Majesty's guards and his own men.[52] Dalhousie's extravagant offer too did not find favour with her. When they found both threats and allurements ineffective, the British Government determined to assume the state of Awadh, chose the option of hostile operation. Brigadier Wheeler marched his troops and halted at Nawalgunj, twenty miles from Lucknow.

Next day, on 2 February 1856, Ali Naqi Khan visited the Residency after the talks with the Queen Mother had broken off. Although the purpose of his visit remained unknown, the Resident on his arrival handed over copies of the Governor-General's letter and the Proclamations A and B for the King's perusal. Outram had spoken of his desire to meet the King formally on 4 February 1856, which was courteously granted by Wajid Ali Shah. Brigadier Wheeler further advanced his troops on the Cawnpur Road, now only eight miles away from Lucknow.

On 4 February 1856, Outram reached Zurd Kothee Palace at eight o'clock in the morning along with Captain Fletcher Haye, the Assistant to the Resident, and Weston, the Superintendent of Awadh Frontier Police. Much to their surprise, the Englishmen found the court deserted and the guns dismounted. The guards of honour at the gate were disarmed and saluted with bare hands. The Resident and his men were received by the King and his brother Sikandar Hasmat to welcome them inside the palace in the most befitting and courtly manner. The conversation started with the King, his brother, Ali Naqi Khan, the Residency Vakil, Mushe-ud-Daulla, his deputy, Shahab-ud-Daulla and Finance Minster Raja Balkishen on one side and the Resident with his team on the other. Queen Mother Aulea Begum and the grandmother (widow of Muhammad Ali Shah Ali) were present behind the purdah.[53]

Zurd Kothee was enveloped in an air of uncertainty and doubt. Outram declared an end to the Treaty of 1801, before formally handing over the draft prepared by East India Company to the King. Overwhelmed and beleaguered, Wajid Ali Shah received the treaty and showed his dismay with utmost dignity that was in keeping with his refined culture. In a brief note the last King of Awadh acquiesced:

> *Treaties are necessary between equals only: who am I, now, that the British Government should enter into Treaties with? The kingdom is a creation of the British, who are able to make and to unmake, to promote and to degrade. It has merely to issue its commands to ensure their fulfilment; not the slightest attempt will be made to oppose the views and wishes of the British Government; myself and subjects are its servants.*[54]

Saying thus, Wajid Ali Shah walked over to Outram, removed his Crown and handed it over to him.

♦

Wajid Ali Shah had shown his solidarity with the British Government, but made no mistake to return his Taj, which was bestowed on his grandfather Ghazi–ud-Din Haidar in 1818 by East India Company. His uncovered head signalled the end of a title, rank, honour and, moreover, the last tradition of an oriental culture. Lucknow witnessed the last pride of a tragic king whose limitless extravagance and indolence had led the British to usurp his crown. Aulea Begum had upbraided her son for his obsession with dance, music and women, saying that his profligacy would one day ring in his ruin. The Queen Mother had earlier indicated her desire to replace Wajid Ali with Sikandar Hasmat or even with the heir-apparent to mollify the British Government, and the King's grandmother preferred one of his stepbrothers, Mustaf Ali Khan, on the throne.[55]

Outram had given the king three days to change his mind before he left the palace. At eight in the morning on 7 February, the assigned day, Outram received a letter from the King, wherein he refused to sign the treaty and was unwavering in his decision. Meanwhile, the King also pensioned off his own troops, police and kotwalees to make room for the British government. Wajid Ali Shah also promulgated two proclamations, one for the Talukhdars, Amirs[56] and landlords, and the other for the Army, urging them to uphold peace and to refrain from insurgency. The people ought to pay revenue to the British Government, henceforth. The King turned down the proposal of the Talukhdars to cross sword unitedly with the British. Outram had no difficulty in taking possession of Awadh, nor did he mobilize the British troops to confiscate the throne. Through a public proclamation, Outram declared the State of Awadh as annexed and as a part of British territory from 7 February 1856. Meanwhile, his efforts to persuade the King for his signature continued through his agents and cronies.

A month after gulping his last 'cherry', Dalhousie retired from his service and set sail for England.

Three

The Oudh Commission and the British Empire

Wajid Ali Shah sailed for eighteen days in the incessant summer heat and reached Calcutta on 13 May 1856. By the time he reached his new home, he was almost burnt out. He took time to recuperate before he could embark on his last mission. Wajid Ali was hopeful of getting justice from the Governor-General in Calcutta and was eager to send his representatives to the Council. Asan Hussain Khan, Mir Aulad Ali and even Mr Patteson, a British advocate of the Supreme Court, came forward to plead for him.[1] But, as expected, the Governor's House in Calcutta paid no heed to the ex-king's appeal and refused to admit his case for hearing. With this, Wajid Ali lost his faith and face as well. His hopes of getting justice in Calcutta remained a reverie, and he realized that he had no other option but to appeal directly to the British Crown. He surmised that Her Majesty would not be deceptive like her people in India and would certainly give a patient hearing to his cause. Wajid Ali Shah started preparing for his journey to England.

This was not to be. The hapless King was disarmed by his doctors, as his ill-health would be an impediment to the exhausting sea journey and he would not be able to withstand it. He was suffering from dysentery and scabies.[2] Moreover, it would be embarrassing for him if he had to return from England empty-handed. The ex-king himself was not very confident of getting justice in the British Parliament. He was losing his heart. Who would dare to cross the dreary waste of 'black water'? The Queen Mother 'with some substance of masculine vigour still left as God had given it'[3] stepped forward to lead the mission. Wajid Ali sighed with relief. It was then decided that the 'Oudh Commission' would be led by Moulavi Masih-ud-Deen Khan as his Mukhtar[4] and Envoy Plenipotentiary, accompanied by the ex-king's brother, General Saheb Sikandar Hashmat, and the heir-apparent Mirza Hamid Ali Bahadur, who was then a lad of eighteen.

The Queen Mother, at the age of fifty-two, was the one who took the revolutionary decision to cross the black water. It was not long before her sojourn in Calcutta that the valiant lady had decided to plead before the British Parliament. Elihu Jaan, her hookah-bearer, narrates the unfolding of events when the Queen Mother took a daring and immediate decision to cross the black water when she came to know that her kingdom was slipping under the hands of Outram. Beating her breast in agony the Queen had cried, 'I will go to England. The Queen of England is also a mother. I will ask her to give me back my kingdom.'[5] The assertion was indeed astounding for a noble lady from a traditional Indian ancestry who would otherwise flinch at the idea of even crossing a river.

The Queen Mother or Malka Kishwar was also known as Aulea Begum. She had a rich ancestry. Her father was Nawab Hisam-ud-Din Khan Bahadur of Kalpi. The Queen Mother was a pious Muslim who read the Quran and could fluently speak and write in Arabic and Persian. Malka Kishwar never bothered to snoop into her son's extravagance and ostentatious lifestyle.

Yet she upbraided her son and held him responsible for the dark clouds that loomed over Awadh. An extremely strong lady, the Queen Mother would never shy away from expressing her mind. Once responding to the clouds of uncertainty, she even dared to express her desire to replace Wajid Ali with Sikandar Hasmat on the throne; and it was she who refused to submit to the temptation when an offer of one lakh rupees per annum was made by the British in lieu of her son's signature on the treaty that was heavily tilted in the favour of the British.

Aulea Begum was religious, but her soul was not free from vengeance. Once she had burnt the face of one of her maids on whom her husband had an eye. She was also suspicious of her son's principal wife (Khas Mahal) who had twice attempted to kill her. But before she set sail, the Queen Mother visited Khas Mahal, in a bid to mend ties and melt the ice.

A steamer was chartered to take them from Calcutta to Suez. It was decided that the Mission would take a break in Egypt before sailing off to Southampton to reach London. As the final date of departure was approaching, more and more people driven by their solidarity, came forward to join the envoy. When the day dawned to leave, the banks of Hooghly came alive and were bustling with hundreds of coolies going up and down the gangway as they loaded the ship. The banks of the river were also full of people who had gathered at the dock to bid farewell to the entourage as they set off to an uncertain destiny. The Queen Mother burst into tears as she saw the people wailing and howling as they were worried about the future that lay ahead for the Mission. Wajid Ali was standing in the verandah of the palace to accept the farewell salaam of his brother and son. Finally, the Queen Mother boarded the ship at midnight, not to move 'like thieves in the dark' in the words of Kaya[6], but to ensure that she was not seen by strangers as was the Islamic custom. She carried valuable gifts of gems-studded rings, diamond necklaces and costly apparel for the British Queen. Next day on 19 June 1856, the steamer *S.S. Bengal*[7] weighed anchor at 7 o'clock in the morning and sailed off with one hundred and forty passengers on board. Lord Canning, who had known of the impending voyage crossed his fingers and simply said, 'Let them go.'[8]

The steamer cruised down the River Bhagirathi (Hooghly) into the Bay of Bengal and turned south towards Ceylon. Brandon and his wife Mary Ann joined them too. But Major Bird had left Calcutta long before, assuring the ex-king that he would join the retinue in proper time. He kept his word and joined the royal family as they disembarked at the port of Southampton, although another source states that Bird had sailed with the emissaries from Calcutta itself. The Brandons and Bird, Wajid Ali's English envoys on British soil, virtually piloted the mission and acted as interpreters. The steamer touched the shores of Ceylon and journeyed northward to enter the Red Sea through the Gulf of Aden. The *S.S. Bengal* ended its journey at the Port of Suez[9] and the royal entourage travelled on land in carriages till Cairo. They stayed in Cairo for ten days and boarded the *S.S. Indus*, a steamer of the Peninsular & Oriental Steam Navigation Company of England, and sailed off the Mediterranean.[10]

Wajid Ali Shah, in a letter addressed to Queen Victoria, entrusted Moulavi Masih-ud-Deen as his Mukhtar[11] and Envoy Plenipotentiary to express his complaints, while other members of the Commission had no defined role in the presentation. Moulavi Masih-ud-Deen had been a confidant of Wajid Ali Shah since his heyday in Awadh. Moulavi's ancestors had long served the Oudh Crown, but for three generations had worked for the British as mediators and moderators. Masih-ud-Deen himself had been a British servant for twelve years, until he was accused of being an informer of the King of Awadh and expelled, even though the charges against him could not be proved. Awarded the title of 'Khan Bahadur' for his proficiency, Masih-ud-Deen extensively studied the British laws, which helped him to spearhead the Awadhi movement.[12]

The Oudh Commission reached Southampton from Alexandria at five in the evening on 20 August 1856 after touching Malta and Gibraltar. The Commission was received by a huge crowd with great applause. A gala reception was held and had been pre-announced by Wajid Ali's hired English delegate Mr Bird, who was in London to set forth a political ground. *The Times* vividly illustrated the tremendous curiosity amongst the Britons to get a glimpse of the oriental royalty.

> *The disembarkation of these illustrious individuals has excited the greatest curiosity, and a vast number of people congregated in the docks to witness it. The Queen-Mother was brought on shore in a sedan-chair, closely veiled, and the same seclusion was observed in reference to the landing of her daughters [female attendants].*[13]

The crowd burst into applause as the ex-king's brother and the heir-apparent waved to them from the carriage.

Brandon rented the Royal York Hotel from one Mr White at Southampton at a cost of one hundred pounds for the royal retinue for ten days. The Mayor of the city took all initiatives to ensure that the Queen remained out of public gaze as she was being transferred behind a cordon of white curtains from the ship to the hotel. Bird addressed the gathering in front of the hotel and explained the reason that had induced a fifty-two-year-old lady from Eastern royalty to sail to England. She was here to seek justice and to regain her son's lost throne and kingdom. No matter how plausible was Bird's oration the British crowd was divided in its opinion. The role of the English newspapers towards the colourful but politically challenged mission was quite different and did not reflect the emotions of the British people. Articles tried to impress that the British were driven by curiosity rather than by political conjectures.[14]

The reception hosted by the aristocrats of Southampton was fairly courteous. Three days after the Queen Mother disembarked at Southampton, a delegation of British aristocrats visited the royal emissaries along with Mt Andres, the Mayor of Southampton. Only the respected ladies were allowed to meet the Queen.[15] The dignitaries were received by the Brandons, Major Bird, Sikandar Hashmat and Mirza Hamid Ali Bahadur. The Queen Mother held a durbar with the respected ladies and Mrs Brandon was the interpreter. The Queen modestly apologized before everybody for not being able to speak in English. This was probably the first zenana durbar[16] being held on the British soil.

The time had come for the embassy to leave Southampton for London. A special train was arranged for the entourage. The delegation left Hotel Royal York at 6 o'clock in the evening on 30 August 1856, in twenty hired cabs, while the Queen Mother left in a carriage.[17]

The train reached London on Sunday, 31 August 1856. The excitement that was palpable at Southampton railway station had subsided by the time the delegation reached London. Only a few people could be seen on New Road in front of Harley House, where Brandon had arranged for the Queen to stay. There could be three reasons for it. Firstly, Queen Victoria with her frontline ministers was out of town. Secondly, the government officers or representatives of the East Indian Company found it imprudent to give a formal reception to the emissaries; thirdly, apprehending an unwarranted public clamour against the Indian Government, the British authority had decided to avoid publicity of the ex-king's delegation. The Queen Mother with her thirty female attendants reached the mansion to live a secluded life with all the window blinds constantly drawn down. Harley House, the former residence of Duke of Brunswick on New Road, was rented for one year at a cost of £550. Some of the adjacent houses were also rented to accommodate the rest of her retinue.[18] A letter was sent to the directors of the East Indian Company by one Jalees-ud-Daulah, a musahib[19] of the Queen's entourage, announcing their arrival.[20]

Malka Kishwar had to test her endurance for ten long months before she could pass though the doors of Buckingham Palace. The day when the Dowager Queen of Oudh had her first meeting with Queen Victoria on 4 July 1857, Sir Henry Lawrence, the Chief Commissioner of Oudh, sacrificed his life in the Residency of Lucknow, fighting against the mutineers of the Great Rebellion.

Ever since they arrived in London, the Awadh emissaries tried their best to mobilize campaigns to win over the Company's directors, Members of Parliament, the British Queen and even the common people of Britain. Initially the response was disheartening. The direct appeal of the Queen Mother to the directors and the Board of Control did not cut any ice and was rejected. The Queen Mother adopted an innovative strategy of holding a zenana durbar on every Thursday. The response was better, and the durbar was attended by eminent dignitaries, ladies of rank and even attendants of the British Crown. The publishing of Major Bird's pamphlet *Spoliation of Oudh* in 1857 and his anonymous work *Dacoitee in Excelsis* in the same year spurred a series of propaganda. The endeavour of the Indian emissaries was not totally unsuccessful; rather the Commission was triumphant in creating a public clamour in its favour. The British press, on the other hand, tried to advocate that the Commission's aim was to defame the colonial government in India. Clearly the Commission was seeking to defend the Oudh king's licentious lifestyle, whereas the British found it totally abhorrent.

The Indian Government under the British East India Company was subservient to the controls of the British Parliament. The authority bestowed upon Lord Dalhousie by the Board of Control was not beyond criticism in the House of Commons.[21] The British were known to be honest and trailblazers in dispensing natural justice. The Honourable Members of the House of Lords could not defy the indictment of deceit brought against their Indian counterpart, which had vilified the nation. The validation of the Treaty of 1837 and its applicable clauses in this context became the most burning issues in the debate. The treaty in question was solemnly entered into and executed, but was set aside by Lord Dalhousie, as the agreement was a serious impediment to his policy of annexation. Thus, the endless debate continued without a plausible conclusion. Many columns had been devoted in the English dailies to the inquiry. The Oudh question remained scrupulously neglected and soon went out of mind. Nevertheless, the gracious Queen had five million more subjects and thirteen hundred thousand pounds more revenue than she had before.[22] This fact could not be denied.

Four months after the debate ebbed out, the Oudh

Commission had its presence felt on the British soil, leading to an unanticipated public clamour. But the members of the Houses were seasoned practitioners of public relations. On one hand, they pretended to lend an ear to the public clamour and on the other they unleashed the British press against the Oudh Commission. *The Oude Blue Book 1856*, officially called *Oude: Papers Relating to, Presented to Both Houses of Parliament by Command of Her Majesty, 1856* was the most controversial paper ever published on British policy during the Company's days in India. It was presented to both the Houses of Parliament by command of Her Majesty after the House debate on 10 April 1856. The paper was published by the Board of Directors of the East India Company to describe its viewpoint to the British Parliament. In it were framed a series of charges against the King for his dereliction of duties. The report was nothing but a collective 'fiction of official penmanship'[23] by some prejudiced contributors such as Richmond, Sleeman, Dalhousie, Outram and others.

The memory of the historical debate of the Lords held on 10 April 1856 and the subsequent issue of *The Oude Blue Book* was fading into oblivion. In the midst of all this, a fresh debate in the Court of Proprietors of the East Indian Company held at Leaden Hall on 24 September 1856 kindled the hope of the hapless Indian emissaries. The boisterous oration of the proprietors Messrs Lewin and Jones at Leaden Hall during a Quarterly Court of the Company practically jolted the country into reality that their complacency was unwarranted. Jones argued that:

The King has been charged with being guilty of vices and debauchery; but he [Mr Jones] was told on good authority

> *that few people were more moral than the King of Oude in that respect.*[24]

Although viewed by the British press as 'vulgar and ill-conditioned speeches to lower the East India Company in the eyes of the public', the statements carried enough weight to mould the public opinion against the impiety of the Company. Lewin stated that:

> *In a season of extremity (1815), when the rule of the East India Company was waning, its treasure exhausted, and the Government of India unable to borrow money…opened its coffers with a loan of 2500000…and subsequently in 1825, under similar exigency assisted the East India Company with a further loan of 1500000 and again in 1842…with a further loan to relieve the pressure of the Indian treasure.*[25]

The Oudh Commission engaged Gregory Skirrow & Company, a British law firm to solicit its support in getting copies of relevant papers from the Company that spoke of the charges framed against them. The solicitors had to persuade Parliament to release these papers after their appeal was denied by the Company. The papers truly helped the Commission to refute charges framed against the King to justify the annexation.[26] Possibly, *The Oude Blue Book 1856* came into the hands of Wajid Ali Shah at Metiyaburj during that time. The preface of Wajid Ali Shah's *The Oude Blue Book* testifies that he had to ship his defence arguments from Metiyaburj well after sending off his Commission. Wajid Ali's reply was initially in Persian and later translated into English. This version had seven chapters covering fifty-eight pages. The ex-king spent lakhs of rupees to print three hundred copies of his 'reply' in English and to send them off to England for widespread distribution amongst interested readers and also Her Majesty Queen Victoria, Prince Albert and the British Prime Minister. The public sentiment took a 180-degree turn in favour of the ex-king as soon as the 'reply' reached London, probably on 12 December 1856. In a farman[27] sent alongwith, the ex-king delegated his authority to his brother Mirza Sikandar Hasmat, Moulavi Masih-ud-Deen and Major Bird to represent him in the British durbar.

Oudh emissaries decided to meet the directors of East India Company, who according to the Governor-General of India had ordered the Indian Government to abrogate Oudh. Major Bird and Moulavi Masih-ud-Deen were entrusted to open a dialogue for reconciliation. Incidentally, one day the royal emissaries met General Outram at Sydenham Palace on 11 October 1856. Outram was in London at that time and showed courtesy by visiting the royal family at Harley House, expressing himself as, 'Outram who has taken your kingdom, is present!'[28]

An envoy of royal princes, Moulavi Masih-ud-Deen, and Major Bird were greeted by the Chairman and Directors of the Company as they reached the portico of the India House, the Headquarters of East India Company, on 19 January 1857. Moulavi Masih-ud-Deen gave an eloquent speech in favour of liberation and challenging the annexation. His articulacy mesmerized the audience who could hardly counterpoise his arguments. The Oudh Commission's appeal was diplomatically referred to the Parliament by the Board for final judgment. On 21 January 1857 the directors paid a visit to Harley House and offered a pension of five lakh rupees per annum and an annual Jagheer[29] of ten miles of land surrounding Lucknow to the King of Oudh. The directors had reasons to believe that out of hundreds of misdeeds pointed out by Colonel Sleeman in his report only few were correct and, therefore, the directors came forth with such recompenses. The Moulavi forwarded the offer to the ministers and to the Members of Parliament as evidence to prove the innocence of his Master.

Finally the long wait for Wajid Ali Shah's envoy came to an end when Her Majesty—the Queen of England admitted the Queen Mother to an audience on 4 July 1857. This incident, which was happily picked up by the media, finds mention in Victoria's personal diary. The British Queen graciously received the 'Queen of Oude' in Buckingham Palace and took her inside for a special zenana durbar[30] which was unique in the history of England. The Queen Mother of Oudh was veiled and wore a robe made of gold tissue. She shook hands with Queen Victoria and sat on a similar chair opposite her. She was accompanied by her son and Moulavi Masih-ud-Deen, and the delegates from the British side included Prince Albert, the Prince Consort, Mr Vernon Smith, the President of the Board of Control, and Sir G. Clark who was the interpreter. The British delegation entered from the back and stood at the rear end facing the back of the Dowager Queen of Oudh. Only Queen Victoria's eldest son, the Prince of Wales, was allowed by the Oudh Queen to stand beside his mother. Finally, the Queen of Oudh removed her veil and handed over a letter from Wajid Ali Shah and a handful of ornaments, including pearls and precious stones to Queen Victoria. The British Queen was extremely courteous and addressed Malka Kishwar as the 'Queen of Oude'.[31] Her Majesty's reception was magnanimous and benevolent enough for the dowager queen of a state, which had long been abrogated by Her Majesty's own government.

The dialogue was opened by Malka Kishwar, where she aired her views and regretted the British debauchery to confiscate the

Kingdom of Awadh and oust a royal family, which had been faithful allies for a century. Her son was innocent but fell victim to the Governor-General's greed of engulfing native states on flimsy grounds. The hapless King had adopted reforms that would favour his subjects, and were in keeping with the ideas professed by the government. The King stood by the government in need to bail out financial crisis. Yet he was forced to lose his crown. The argument had strong merits but failed to cut ice. It was inconceivable that the British Crown would recommend the Indian Government to relinquish its claim over Oudh. The durbar was courteously adjourned and postponed till the next day. However, the 'next day' was not destined to come. The unexpected news of Wajid Ali's arrest in Calcutta bewildered the emissaries and soon the Oudh Commission melted into obscurity. Queen Victoria could not warrant an audience to the emissaries of an ex-king who had reportedly instigated his people to revolt against the British Crown. The British were shocked by the mutiny of the sepoys and the arrest of Wajid Ali Shah. They lost their sympathy for the Oudh Commission and started to disbelieve them.

Wajid Ali Shah was taken to Fort William as a state prisoner on 15 June 1857 and the news of his arrest reached the shores of England on 5 July. The moment was significant for his emissaries in London. A loss of confidence was already intensifying amongst the British against their representatives who were ruling India under the East India Company. The spoliation of Oudh by the Company's servants and its effect in the minds of the justice-loving people created a wave of empathy, which was unprecedented. Lord Canning was struggling hard to justify the annexation of Oudh. But luck favoured him. The complete volte-face by the British public in England after the mutiny came as a heaven-sent opportunity for Lord Canning. Their lack of support to the Indian cause was exactly what Canning was hoping for. As it so happened the mutiny was at its peak in April 1857 and Canning got a golden opportunity to accuse Wajid Ali Shah in Calcutta as an accomplice to the great misery caused to the British who were living in India. The all-powerful colonial government did not feel that it had any obligation to prove the ex-king guilty, or even to admit the petition filed by the ex-king for justice. The effect was instantaneous. The Governor-General was able to invalidate the British sentiment that had been in favour of the ex-king of Oudh. He put him behind bars and spread the rumour that Wajid Ali Shah had instigated the sepoys and was therefore responsible for the mutiny against the British Government.

A high-pitched debate broke out in the Houses of Parliament as soon as the news of the British carnage in Indian territory came in. The debate in the House of Commons held on 27 July 1857 was more interesting. Mr Benjamin Disraeli's boisterous oration against the spoliation of Oudh leading to a 'national revolt' is worth mentioning. Although Vernon Smith, President of the Board of Control, responded to Disraeli's three-hour-long oration and tried to justify the annexation by stating that there had been a marked improvement in the lives of the people of Oudh since the annexation, he was not able to convince the audience. On the contrary, the British scheme to imprison Wajid Ali Shah with an ulterior motive became apparent in his explanation. Smith denied that the recent outbreak had any connection with the annexation of Oudh.[32]

The Oudh Commission, as a last resort, submitted an appeal titled *Petition from the Queen and Princes of Oude* to the British Parliament, which was presented before the House of

Lords by Lord Campbell on 6 August 1857. Digressing from the Commission's fundamental claim of reinstating the confiscate kingdom, the royal family of Oudh spent more words to prove themselves (and the King) innocent of the recent mutinous outbreak. The Commission expressed its sincere regret over the recent tumult and once again solemnly assured the fidelity of royal family to the British Crown. The Commission strongly sought justice from the British Parliament for detaining the King without any charge. The Commission requested the Parliament to divulge the charges framed against the hapless King and by whom and on what authority were these charges levied, so that he could get a fair opportunity to refute them.[33]

According to Lord Campbell, the Chancellor of Exchequer, the prayer was justified but Lord Campbell had to excuse himself for submitting the petition before the Lords since the pleas of the royal family of Oudh were rejected on the flimsy ground that the word 'humble' had been omitted throughout. The absurd issue was raised by Lord Redesdale who said that since the petition used the word 'pray' instead of 'humble pray' the Lords could not receive such a petition. The Oudh emissaries had to learn from *Times of London* on Saturday, 8 August 1857 that:

> *The petition from the Queen Dowager and the Princes of Oude, which was presented on Thursday by Lord Campbell to the House of Lords... their Lordships declined to receive on account of an objection having been taken by Lord Redesdale, because it did not style itself 'the humble petition'.*

The petition stood withdrawn and thrown out forever.[34]

Members of the Commission were stumped. They were shocked at the unfolding of events. Hundreds of petitions containing thousands of signatures were submitted before

Her Majesty and the Parliament, pressing for the release of Wajid Ali Shah, but in vain. The British public rebuffed the Oudh's sentiment as the mutiny of 1857 broke out. The Oudh Commission proposed to re-conquer Awadh from the mutineers under the leadership of the heir-apparent with the help of the British soldiers in the name of the Queen of England. The proposal was put down without much thought.[35]

Funds started dwindling since the last support of over four thousand pounds, which the ex-king arranged to send in October 1856, while in prison, was almost exhausted. The appeal for a grant made to the Directors was rejected for obvious reasons. Soon the royal family found itself spiralling towards debt, which further splintered them. The family vacated the Harley's House and a small country home was rented for the Queen. The retinue started to scatter and members rented four small houses on Warwick Road.[36] Finally a sum of seventy-two hundred and fifty-six pounds came from Wajid Ali Shah in January 1858 and the entourage breathed a sigh of relief.[37] Meanwhile, internal conflicts were brewing. Insurgency was breeding amongst the most trusted men. Moulavi Masih-ud-Deen challenged the leadership of Begum Malka Kishwar and wrote to the Directors of the Company to ignore all the communications coming directly from the Queen. The disheartened Begum decided to go back to Calcutta via Paris and on her way she wished to visit Mecca. The British Government, to add further insult, declined to issue a passport, even as the French Government issued it. The British Foreign Office, in a flurry of correspondences, insisted upon the Indian emissaries to apply for passports as British citizens, so that any such acknowledgement on part of the Queen Mother would imply acceptance of British annexation of Oudh. 'Does the Queen Mother of Oudh ask for a passport as a British subject?' was their question.[38]

The Queen went to Paris where she breathed her last on 24 January 1858. In Paris she was critically ill, but did not allow any doctor to see her until death was imminent. The ailing Queen was last attended by Dr Royar, Emperor Napoleon's physician, and a prayer was sung at her deathbed.[39] Mirza Sikandar Hasmat, Mirza Hamid Ali Bahadur and Moulavi Masih-ud-Deen were telegraphed from London and full Mohammedan funeral rites were extended. The funeral took place a few days after the death. It was a grand procession, a scene very unusual in Paris. Eight members of her entourage carried the coffin to the hearse, which was covered with silver tissue and drawn by eight white horses. The hearse was preceded by a carriage carrying the priest and was followed by her son Prince Sikandar Hasmat, accompanied by General d'Orgoni and Captain Lynch. A large procession on foot and a convoy of ten mourning-coaches, carrying ministers of the French Empire, Turkish Ambassador Haidar Pasha, Iranian Ambassador Farukh Khan and other men notable in science and literature. A huge crowd assembled in the Rue Lafitte to witness the procession as it reached the Persian cemetery of Père la Chaise where the body was interred.[40] A monument was erected over the tomb, inscribing:

> *In memory of Malka Kishwar, Queen of the Kingdom of Oude, died at Rue Lafitte, aged fifty-three years.*[41]

A month later, Prince Mirza Sikandar Hasmat, Wajid Ali's brother, died in Paddington, London, on 25 February. His body was taken to Paris and laid beside his mother.

While the funeral was underway in Paris, the heir-apparent Mirza Hamid Ali Bahadur was busy fighting a legal skirmish against Moulavi Masih-ud-Deen to provide leadership to the

Oudh Commission, so that he could take control over the remaining fund. The Moulavi was eventually compelled by the British Court to refund four thousand pounds to the young Prince despite solicitation of a famous advocate Mr T. J. Angell. Following a futile petition before the British Parliament, the Prince left London and returned to Calcutta on 29 September 1859, via Marseilles and Alexandria.[42] Mirza Hamid Ali Bahadur settled in Metiyaburj and died during his father's lifetime.[43] When Moulavi Masih-ud-Deen was dismissed by Wajid Ali Shah from his mission in 1859, he settled in Britain and married an English woman by the name of Miss Bilk. After his futile endeavour to get employment or a pension from the British Government, Moulavi left his wife and returned to India in 1863.[44] John Rose Brandon and his wife sailed off to New Zealand in 1858 and spent the rest of their lives there. Major Bird stayed back in England. Bahran Nissa and her husband left Paris for Mecca after the Queen's death and came back to Lucknow.[45] Some members of the mission decided to settle in Britain and did not return.

The Oudh Mission ended with Wajid Ali Shah still remaining the most misunderstood man. It turned out that Wajid Ali Shah's faith in the British people was futile. A sudden twist of fate had changed his life and he was taken away from the throne of Awadh to a different destiny in Calcutta, forever.

Four

The First War of Independence

While the Oudh Commission was striving hard to craft a public clamour on British soil against political deception and British snobbery, signs of a mutiny were brewing in India. The seed was already sown by the discontented sepoys from Awadh. These sepoys comprised an overwhelming number in the Bengal Army and their ire was threatening to mount a colossal furore against the British masters in a cantonment that was not more than twenty miles from Wajid Ali's riverside abode in Calcutta. Mangal Pandey, a sepoy of the 34th Bengal Native Infantry of Barrackpore, raised his musket against his superiors Lieutenant B. H. Baugh and Sergeant-Major Hewson and started an open mutiny single-handedly on 29 March 1857. Pandey's rebellion was devoid of any personal interest. His crusade was indicative of a serious remonstration to protect Hinduism and Islam against the British wiliness of converting people to Christianity.

Pandey's execution in open view of assembled troops on the parade ground of Barrackpore created an intense agitation among the sepoys who were stationed at Lucknow during the annexation and had witnessed British deceit as an affront to their honour.

The insurgency began, with the sepoys urging Bahadur Shah

Zafar, whose power was then restricted to the Red Fort and surrounding areas of Delhi, to lead their movement. After much hesitation, Bahadur Shah, at the age of eighty-two, consented to their proposal and was proclaimed the Emperor of India on 13 May 1857.

The grounds for a mutiny had already been paved in Lucknow and conflicts of interest were intensifying after the confiscation of Oudh. The British were showing their true colours. The Talukdars[1] had lost their lustre and their authority as well. Immediately after the annexation, the British started posting European officers, both civil and military, throughout the territory of Awadh and the process of levelling began. Even as the Talukdars took to their guns, it was done with diffidence, as they were not warriors as such. They belonged to the sophisticated elite class and despite the threat some of them could not give up their indolent lifestyle.

The persistent vandalism was not unknown to Wajid Ali Shah and his mind was never peaceful. While at Garden Reach in Calcutta, the ex-king came to know how his ancestral properties and edifices had been razed to the ground, his animals had been auctioned, armoury had been looted, his godowns had been broken into and the grand collection of English books in his library had been vandalized. Coverley Jackson who had replaced General Outram as the Chief Commission on 8 May 1856, unabashedly used the office of the City Magistrate Major Carnegie in the state-sponsored loot. Carnegie issued an order to stop all payments to the ex-king's family from the royal fund, which had been left by Wajid Ali before he went to Calcutta so as to meet necessary expenses of his family. But the most immoral act, which forced the ex-king to send a written complaint to the Governor-General in Calcutta on 14 September 1856, was a notice to the women residing at Chutter Manzil to vacate the building without making an alternate arrangement for them to stay.[2]

The British turned a deaf ear to the ex-king of Awadh. Major Carnegie evicted the women from Chutter Manzil and threw out their belongings. The magnificent building of Furrah Buksh Palace had been turned into a kennel and a stable. The ancestral jewels and ornaments of the Queen Mother were excavated from the hidden tank and looted. An insulted Wajid Ali Shah protested once again to the Governor-General, but all was in vain.[3]

The Talukdars of Awadh were apprehensive of losing power after the annexation and soon their fears rang true. The British ordered complete disarming and demolition of the Talukdars' forts scattered all over the countryside of Awadh. The Talukdars were all-powerful in the state of Awadh and possessed more than two-thirds of land in the countryside. Some of them even owned paid foot soldiers and cavalry, varying in strength from two to three hundred to nearly twelve hundred. They had the power of a collector and that of a magistrate to hold darbars[4] and issue orders, so long as they accepted the lordship of the Badshah.[5] The Talukdari system was virtually put to an end by the British with the implementation of 'Summary Settlement' to alleviate the peasants from the coils of extortion and to settle land with the actual owners of soil. However, there was something deeply flawed in the revenue assessment system and eventually the peasants were burdened with obnoxious taxes levied on stamps, petitions, food, houses, eatables, ferries and opium.[6] With the abrogation of the Talukdari system, soldiers and courtiers of the Talukdars turned jobless and soon became political rivals of the British command.[7] The peasants sided with their old masters to create a joint tumult against the British.

The oppressed foot soldiers of the feudal heads were now ready for a clinching revolt against the tyrannies of colonial power.

The people of Awadh were restless. The confiscation of the kingdom and subsequent deposition of Wajid Ali Shah to Calcutta had far reaching military consequences since Awadh was a major area from where most of the sepoys of the Bengal army were recruited. The sepoys of the recently disbanded 34th Native Infantry after the Barrackpore incident returned home to Awadh, discontented and frustrated; however, they got a now rousing welcome from villagers who now revered them as martyrs. The notion of greased cartridges had been planted by the high-cast sepoys to their brethren. The rebellious Talukdars, the hapless peasants and the disbanded sepoys (also known as 'peasants in uniform') came together and united on the eve of a great rebellion against the colonial power. The first rebellion was noted on 30 May 1857 when the sepoys of 13th, 48th and 71st Native Infantries and 7th Light Infantry, stationed at Lucknow, defied the government. However, the rebellions were suppressed by Sir Henry Lawrence who replaced Coverley Jackson as Chief Commissioner on 20 March 1857.[8]

On 4 June 1857, a rebellion was recorded at Sitapur, followed by another at Faizabad, and then in succession at Daryabad, Sultanpore and Salon. On 30 June, Lawrence came to know that a large group of rebels had assembled in the north of Lucknow. The rebels were openly inviting the authority to large-scale open warfare. The Chief Commissioner himself took part with the British 32nd Regiment on Foot, along with some loyal soldiers of 13th Native Infantry and a group of Sikh and European cavalries, and confronted a well-organized force of mutineers during the hottest days of summer.[9] The battle took place at Chinhat and the insurgents outnumbered the British army by a ratio of six thousand to six hundred. Lawrence had to face an unexpected defeat.

The British administration virtually collapsed in the periphery of Awadh, and the usurpers pushed the colonial authority to the limits of Lucknow. The Battle of Chinhat further curbed the British to stay within the Residency's compound. The British troops, civilians and all other Europeans residing in Lucknow swarmed inside the Residency for shelter as administration of the state slipped out of its hand. The historic siege of Lucknow thus began on 1 July 1857, confining three thousand Europeans inside the Residency. In course of time, the rebels received large-scale reinforcements from the Talukdars.[10] The Talukdari settlement engineered by the British had backlashed, driving another nail in the coffin of the British Raj. Coverley Jackson's hasty approach to abrogate the rights of the Talukdars splintered them further. The British tried their best to diffuse the muddle by bringing in Henry Lawrence as Chief Commissioner. Lawrence was perceived to be somewhat more sympathetic to the landed gentry. However, it was already too late and within a few months the revolt broke out.

A state of complete pell-mell engulfed the city of Lucknow. The insurgents sanctified violence and vandalism in the name of freedom. The rebels, who were without a leader, took to looting and plundering on a large scale, not even sparing the native elite. The rebel forces plundered singers and the musicians too. Shops were ransacked in the Chowk. Thousands of English books, which were looted from the library of General Martin College and Royal Library, were burnt to ashes or thrown into the ponds.[11] There was complete anarchy, the law and order machinery had collapsed and such lawlessness had never been witnessed before. The military command of the insurgents was in the hands of Raja Jai Singh, the Názim[12] of Azamgarh, who first realized that the ecstasy would soon evaporate unless the Indian revolutionists could find a regal idol in front of them.[13] The revolt was taking a wrong turn. The throne was vacant. Mirza Hamid Ali Bahadur was still in London along with the Queen Mother. The Raja proposed Birjis Qadr, the eleven-year-old son of Hazrat Mahal, to be declared as the Nawab of Awadh. Consent was sought from the begums of Wajid Ali Shah in Lucknow and from the Talukdars. Coronation of Birjis Qadr as the Nawab of Awadh was approved by Bahadur Shah Zafar, granting him the rights to rule over the province on behalf of the Mughal Emperor. The Nawab was crowned with a gun salute on 5 July 1857, the day when the news of Wajid Ali Shah's arrest reached the English shores and drove the final nail in the coffin of Oudh Commission.

Hazrat Mahal who was hitherto trying to consolidate her son's position as his father's rightful heir, was not prepared initially to let her son hold the flag of mutiny and be remembered as a martyr. Mohammadi Begum, being a courtesan in her first life, entered the harem of Wajid Ali Shah as a begum and was bestowed the title of Hazrat Mahal after the birth of Birjis Qadr in 1845.[14] The spirited lady took charge of all affairs in Lucknow after Wajid Ali Shah had chosen to settle in Calcutta, despite her separation from the Nawab. Her fortunes were revived when her minor son ascended the throne as the undisputed Nawab of Awadh. Birjis Qadr declared himself to be an independent ruler after his coronation and coins were also struck in his name. But the Begum was the real power behind the throne, holding the strings of control most effectively. During her ten-month-long rule as regent, Hazrat Mahal had held regular durbars even in times of turmoil. Hazrat Mahal's innate quality of leadership helped her to lead the kingdom from the very first day, even before she emerged as regent for her minor son. She regularly presided over the council of war and personally directed the army, mounted on a war elephant. This wife of Wajid Ali Shah's is remembered as an immensely brave character in the Indian history of freedom struggle as she fought one of the most significant colonial wars of nineteenth century and did not surrender to the British masters till her last breath.

The seizure of Lucknow took its first toll on 4 July 1857, when Sir Henry Lawrence succumbed to a grievous injury caused by a fragment from an artillery shell. The shelling on the Residency and placing of snipers by the sepoys under Begum's leadership further alienated many innocent European civilians locked inside the 37-acre compound of Lucknow Residency. The combatant force within the Residency could not be more than seventeen hundred, while the rest were civilians. The baton of command was passed on to Colonel Sir John Inglis after Lawrence. Inglis continued the struggle to keep the rebels at bay, while Major Banks succeeded as the Chief Commissioner.[15] Major Banks was killed when a lethal shot pierced his skull on 21 July and was succeeded by James Outram once again, as the Chief Commissioner of Awadh. Outram was summoned from England after he returned from the Anglo-Persian War. Although the rebels outnumbered the British combatants, it was the lack of a unified and concerted attack, which prevented them to flank the last post of Residency. It was not until 23 September 1857 that the rebellion first heard the cracking of gunfire on the other side of Lucknow, and two days later the first rescue operation led by Sir Henry Havelock as chief commander and Sir James Outram broke all barriers and entered the Residency by nightfall.[16]

60 • *Pearl by the River*

The British force encountered a tough battle in Alambagh on 23 September 1857.[17] The casualty was heavy and the colonial force lost one hundred and ninety-six lives, while five hundred and thirty-five soldiers out of two thousand men left the field wounded on that eventful day.[18]

Although Havelock and Outram fought their way through to the Residency, it was impossible for them to release the detained civilians; instead, they themselves got trapped and remained besieged in the Residency. The first relief of Lucknow virtually failed at the cost of several lives, the only consolation being that the British troops occupied some of the adjacent palaces like Chuttur Manzil and Farhat Bakh and freed Alambagh from the clutches of the mutineers.[19] Wajid Ali Shah, lying in his murky cell of Fort William, must have got some solace from the news that Outram was besieged inside the Residency by his own people. Supply lines were cut off and the air inside was laden with the agony of wounded defenders. The catastrophe was equally appalling on the other side as more than five thousand rebels had been either killed or wounded in encounters.[20]

The peril went on till November 1857 when a second relief was attempted by the British with Lieutenant General Sir Colin Campbell at its helm. Outram firmly believed that re-establishment of the British rule would remain a reverie till the capital of Awadh remained in the hands of rebels.[21] Symbolically, Lucknow emerged as the only seat occupied by the rebels after the relief of Delhi and imprisonment of Bahadur Shah Zafar by William Hodson on 22 September 1857. As the siege of Delhi was cleared off, the rebels swarmed into Lucknow in response to the appeal of Hazrat Mahal in the name of Khuda.[22] The rebellion force swelled to more than fifty thousand[23] but still lacked a unified leadership to direct their activities. On the other hand, Campbell was left with five thousand soldiers at best.[24] The troops marched forward and triumphed over the rebels at Dilkhusha Park. Then they crossed the canal near river Gomti on 16 November and reached an enclosure called Secundrabagh,[25] which was surrounded by strong masonry walls. A tough battle was fought to capture Secundrabagh.

Shah Nafaj, a massive mosque on the road to Residency, came under British control by nightfall on 16 November.[26] Meanwhile within the Residency, Havelock and Outram, encouraged by the success of Campbell's army, secured their position at Chutter Manzil, which was already under their control and broke open a wall to establish a link with the British relieving force.

Campbell's last resistance was at Moti Mahal. The British troops stormed into Moti Mahal on the morning of 17 November 1857 and captured some adjacent houses and brought them under British control. After repeated efforts, the defenders led by Havelock and Outram and the relievers led by Campbell finally united their forces. The British triumph over Lucknow and the liberation of the besieged Residency was a watershed moment in India's history of freedom struggle, which re-established the British rule once again in India. The second relief of Lucknow produced 24 Victoria Cross winners on 16 November 1857, the largest number won in a single day.

The British strength was further reinforced on 11 March 1858 when the Nepali Gurkha Contingent under the leadership of Jung Bahadur joined the force.[27] Lucknow remained predominantly under the natives' control, till a brushing operation was conducted by Campbell in March 1858. A tough fight took place at Begum Kothi on 11 March 1858 and eight hundred dead bodies of the natives were counted inside the Kothi.[28]

Finally, on 21 March 1858 the British force won the epic battle under Sir Colin Campbell and released Lucknow from the clutches of the rebels.

The leaders of the Sepoy Mutiny did not have absolute control over the sepoys and this was the main reason for the failure of the uprising. There was a dearth of autonomy in the execution of orders. The bravery shown by Hazrat Mahal soon evaporated in the shoddy annals of Indian history of freedom struggle. The native vigour was colossal but not wily enough to conquer the superior military power of the Britons. They had the will but lacked the adroitness of the colonials. Lucknow was freed from the rebels, but it did not mean that Awadh was back in control. The rebels were expelled from Lucknow, but they hung around in the periphery, waiting for an opportunity. The fall of their strongest foothold, which was in Lucknow, had thrown the rebels into uncertainty and they now lacked the confidence to launch a frontal strike.

With the fall of Lucknow, Hazrat Mahal and her minor son Birjis Qadr were forced out of the capital. Nawab Sharf-ud-Daulla cautioned the Begum about Campbell's force knocking on the doors of Kaiserbagh.[29] Time had come for the Begum to leave. On the evening of 15 March 1858, the Begum and her son left Chaulakhi Kothi[30] of Kaiserbagh and shifted their base to the fort of Baundi (in district Bahraich). It was in this palace built by her husband that the Begum endured her life's biggest challenge, which she fought almost single-handedly from May 1857 to March 1858. As soon as the Begum deserted Kaiserbagh, the British soldiers ran amok and rampantly plundered the palace, only leaving behind such items as marble statues, furniture, massive jade bowels, which the soldiers found difficult to move. Hazrat Mahal, anticipating the British vandalism, took along with her as much of the royal jewels and ornaments as she could. Nevertheless, it was not the loot which damaged the palace as much as the Britishers' vicious attempt to demolish Wajid Ali's dream abode. It would have been an excruciating experience for Wajid Ali Shah to witness the crumbling of his favorite palace in front of his own eyes. Perhaps, he was lamenting the loot of Lucknow and his favourite palace from a forgotten corner of Fort William.

The death sentence was written on the day when the Secretary to the Governor of India said, 'As to buildings in Lucknow, the only one that I think it might be well to level to the ground is the Kaiserbagh as that is the palace where our chief enemies have resided during the rebellion.'[31] Hazrat Mahal's Chaulakhi Kothi was amongst the ill-fated structures, which were razed to the ground.

The ember was still alive in her heart and the Begum actively fostered her aspiration to strike back from her exile. She bought heavy guns, gathered together armed men and had fifteen to sixteen thousand followers at Baundi.[32] The Begum began to operate in the trans-Gogra region supported by the rajas of Gonda and Churda. She was joined by Nana Sahib and his brother Bala Rao, who had left Kanpur and joined the struggle in Awadh.[33] Although the British took control over central and southern parts of her kingdom, the northern part of Awadh remained hostile till the end of 1858. The period witnessed a series of sporadic outbreaks by the sepoys of Talukdars and other feudal lords, all united under Hazrat Mahal. Under her banner, famous revolutionaries of 1857 such as Nana Rao, Bala Rao, Moulvi Ahmadullah and Beni Madho fought the British. The turbulence went unchallenged till the scorching heat of summer finally slackened.[34]

Steadily, the British force intensified in the northern territory of Awadh, bursting into action under Lord Clyde in the middle of October 1858, to mop up the last rebel of the state. The Talukdari bastions dwindled as the British crackdown was hard to challenge. More number of feudal lords surrendered before the British supremacy. But Hazrat Mahal was determined not to surrender to the British and left the fort of Baundi in December 1858 with some of her faithful followers and took refuge in the jungles of Himalayan foothills.

Queen Victoria's proclamation issued on 1 November 1858 marks a watershed moment in the annals of Indian history, representing the momentous end of East India Company's dominion on Indian soil. This resulted in complete transfer of power from East India Company to the British Government. For more than a century, India had been under the administration of the British East India Company. The Indian subcontinent was fractured by the activities of competing local rulers, some of whom allied themselves with the British colonizers for their own gain and to preserve their own power. Deceit and dishonesty, along with efforts to blindly Westernize eventually undermined the authority of the British East India Company, leading to the armed revolt of 1857. As the turbulence settled, British Parliament passed the Government of India Act 1858 (formally called An Act for the Better Government of India), which transferred authority of India to the Crown.

After the British restored their hegemony in late 1858, Nepal became the destination for fleeing rebels so as to avoid arrest. By the end of 1858, Hazrat Mahal had lost most of her supporters and was forced to seek refuge in Nepal. Jung Bahadur, the Maharaja, had been a confidant of the British in the Great Uprising of 1857 and had provided the British army with fifteen thousand troops to fight the second battle of Lucknow. Jung Bahadur returned to Nepal from Lucknow in March 1858 but continued to aid the British in moping up the rebels who sought refuge in Nepalese Terai. The British recognized Jung Bahadur's authority after he staged a coup against the king of Nepal, declaring himself de facto ruler of Nepal. The Maharaja had to be subservient to the British Crown. Being a trustworthy ally of the British Government and knowing well the consequences that might result from it, Jung Bahadur took calculated risks of housing Hazrat Mahal, Birjis Qadr, Nana Sahib and his brother Bala Rao as political émigrés in Nepal from time to time.[35] Moreover, the British troops forced the rebels out of Indian territory and did not want them to come back. Permanent asylum was bestowed on Hazrat Mahal and Birjis Qadr on 17 April 1860, in lieu of a written undertaking that they would neither get involved in intrigues nor would they engage any servant without the permission of the Maharaja.[36] The Begum's own troops were driven out from Nepal in order to clip her wings.

Initially, the Nepalese Government was most reluctant to provide shelter to the Begum and coerced her to enter into a treaty and call off her armed race. In a stern letter, Jung Bahadur advised her either to accept British command or to prepare to fight the Gurkha troops. Thus, he wrote on 15 January 1859:

I inform you that if you should remain within my territory the Gurkha troops will most certainly...attack...you. Be it also known that the Nepalese State will neither assist, show mercy to, nor permit to remain in its territories...[37]

Implicit in the advisory was a veiled threat to acknowledge the British sovereignty or to face trouble. The Begum remained indifferent and refused to submit before the British supremacy. Jung Bahadur had to change his words and give asylum to the Begum under stringent terms. Nevertheless, it was not possible for him to expel the rebels who had swarmed the border in large numbers.[38] The British could not exorcise the ghost of 1857 from their minds and wanted to return the Begum's lost dignity in lieu of her unconditional acquiescence:

> *The Begum Hazrat Mahal will receive all the consideration which is due to her as a woman and member of a royal house. But political power she shall never have and she will do wisely to secure by prompt submission a generous treatment and an honourable position for rest of her life.*[39]

Unlike her ex-husband, the Begum lived in exile but refused to compromise with the British. Even after the mutiny quelled, the Begum tried to sway Jung Bahadur and to rouse people into rebelling against the British command. While leaving Lucknow the Begum brought with her her immense wealth, which she spent entirely to sustain her ten thousand adherents. In Nepal, she lived the life of a commoner for twenty-one years till her death in obscurity in April 1879. There was not even sufficient money to build a modest mausoleum on her grave. She was stubborn enough to not accept the royal pension of twelve lakh rupees.[40] This fact was stated by Sir H.W. Russell[41] in his applausive words,

> *She declined to tactically renounce the rights of her son by accepting a British pension. She was a better man than her husband and lord.*[42] *However, Jung Bahadur conferred on her a meagre pension of five hundred rupees per month.*[43]

There was a time when war had thrown the British out of gear and Outram had tried to reconcile with the Begum, offering to restore her vast territories, only to buy peace.[44] Wajid Ali Shah would have never dreamt of such a warm response from the usurpers of power. Surely he was proud to hear from one of his wives, Sayada Begum who wrote to him from Lucknow:

> *Hazrat Mahal showed such courage that the enemy was terrified. She has brought name to the Sultan Alam,*[45]

or when Begum Sarfras wrote to Akhtar Mahal in Calcutta,

> *I did not know Hazrat was such a brave lady. Seated on an elephant she led her troops against the English without any fear.*[46]

In exile, Hazrat Mahal heard the news that her most trusted General Raja Jai Lal Singh and Babu Ram Bakhsh had been tried and hanged. Her confidants Loni Singh and Digvijai Singh were transported to penal settlements in Andaman.[47] Her people either died fighting or were executed by the British. Mammu Khan, her pre-marital paramour and chief adviser after her assumption of power, surrendered to the British and was eventually hanged as well.[48] Just before her death in 1877, Hazrat Mahal had wished to go to Metiyaburj to her ex-husband but was debarred by the British Government from doing so.[49]

Nevertheless, till her last breath Hazrat Mahal strived to keep the torch of liberty burning.

Five

Wajid Ali's Gloomy Days in Fort William

The bullet, which popped out of Mangal Panday's musket, grazed the English duty officer and slammed into the minds of Indians to kindle discontent in the northern realms. The ember soon swelled into an inferno, burning through the British smugness across Delhi, Mathura, Faizabad and Lucknow. The heat was felt by the European aristocrats in Calcutta. It jolted them from their peaceful slumber. Hitherto the capital city of Calcutta had been a safe abode for the whites. The ghost of mutiny was exorcised by the government with the public execution of Mangal Pandey and the subsequent disbandment of the 34th Native Infantry at Barrackpore.

George Bruce Malleson, the distinguished British commentator, was in Calcutta when Calcuttans first tasted the sting of the poignant tumult in 1857. Fourteen June was a Sunday and Malleson, like all other Europeans, had just returned home from the church at Fort William. The morning had been clear and bright. It was four in the afternoon when the sounds of trampling horses and rolling of carriages roused Malleson. He could not believe the sight in front of his eyes.

Panic-stricken Europeans, in a bid to escape an unknown massacre, fled to seek shelter inside Fort William; others rushed to the docks on the eastern bank of the Hooghly to board the ships before they sailed out. This was certainly neither expected nor anticipated by the English masters. Malleson found that many of his neighbouring houses in Chowringhee had been abandoned and the high officials had sent their families on board the ship. In the suburbs, most of the houses belonging to the Christians were deserted. Horses, carriages, palanquins and vehicles of every sort were used to transfer the fugitives. Malleson feared an upsurge of potentially catastrophic dimensions in his eyewitness account published in *Red Pamphlet*.[1]

There was more than a grain of truth behind the alarm bells that rang on 'Panic Sunday'. General Hearsay smelt the whiff of an insurgency brewing in Barrackpore cantonment and taking no chance to precipitate trouble, the General summoned the 78th Highlanders from Chinsura, who reached Barrackpore at daybreak on the eventful day. The 78th Highlanders were marched along with the native regiment with full arms. The native sepoys were asked to ground their arms, which they did without any resistance. But the wildest rumour which spread was that the native sepoys of Barrackpore regiment had revolted. That the sepoys had killed all the Europeans in Barrackpore and Dumdum, and were marching forward to Calcutta. The fever reached a crescendo until it was confirmed that the native troops were disarmed in Barrackpore, Dumdum and in Fort William, and the state of affairs was under full control.[2] The night was still a nightmare and many Europeans posted sentries as safe guards, or slept on the sofas with their pistols loaded besides them. Major General Sir Williams Cavenagh of Fort William best describes the night of 'Panic Sunday', 'I never saw Calcutta so quiet; now and then a figure clothed in white flitted past me, and I met a patrol of volunteers, otherwise it was like a city of the dead.'[3] The government had enrolled corps of volunteers on horseback and on foot to patrol the streets and mounted guards at different points at night.

The fight against an invisible enemy went on for a long time. Rumours flew thick and fast as the native servants filled the ears of their European masters. They were very scared of the final outcome.[4] Canning, of late, had realized that the British capital of India was no longer a safe haven for the Europeans. Home Secretary Cecil Beadon's words of assurance on 25 May that 'everything is quiet within six hundred miles of the capital'[5] were exaggerated and had misled the government. News of armed mutinies and massacres in Lucknow, Azamgarh, Benaras and Allahabad filled the air of Calcutta, and added to the worry regarding the city's fragile safety infrastructure. Canning paid no heed to Beadon's assurance; rather he was desperate to summon a European regiment to Calcutta in early June and put together a cadre of voluntary corps from the willing citizens of Calcutta. Beadon's misplaced confidence was once again rebutted by Mr J.P. Grant, a member of the Supreme Council, through his apprehensions expressed on 10 June. He was categorical in his warning, 'In reality as well as in appearance we are weak here [Calcutta].'[6]

Apart from the Native Infantries, Grant's other worry was that he had no idea about the number of armed men at Garden Reach under the deposed king of Awadh. Rumours were spreading like wild fire that the ex-king's men had gained unlimited right to plunder the supposedly protected suburb and had turned the Europeans into pitiable inhabitants. The tone of the native press was disdainful and the mood changed against the British Government after the Meerut outbreak. These adversities culminated in incessant anxiety and formed the base of flimsy charges against the ex-king.

Grant's scornful portrayal of the ex-king of Awadh as a potential threat to the peace and tranquility of Calcutta irritated the Governor-General more than the incessant danger of the Barrackpore Native Infantry. The decision to confine the ex-king was taken on 14 June 1857. Instead of delving into the morality of the situation, Canning planned upon two basic results. Firstly, if Wajid Ali was detained then his followers would simply disperse as they did not have a leader in sight and in this way a mutiny could be averted. Secondly, the colossal public furore against the British debauchery in India and the wave of sympathy in favour of the deposed king aroused in London by the Oudh Commission could be quashed. Rather it would appear to the British Parliament as a safeguard adopted in public interest by the Indian Government to thwart the usurpers of power from an undesired but preventable siege of Calcutta. While planning was underway, an incident took place on the night of 13 June, the day before 'Panic Sunday', which gave enough reason to Canning to enforce the plan. On 13 June 1857, a young Muslim boy called Abdul Subhan was caught spying inside Fort William. He divulged his identity as an agent from Garden Reach who had been assigned the task of unravelling the relationship that existed between the Europeans and the native troops in the garrison stationed at Fort William. He was to find out if the native troops would side with the assailants in the event of an attack. On interrogation he confessed that Bahadur Shah Zafar, the titular Emperor of India, in connivance with Wajid Ali Shah was preparing to oust the British from Calcutta.[7] It was revealed from his deposition that apart from the sepoys of Calcutta and Barrackpore garrisons, four hundred of the ex-king's dependents were preparing for an upheaval in Calcutta.[8]

On 15 June 1857, Lord Canning sent Mr G. F. Edmondstone, Secretary to the Government of India, with an arrest warrant to take Wajid Ali Shah and four of his close confidants into custody. A team of five hundred men of the 53rd Regiment[9] under Colonel Powell, some artillery, bodyguard line of the Governor-General, along with Commander Foulerton's naval force boarded the Semiramis and reached Garden Reach early in the morning.

Initially shocked and eventually dismayed, Wajid Ali Shah realized that destiny was prodding him to face the second challenge of his life. Canning was extremely modest in his words yet implicit in his brief letter was a disguised threat to the deposed king.

The operation was so smooth and sudden that the ex-king's followers had no other option but to accept their own humble circumstances as an episode linked to their kismet.[10] The King was taken by utter surprise and all his efforts to plead innocence fell on deaf ears. His house and grounds were searched and about six hundred men and a thousand stands of arms were discovered and seized.[11]

Wajid Ali Shah was arrested on the charge of conspiracy against the British Government and instigating insurgency amongst his armed followers. He was accompanied by Mujahidaullah and Diwanat-ud-Daullah[12] in a carriage, which drove in through the Coolie Bazaar Gate of Fort William.[13] The ex-king of Awadh behaved in the most dignified manner customary to him. While he protested the English iniquity, he surrendered to go wherever the Governor-General might think as right. As soon as Wajid Ali's carriage disappeared from the horizon of Garden Reach—the seed of rebellion in Calcutta, had there been any, faded into obscurity. The convoy reached Fort

William at 8 o'clock in the morning, the onset of a beleaguering episode in the life of the banished king. The edifying narration of Sir Orfeur Cavanaugh, the Town Major in Fort William, embodies the aftermath of the ex-king's arrest. Cavanaugh, who was present at the confidential late night meeting with Lord Canning where the bold decision of Wajid Ali's arrest was taken, was given the charge to accommodate the ex-king in Fort William. At four in the morning, Cavanaugh rode to Fort William and directed the garrison surgeon to vacate his quarters at Coolie Bazaar Gate to house the arrestee and his party. There was bad news waiting for Cavanaugh—the spy from Garden Reach had somehow managed to escape from the cell where he was confined.

Edmonstone and his troops returned to Fort William at 8 o'clock in the morning but the ex-king was detained until 2 o'clock in the afternoon before he was finally allowed to settle in his room. Cavanaugh's personal account indicates that the panic caused by the mutiny in Calcutta did not lessen with the detention of Wajid Ali Shah. On the contrary, the shadow of a mutiny was looming large to besiege the fort and set the detained King free from custody. It was again a sleepless night for Cavanaugh as he could smell the threat. The sheer presence of the banished King in the Fort could herald a mass movement against the British power. The security of the British bastion was called into question due to the escape of the spy. It would not be a difficult task for the ex-king's secret agents to set fire to the arsenal and to blow up the magazines. On the same night, the duty officers at Water Gate of the fort got suspicious and seized a carriage that had been waiting during odd hours with two natives. On scrutinizing some papers, which the sentries had found in the carriage, Cavanaugh had reason to believe that the natives were agents of the ex-king of Awadh and were engaged to pass information about the British troops. Nothing apparent could be proved against the two men and they were eventually set free. Cavanaugh obtained permission from Lord Canning to inflict corporeal punishment, on any unknown person seen loitering inside the fort. No sooner had this happened that two natives were detained for strolling inside the compound and spying into the proceedings of the ordinance officials.

Cavanaugh was compelled to call for capital punishment, as the detainees were hell bent not to answer any questions. The execution was meant to serve as an example and to prevent trespassing by unwarranted people. The whole month of July 1857 was anxiety-ridden, with disturbing news coming from Lucknow where the siege of Residency had begun. Apprehensions were rife of a similar revolt to precipitate on the occasion of Eid and Muharram. There was an increased rush to the gun-makers and more ammunitions were being sold in Calcutta than ever before. Stringent regulations were imposed to curb the sale of firearms to the natives as some of them were suspected to have hoarded firearms and ammunitions to utmost capacity.[14] On 24 July 1857, the arrest of some Mohammedan conspirators worsened the situation, with heads of the Mohammedan community alarmed at the situation. More and more troops set sail from England to replace the native infantries from the garrison. The British Government found it difficult to accommodate the newer military entrants in Calcutta and most of the public buildings such as Town Hall, Suddur Court, Free School, Mohammedan College, Ordinance and Commissariat Store Houses were converted into temporary barracks.[15] Thus, panic took root in Calcutta with the apprehension that an upheaval of catastrophic dimension similar to Lucknow would take place here too.

As Wajid Ali Shah strolled the corridors of Fort William to his cell, the memory of an unfortunate incident dismayed his heart. The air was heavy with the distressing sighs of his predecessor Wazir Ali Khan who took his last breath in a murky cell of Fort William. Wazir Ali had ascended the throne in 1797 as Asaf-ud-Daulla's son and heir. Questions were raised by the British scandalmongers in connivance with his uncle Saadat Ali, challenging the legitimacy of Nawab—Wazir's birth. But the cause of his ill fate lay elsewhere. Wazir Ali Khan defied Governor-General Sir John Shore's stringent policies and fell victim to the British fury. To add fuel to the fire, Bahu Begum, the widow of Suja-ud-Daulla and her cohorts-nobles of the royal court signed a letter addressed to the Governor-General to confiscate the throne of Wazir Ali Khan. Finally in 1798, four months after his accession, Wazir Ali Khan was deposed and exiled to Benaras, while his brother Saadat Ali Khan was raised to the masnad.[16] Wazir Ali was also granted a liberal pension by the British authority.

Wajid Ali Shah's name and fate had a striking resemblance with his predecessor, the only difference being that Wazir Ali never surrendered to his destiny. The deposed Nawab had murdered Mr J. F. Cherry, the British resident of Benaras and revolted with several thousand of his followers, killing some European officers. Eventually, he was routed by the British army. Wazir Ali spent the last seventeen years of his life in the dungeons of Fort William, where he breathed his last.[17] He was interred in the Muslim burial grounds of Kasia Bagan in Calcutta and remains in oblivion.[18]

Whilst the European populace in Calcutta was deceived by the proverbial lull before the storm and were striving to ensure safety, the Bengali aristocrats were seething with discontentment about their security. Unlike the Talukdars of Awadh, the Bengali Zamindars[19] and aristocrats of mid-nineteenth century Calcutta hitherto conferred full confidence on the British policy to thwart the sepoy upheaval. Traditional hegemony had made them complacent and they had overlooked the serious divide between the British polity and the ideology of a highly spirited sepoy uprising that had dimmed the European pride in the whole of northern India. The arrest of Wajid Ali Shah could not cut the slightest dent to their habitual smugness. In the snooty circles of Calcutta, the British continued to be the most trustworthy custodians.

The vernacular newspapers were able to express their bewildered state of mind. According to the *Sambad Bhaskar*, 'a wave of terror engulfed the city and the hapless residents concealed their ornaments inside the floors and within the walls (20 June 1857).'[20] *Bhaskar* further reported a severe inflation of the prices of foodgrains that had been done to feed the hungry soldiers. The unnerved rich elite hoarded rations that would suffice for six months while the baffled middle class survived on mangoes and jackfruits, which were relatively cheaper. Naturally, the misery was worst amongst the poor. The news of Wajid Ali Shah's arrest came out in *Bhaskar* on 18 June 1857 in detail. The local daily was sympathetic to the ex-king but did not reveal the motive behind his arrest.

The Bengali babus[21] who had just started to spread their wings in the western sky and were rubbing shoulders with the European elite, turned a blind eye to the nation wide stir against the British. Mangal Panday was not a Bengali, but a Brahmin from Awadh. His martyrdom failed to make a dent in the Bengali social circle. The Bengali aristocrats, aspiring to have more Europeanized sensibilities than the traditional Indian style of life, sided with the Raj, and emerged as a united ally to accomplish their goals of life. Rather, it was the non-Westernized Mohammedan community, having their roots in Awadh, that actively fostered a sense of patriotism with the single-minded determination to set their King free. On their part, the Bengali babus tried to project the positive side of the British reign and how it would save the Hindu culture and civilization from the oppressive Muslim infidels.

To celebrate the victory of East India Company in the Sepoy Mutiny and the subsequent assumption of the imperial power by the Queen, Radhakanta Deb of Sobhabazar royal family hosted a lavish party at his palace, which was attended by three hundred guests, including the top-notch British officers of the city. [22]

But irrespective of how Bengali babus were striving to mollify the British Raj, Europeans staying abroad viewed the upheaval as a widespread conspiracy spinning around the deposed king of Awadh and his cohorts. One of the main reasons for this belief was that the bulk of the sepoys in Bengal Army were recruited from the ex-king's dominion. The English press was seething with resentment and so were the people of England. The news of Wajid Ali Shah's arrest reached England on 5 July 1857 and created a clamour, which washed away all the public sympathy that the members of the Oudh Commission had gathered. The British press reacted to this news but the local media in Calcutta remained silent—thanks to Canning's caveat.

It was a terrible blow to the Europeans in Calcutta. The incident marked an end to their endurance and evoked feelings of repugnance towards the British Government. London's *The Morning Chronicle* testifies to a meeting of the Europeans in Calcutta, which was held at the Chamber of Commerce on 3 August 1857 with Sir A.D.H. Larpent in the chair, where a petition addressed to the British Parliament concerning the present tumult and the insecurity prevailing in Calcutta was drawn and signed. A strong message of no confidence against the British administration of Calcutta was voiced to the Lords and the Commons. The inconvenience of the Chamber had driven one more nail into the coffin of East India Company's complacence.

When Wajid Ali Shah was walking past the doors of Fort William, little did he know that he would be doomed to the life of a prisoner for twenty-five long months before he could walk out a free man. The horrific days in a desolate milieu dredged up the literary insight of the banished king and the genesis of a new era. *Masnavi Huzn-e-Akhtari*, meaning 'Sorrows of Akhtar', his autobiography was penned in the cells of Fort William. This book embodies a poignant narration of his misfortune and a testimony of his life. His narrative reveals that he was housed in a dingy room in the centre of the fort, infested with insects and mosquitoes. He could hardly see the light of day or meet his own people. The behavior of the staff was atrocious. Conversely, he appreciated the courtesy shown by Cavanaugh who helped in making his life a little comfortable. Nevertheless, he cried for justice, testifying his innocence and loyalty towards the British. He wrote several letters to Canning pleading for his release.

Wajid Ali Shah's appeal to Canning eventually bore fruit. In July 1857, he was removed from his cell and housed in the erstwhile Governor house built inside the fort in 1802, while Ali Naqi Khan was accomodated in the Royal Barrack, both guarded by the Europeans.[23] Canning, in a letter, explained to the ex-king that arrangements were thus made to protect him from the 'insurgents'. However, the government would make all arrangements at its own expense for the King's comforts. To ensure security, the government would look for a safer residence as soon as the situation was brought under control. Till then, the ex-king would live in the fort with full dignity and comfort, free from anxiety. Canning did not give a false assurance. Wajid Ali was immediately provided with all comforts of life. He was allowed to have food brought from his residence, but under a strict vigil. Wajid Ali wrote that he was given a pulling fan in his room and that ice was supplied in the summer months to keep his room cool. Servants were provided to take care of his personal needs and their conduct was watched closely. *Huzn-e-Akhtari* mentions that altogether thirty-three attendants used to stay with him in the fort. Of all the detainees, only eighteen were allowed to stay with him. He specially mentioned some of them in custody, like his physician Tabib-ud-Daullah who managed to get himself freed, leaving the ex-king bereft and lonely in his cell. One Mahatamim-ud-Daullah went insane and was released. Fate-ud-Daullah, the ex-king's teacher died in custody. The banished king admired his people and their faithfulness amidst the unbearable misery. However, he was silent about Ali Naqi Khan, possibly because he was quartered elsewhere.

G. B. Malleson of the Bengal Army, who often criticized the government for giving greater value to the lives of their enemies than to the lives of the English troops, strongly suspected that Ali Naqi Khan was in cahoots with the intriguers. The banished king played innocent, as he had been. Malleson's narration in 1857 testifies Ali Naqi Khan's covert role in supporting the insurrection as a measure of retaliation for the seizure of Awadh, leaving the road of legal justice and taking the path of armed revolt. It was also proved beyond doubt that the conspiracy was organized and arranged at Garden Reach. He had left no stone unturned to communicate with his allies even from his custody.[24] More controversy was spinning around Ali Naqi Khan than the ex-king himself. The British Government had been suspicious of him since his heyday in Lucknow. There was gossip that Wajid Ali Shah himself was wary of his Prime Minister's treacherous mind and that it was only to avoid being assassinated that he had married Ali Naqi's daughter.[25] Wajid Ali's eldest queen, Khas Mahal, was also the niece of Ali Naqi Khan. Thus, Sleeman had remarked that for his own interest, Ali Naqi would keep the King alive. Ali Naqi Khan remained with the ex-king forever and shared his misery equally, if not more, to face the British trial. Nevertheless, Wajid Ali's Prime Minister could not get rid of his shades for the rest of his life. With the threat of insurgency looming large, Ali Naqi Khan remained the prime suspect to the British intelligence.

The news of Akhtar Begum giving birth to Wajid Ali Shah's son was a harbinger of ecstasy. His second wife was the daughter of Ali Naqi Khan. The banished king was eloquent to describe the mesmeric beauty of his seventeen-year-old wife in his *Masnavi* and bewailed her absence. While in custody, the King also came to know about the great mutiny. *Masnavi Huzn-e-Aktari* proudly extolled his twelve-year-old son Birjis Qadr and his valiant mother, Hazrat Mahal, for leading the great war of freedom against the British.

Arrangements were not bad, if not lavish. Before entering his cell in Fort William, the ex-king had deposited his jewellery and valuables in the Company's treasury in Calcutta to avoid being looted while he was in custody.[26] He was allowed by the authority to spend his money in custody, to meet his own obligations and to pay his attendants. The ex-king was committed to support his emissaries and his family in England.

The resources were dwindling and were soon reduced to only a lakh of rupees.

It would be wrong to attribute only malign motives to the British authority, rather no stone was left unturned to keep the detained king in a jovial mood. But Wajid Ali's days in the fort were full of misery and grief. In *Masnavi* he lamented, 'My health is giving up, my hair is falling, my eyes remain laden with tears and my mind is becoming restless. I have lost all my power and can not take food in my hands.' Anguish added to his dismay, when he received the news of the deaths of his mother and brother abroad. A deep-rooted sorrow locked up inside of him. There was no poetry, no music, no romance and no wife in his life.

The lines of *Huzn-e-Akhtari* lamented the pangs of separation. His heart burnt and his eyes wept. He somberly remembers the sweet memories with Khas Mahal, the mother of his heir-apparent and his other consorts, Begum Malka-e-Mulik, Begum Mahbub-e-Khas, Begum Jaane Jaan, Begum Mumtaz Alam, Kaiser Begum, Khujista Mahal, Zafri Begum and lastly Akhtar Begum.[27] But a single twist of fate had taken him away from his begums to a different world. The King loved Zafri Begum as much as he loved his favorite poems of Firdausi. She would send him paan in the jail as a token of her love, but her devotion did not last forever. Zafri Begum stayed with him for seven years before her passion was exhausted. Khujista Mahal too left the king to marry a man in Calcutta and later left for Lucknow. Kaiser Begum too went back to Lucknow. Wajid Ali wrote that she was not his married wife but it was her invincible love that had drawn her to Calcutta. He gave in to his destiny, as his begums left him one by one. It was only Khas Mahal who remained with him till the end with loving care and she never forgot to send him his meals and five paans daily in the prison.[28] The King lamented for not being able to see her face but could feel her presence in the lock of hair she sent him as a token of her love.

An interesting account of the ex-king's prison life was brought out by The *Caledonian Mercury and Daily Express* (Edinburgh, Scotland) on Tuesday, 6 September 1859. The British daily illustrates the ex-king to be extremely abstemious who had denied himself from many pleasures which even the authority would have permitted. He spent most of his time writing poetry, painting portraits[29] and writing letters to his begums who lived in Lucknow and in Garden Reach. He loved to send valuable souvenirs to his begums. He was fond of toys and spent much money on them. Nothing could give him more pleasure than to sit and watch the circular movements of automatic toys set in motion by him. He was particularly very skeptic of being intruded upon and Colonel Cavanaugh was extremely rigid in allowing anybody, irrespective of their rank, to enter into his room or in any other way to incommode him. Ali Naqi Khan was less comfortably situated. He was always reserved and devoted most of his time to reading the Quran.

Wajid Ali Shah's romantic side is best reflected in his letters of love, which he wrote to his wife Iklil Mahal in Lucknow. His *Tareeh-i-Mumtaz* mentions a series of twenty-nine letters addressed to Iklil Mahal from Calcutta, and some of them were written while he was in his cell in Fort William. The entries testify Begum's rich ethos and her literary talent in writing poetry. Iklil Mahal was also a good singer and in many of his letters the banished king sent her his own gazals to sing. In one of his letters the King composed a few lines of a Persian verse and sent it to the Queen to conclude. And so it went on.

Wajid Ali dreamt of compiling a masnavi of his letters of love to Iklil Mahal and wished to name it *Kitab-e- Masnavi*.

While Wajid Ali Shah was taking his romance to a new scale in his letters, the British Government was busy making new plans to curb the rebellion. The control of Lucknow was restored and the fire of mutiny seemed to have been extinguished. The death of Queen Mother and Mirza Sikandar Hasmat put a natural end to every entreaty and hope of Oudh Commission in London. Moulavi Masih-ud-Deen's talks ended in a fiasco. The public clamour in London was swaying largly in favour of the Indian Government. On 1 November 1858, the famous proclamation in the name of the Queen transferred the sovereignty from the company to the Crown. Canning, the first Viceroy of India under the British Government, could have found no better opportunity to kill two birds with one stone—the native rebels and their idol Wajid Ali Shah. Nevertheless, the twenty-five-month-long incarceration had put to the test the banished king's hope of reclaiming his lost kingdom. The ex-king was there but the kingdom was gone, leaving behind several mouths to feed. The hapless emissaries in London had been struck by the austerity of penury. A crisis vis-a-vis delpetion of funds was bound to beseige Wajid Ali Shah sooner or later. His followers in custody, having their own agenda, persuaded him to accept the British terms and live happily. Those who were close to the ex-king in Calcutta, and envious of Masih-ud-Deen's success in London, were scared of losing their identities lest the hegemony over Lucknow was restored. Wajid Ali favoured Moulvi in the beginning, but later changed his mind. He preferred to go by the words of his men than to wait indefinitely for Masih-ud-Deen's victory over the British Government when the threat of his destitution was quite evident. The banished king was ready to annul his claim in

London in lieu of his monthly allowance of one lakh rupees as promised by the government, to be paid retrospectively from the date of annexation. The British accepted his proposal with a caveat to disburse his allowance from the prospective date of his release from the custody. The refusal to accept the allowance by the King during annexation and also the deprivation of a large portion of revenue from Awadh for the period of the mutiny from which the stipend was supposed to be paid, were enough reasons for the British to deny the commencement of allowance from a previous date. Moreover, the British bargained to drop the annual allowance of three lakh rupees, which was proposed for the upkeep of his retinue.

On Saturday 9 July 1859, Wajid Ali Shah came out of his austere cell of Fort William after twenty-five months of excruciating imprisonment. The *Caledonian Mercury* and *Daily Express* narrate his ecstasy at being given back his freedom. His liberation was announced by Col. Cavanaugh and Major Herbert with much delight and courtesy. The ex-king was so excited that he immediately ordered that his evening meal, which had already arrived from Garden Reach, be taken back. But he offered his long evening prayer before he left his room. At about half past five, in the glare of the evening sun, Wajid Ali Shah walked out of his cell and upheld his oriental ethos, conveying thanks to the government for allowing him to join his family. At the same time, he regretted the conduct of his wife Hazrat Mahal for siding with the rebels and for making use of his son, Birjis Qadr.[30] The latter remark underscores a complete deviation of his earlier soliloquy in *Huzn–e-Akhtari* wherein the ex-king eulogized his wife and son for their relentless struggle for freedom. Wajid Ali drove off in an open carriage, accompanied by Major Herbert, while the retinue followed behind.[31] Lord Canning decided to release his monthly stipend from that day itself.

Immediately, the news of his release was sent to London by the Indian Government with a sigh of relief. But Masih-ud-Deen was enraged at the turn of events. He was not prepard to relinquish his long endeavour when success was not a distant dream. Masih-ud-Deen pleaded before the Parliament that the King had been coerced to accept the truce under pressure in detention and hence the settlement should be ignored. The British Parliament was convinced and adjourned to take a decision. On hearing this at Metiyaburj, Wajid Ali Shah was annoyed with his emissary and announced that he had consented willingly in a sound state of mind only after his release and saying so he immediately dismissed Moulvi Masih-ud-Deen from his power of attorney. Masih-ud-Deen had no other way but to give up his dreams. His last hope of reinstatement of the Kingdom of Awadh was annulled forever.[32]

The appeasing words of Wajid Ali Shah in his letter to Canning after his release, dated 5 October 1859, had greased Lord Canning's ego. Wajid Ali Shah was allowed to retain his title of 'King of Oudh' till his death and also the pecuniary allowance. The King was allowed no jurisdiction within his estate but legal processes within its precincts would be served by an officer who was appointed as Agent with His Majesty by the British Government. In March 1862, an act was passed to exempt the King from the jurisdiction of criminal courts, except for capital offences. He was also exempted from appearance as a witness in any court and to provide for his examination through the Agent to the Governor-General.[33] It was officially intimated that separate provisions would be made for the King's wife Hazrat Mahal and his son Birjis Qadr, in the event of their surrender. However, the Viceroy declined to sanction three lakh rupees per annum, which was proposed for his guards and watchmen. Ali Naqi Khan was conditionally released from imprisonment at the same time.

The arrest of Wajid Ali Shah had not evoked much sympathy amongst the elite of Calcutta. The influential Bengali babus, supposedly closer to the British power, paid no heed to the banished king's controversy. No entry is found in the contemporary Bengali literature to testify the Bengali babus' concern over the British rapacity and debauchery.

The banished king had to fight a lonely battle to survive in the city of Calcutta.

Six

Wajid Ali Shah Establishes 'Chota Lucknow' in Calcutta

Nineteenth century colonial Bengal witnessed a grand era of British Orientalism and Bengal Renaissance that began in the backdrop of European ideas and oriental education movement. The consequent debate that took place between the Orientalists and Anglicists to establish the highest intellectual standards momentarily abated the effects of the Sepoy Mutiny, during which intellectual Calcuttans had been reluctant to side with the mutineers. The city boasted of Europeanized intelligentsia. It was conversant with Western culture and responded to it. Thus, it had the wherewithal to bring forth a renaissance in Bengal. Yet, it was basically a Hindu dominant awakening. Muslim traditional ethos and sensitivities did not touch the hearts of Bengali intelligentsia of nineteenth century; rather the Muslims preferred to stand outside as an external proletariat, as did the non-urban Hindu society. The Bengali bhadraloks (elite folklore) deeply engrossed in western mores, kept away from traditional Muslim aspirations. Wajid Ali Shah, a renowned proponent of traditional Orientalism and ethos, suddenly found himself outside the orbit of the Bengali clique.

King Wajid Ali purchased a large riverside estate in Metiyaburj in the south-eastern fringe of Calcutta, with the permission of the British Government.[1] Here, he began to construct a city that would one day be an extension of Nawabi Lucknow. The King spent lavishly from his income of one lakh rupees per month and continued to live in an extravagant fashion. A beautiful township sprawled in Metiyaburj that has often been described as Chota Lucknow.

Sharar, a contemporary court historian, wrote that the King was provided with a palatial building in Metiyaburj by the British to live in, which he named Sultan Khana. He was also given two other mansions later, named Asad Manzil and Murassa Manzil.[2] The King, an expert in architecture, had several apartments constructed to house not only his entourage but also the innumerable womenfolk. The edifices were surrounded by beautiful gardens and lawns. Sharar identified some of them as Qasr ul Baiza, Gosha-e-Sultani, Shahinsha Manzil, Shah Manzil, Nur Manzil, Tafrih Baksh, Badami, Asmani, Tahaniyat Manzil, Had-e-Sultani, Sad-e-Sultani and Adalat Manzil. In addition, there were several beautiful houses surrounding Sultan Khana for his wives. There were many single rooms and cubicles on the banks of the Hooghly river, which offered a breathtaking view of the river. The interiors were well furnished with silver bedsteads and carpeted flooring. A team of cleaners was engaged to keep everything spotless. Gardens and lawns were well-maintained and designed in various geometrical shapes to give them an aesthetic appeal. Shops with the finest varieties of goods were set up for about a mile along the municipal road, where the palace employees also lived. A guardhouse was built near the gate of Sultan Khana where drums were beaten to mark the hours.

The Sibtainabad Imambara was built in 1864 and had an impressive gateway, which was sculptured with double mermaids. This was the emblem of the royal family. Other monuments of religious interest included the Baitul Naajat or the Chota Imambara; the Begum Masjid where one of the King's mutá wives was buried; Quasrul Buka or 'house of mourning'; and his personal Shahi Masjid within the compound of Sultan Khana. Quasrul Buka was the first Imambara built in Metiyaburj. The imperial splendour of Metiyaburj was called 'Garden of Eden on earth' where both Indians and Europeans would be filled with wonder.

The King's memories of Lucknow were fading fast. The Hooghly had entwined his heart with deep and enduring bonds, which appeared to him familial and destined to grow further. The water of Gomti and Hooghly bore testimony to the flow of the King's life. Calcutta was new to him and so was the culture of Bengal. The King penned:

Äb nishane isk
Kalkatta me garwa chahiye
Husn-e-sharhre Lucknow
Hurdam ujane chahiye

Meaning–

> The love that I have for my country should be poured in Calcutta. This place should be filled with all the splendours of Lucknow.[3]

The King's Chota Lucknow was the gem of his eyes, his pride and ego, and his success in touching the arrogance of the snooty bhadraloks of Calcutta. His 'kingdom' was symbolic of his crusade against the colonial rapacity. With the giant shadow of Anglicism looming large on the horizons of Calcutta, Wajid Ali Shah's fervour of traditionalism remained unwavering and steadfast. He continued the tradition of holding durbars in the

Mughal style in a remote corner of Calcutta. It was symbolic of the time-honoured Mughal conventions that were so important to him.

Metiyaburj had replaced Lucknow in his heart. The King wrote:

> *Rawana hoti hai*
> *Saree nakhat*
> *Zahur ifroz de hai daulat*
> *Khuda ne chaha to ahele gurbaht*
> *Badalte hai hum batan batan se-*

Meaning–

> All the splendours that I had, are now washed away. The advent of poverty is also wealth if God wishes to the migrant. I exchange my native place with Calcutta. (Lines from Qamr Mazmoon, written by the King in Fort William.)[4]

In another of his poem he confesses:

> *All signs of adversity are about to bid ado,*
> *And penury is indeed a blessing,*
> *God willing my fellow refugees...*

I intent to exchange my native place with the new one.

This was indeed a blessing in disguise. The King thought that even if he goes back to Lucknow he will have to feed so many of his people, which is not possible now in his state of penury. So, God has given him Calcutta to stay and therefore he wants to make up his mind to give his everything to Calcutta. The above verse taken from *Qamr Mazmoon*, written by the Nawab himself, shows his changing mind during incarceration.

In Metiyaburj, one could sense the same bustle of activities as in Lucknow. People spoke the same language, recited the same style of poetry, had the same conversations, enjoyed the same wit, witnessed the same cockfighting and relished the same opium. Even the shopkeepers and moneylenders were from Lucknow. People could freely stroll around the parks and zoo; often a lucky man would catch a glimpse of a charming lady peeping from the windows, or would hear a recital of an eloquent shayari.[5] The tazia of Muharram was never so enchanting as it was there. Even the British would come to Metiyaburj to witness the fascinating show and join thousands of people gathered there. People discovered a new Lucknow in Metiyaburj. The King did not hesitate to spend copious amounts of his wealth so as to keep the glitter of Lucknow alive on the banks of the Hooghly. The Durbar Hall here was witness to the brilliance of Lucknowi gharana, and enjoyed by the connoisseurs of music amidst Calcutta's elite.

Tazia was indeed a great show in Metiyaburj and was in no way less enchanting than the one performed in Lucknow. In a demonstration that showcased the past grandeur, the King would lead the pageant from Asmani Koti on the seventh day of Muharram, playing a tasha tied around his neck. Sharar witnessed Wajid Ali Shah's tazia in Metiyaburj and recounts: 'He played the tasha with such delicacy and skill that even people who did not understand music applauded him. I have also seen him playing the dhol.'[6]

Time was announced by playing naubat in Lucknow and the tradition continued in Metiyaburj too. Naubat, the most enchanting of all the bands, was brought to India by the

Muslims. It was a combination of a pair of tabla-like percussions called naqaras and flutes or shahnais. Naubatkhana (permanent stage for naubat) was built over the main gate of the King's estate. A day was divided into eight prahars and each prahar was announced by playing naubat. Only the midnight naubat was omitted so as to not disturb the people as they slept. The tradition was followed in the palace of Metiyaburj as long as Wajid Ali was alive.[7] The mood was indeed captivating and the enchanting melody of the Nawabi naubat blended with the ripples of the Hooghly at the crack of dawn.

The banks of the Hooghly were spectacular and the ships cruising to Calcutta dipped their standards in salute to Fort William. The people basked in the belief that salutes were given to honour their King. A sense of elation was giving way to the previous feelings of love and loss, and the hopeless struggle against destiny. The King was enjoying the fortune bequeathed to him. However, the British politician-author Sir Charles Wentworth Dilke censured the King's extravagance and its ill-effects on contemporary Bengali culture. Thus, he writes:

> *For nine years he has never left his palace, yet he spends, we are told, from £2,00,000 to £2,50,000 a year (more than his annual income of £1,20,000). In his extravagance and immorality the King of Oude does not stand alone in Calcutta. His mode of life is imitated by the wealthy natives; his vices are mimicked by every young Bengalee babu.*[8]

Prof. Garcin de Tassy, a French Orientalist and a professor of Indology, best described him in 1874 as:

> *While discussing the poets, the former King of Awadh, Wajid Ali Shah, should be specially mentioned. He has been living*

> on the banks of Hughli, three miles from Calcutta, for about twenty years. He is fond of music, paintings and poetry. His geets (songs) are sung in the households and streets of Calcutta and Benaras... He has entire jurisdiction over the Palace in which he lives. The number of his subjects is 6,000. All pomp and show of the Royal Durbar, which added lustre to Lucknow, remain still (at Metiyaburj). He never goes out of his palace. He does not visit the Viceroy, although he comes to see him. The King built three palaces for his residence: Sultan Khana, which is the Royal palace, Asad Munzil and Zard Kothi.[9]

The Chinese Mission led by Ma Jianzhong and Wu Kuangpei, which visited Metiyaburj in August 1881 near the end of the King's life, was surprised to see the banished king living happily in a splendid gold and green stone-studded palace at Metiyaburj.

> Dependent upon others, acting slavishly, and living shamefacedly like dung, how could he be peaceful and happy?[10]

Wajid Ali Shah still believed in old-fashioned virtues, and wanted things to be done in style. The township bustled with a thousand sentinels who were paid six rupees a month (though some were paid eight to ten rupees). There were five hundred housekeepers who received the same remuneration, eight clerks who enjoyed ten to thirty rupees a month. There were forty to fifty favoured companions and high officials and each received eighty-eight rupees a month. There were more than a hundred palanquin-bearers and scores of servants as well. Even the relatives of his temporary wives were not deprived of salaries. 'So a town had grown up with a population of more than forty-thousand souls, all of whose livelihood was derived from the King's monthly allowance of one lakh rupees,' writes Sharar.[11] Calcuttans quizzed each other as to where the money was coming from and eventually surmised that the King must possess a philosopher's stone in his vault, which could produce gold simply by rubbing it on iron or brass!

Calcutta's correspondent's account in *The New York Times* vividly portrays Wajid Ali Shah's mimic court on the banks of the Hooghly. The kingdom was small and compact with six thousand subjects who were devoted to the King. The people employed were more than feudal retainers and blindly obeyed their master. The chiefs and the officers of the state had retained the titles they had in Lucknow. Apart from his principal houses, the royal menagerie was worth mentioning. Around the menagerie there were small buildings with marble floors and stucco walls where the King would take a break after a long stroll. Beautifully manicured gardens stretched across the enclosure and were maintained by three hundred gardeners. As the sun would set, the kingdom would be illuminated with small colourful lamps. Exotic lanterns hung from the ceilings, perhaps bought from London's Lowther Arcade. Almost every viceroy chose to visit the palace, while it was the King's pride that prevented him from visiting the Government House. The King's pension of ten thousand pounds and the rent he earned from a native bazaar outside his territory was spent entirely within the four walls of his kingdom. The cost of feeding his animals was five hundred pounds a month. His expenditures were enormous and he saved nothing, nor did he have any wish to do so. He spent his time in the menagerie and in writing poetry. His evenings were enchanting. They were spent in the company of notable singers and dancing girls. No wonder the

King lived a blissful life with his family of thirty-nine Mahals,[12] hundred begums, thirty-one sons and twenty-five daughters.[13]

The flag of Awadh was flying high in the sky of Metiyaburj. The symbol of the Nawabs was a pair of fish. The houses in Metiyaburj bore the piscine icon, which the Awadhi Nawabs revered most. The fish was a holy creature for the Persian saint Kwaja Khijir and much adored by Khusroo Parvez, the Sessanian monarch of pre-Islamic Persia. Saadat Khan, a Persian noble of Nishapur and a confidant of the Mughal Emperor Muhammad Shah, was appointed the Subedar-Nawab of Awadh. He was the first of the Nawabs of Awadh and was given the title of Burhan-ul-Mulk by the Mughal Emperor. Burhan-ul-Mulk established his capital in Faizabad. It was said that while he was crossing the Ganga river on his way from Farukabad to capture Lucknow, a fish jumped out from the water and dropped into his lap. He considered it to be a good omen. Saadat Khan preserved the skeleton of the fish and the valuable memento was treasured by his decedents until Awadh was annexed by the British. Since the time of Burhan-ul-Mulk the fish had become the state emblem of Awadh.[14] Saadat entered Lucknow and seized a palace from the ruling Sheiks. He named it Machhi Bhawan. Some say that the name of the building was given by his successor Safdarjung after the citadel was rebuilt.

Such was the splendour of Wajid Ali's flag that it fluttered higher than the Union Jack in his kingdom of Metiyaburj. *Huzn-e-Akhtari* reveals that five thousand people were living in Metiyaburj before the mutiny, and with more emigrants coming in from Lucknow in search of greener pastures, the population swelled to forty thousand after the war.[15] It was the responsibility of the banished king to provide for them all.

Incredibly, on his limited pension of one lakh rupees a

month, Wajid Ali was well able to keep up for thirty years the same state of affairs and ecstasy as he had been doing ever since his early days in Lucknow. Frederick Wyman, a British traveller, snooped inside the town to discover the mystery. In the narrative of his journey called *From Calcutta to the Snowy Range* in 1866, Wyman was sarcastic in his views whilst describing the banished king.

> *A debauched and prematurely old man—the slave of his parasites; powerless now perhaps for political evil, but potent for such as flows from example; the receiver of a truly royal income, but inextricably burdened with debt.*[16]

Wyman discovered that the kingdom was one of the finest places to see in Calcutta:

> *The visitor to Calcutta who approaches that city by its great water highway, the Hooghly River, will, after passing the long low lines of flat green land immediately above the famed Botanical Gardens, come suddenly upon a series of fantastically-painted villas—some grey, some yellow, some blue—standing in extensive garden enclosures, ornamented more by nature than by art.*[17]

A long line of stable-like buildings stretched across the boundary for the King's men to stay. His palace stood a few yards off. Nevertheless, the picturesque riverbank of the King's township was a pleasant resting place for white-robed and gaily-shawled gentlemen, whose presence was greatly patronized by Wajid Ali Shah. Garden Reach, the sparsely inhabited part of Calcutta in the yesteryears, was now filled with the sound of native horse-carriages and drums, and the crowd of people living in the outskirts of the King's township. The location was chosen by the British Government because it had many advantages over others. Wyman justifies:

> *It was in the outskirts of the town, had ample land accommodation, and was overlooked by the Fort, and in full view of the docks and shipping. Accordingly, a handsome and commodious residence, formerly occupied by Sir Laurence Peel, was appropriated and converted into an abode for his ex-Majesty. Gradually the villas on either side, and facing the grounds, were purchased; lofty walls and high mat fences in time took the place of fragrant and verdant hedgerows.*[18]

From what they could see and notice inside his mimic court, the snooping itinerants formed some ideas. However, the suspicion of a subversive exercise going on behind the scenes by the King's cohorts to usurp power could not be established. The mystery of the King's prodigality from his limited pension was yet to be unravelled.

As water flowed down the Hooghly, the gulf between the kingdom of Metiyaburj and Government House was narrowing. The walls of the enclosure of Wajid Ali's township parted to welcome the Bengali elite and the British lords. The gardens, the menagerie, the palaces, the riverside, and the rich musical assemblage, recitations, classical dance and drama, wooed the outsiders. Soon Metiyaburj became the undisputed cultural hub of Calcutta. The magical city within Calcutta, which offered a niche to people from different class and religious backgrounds, finally gave Wajid Ali Shah critical recognition.

During his long stay in Calcutta, Wajid Ali Shah had come across the office of Viceroys like Lord Canning, Earl of Elgin, Sir John Lawrence, Earl of Mayo, Lord Northbrook and Lord Lytton. Once Lawrence, when he was the Chief Commissioner of Punjab, was rebuffed by the King at Kanpur on his way to Calcutta. Sir Lawrence, still affronted, wanted to see the King in Calcutta. Wajid Ali could not deny the call of the Queen's representative and consented to visit the Government House accompanied by Sir Richard Temple, who later became the Lieutenant Governor of Bengal. The King was afforded due honour and was received by the Chief Secretary at the foot of the stairs. The Viceroy embraced his guest and seated him on a golden chair. Lawrence himself sat on a similar seat facing the King and a jovial conversation in fluent Urdu commenced. Two days later, the Viceroy reciprocated the gesture and paid a return visit to Metiyaburj. The princes received the Viceroy at Khidderpore Bridge. A grand arrangement was made at Nur Mahal by Syed Amir Ali Khan and the King himself. Betel and fruits were offered to the honoured guest.[19] Doves of peace were fluttering high in the sky of Metiyaburj.

Wajid Ali Shah did not have very gratifying memories of Lord Mayo. In 1871, Lord Mayo went to Metiyaburj to meet the King and the latter returned the honour by visiting the Government House the next day. He was greeted by the Viceroy in the Throne Room, and asked to be seated on a throne-chair. In the middle of a discussion the Viceroy left his chair and took his seat in the Presidential chair on the balcony, leaving his guest to sit below. The offended King immediately left the room without making his farewells. He confessed his repugnance, 'to whom could I bid farewell? I saw a corpse lying on that high Presidential Chair instead of a living person.'[20]

The King was courteous and his oriental upbringing encouraged him to respect his guests. In December 1869, when the Duke of Edinburgh (the second son of Queen Victoria) was cruising down the bank of Metiyaburj, a guard of honour was given by a troop of King's soldiers, horses and foot, and by the people of his durbar, whilst the buglers played a welcome tune. But his pride dissuaded him from joining the grand durbar held as a mark of respect for the Prince and lauded by the Maharajas of Gwalior, Jaipur, Rewah, Bharatpur, Alwar, Dholpur, Kapurthala, Hathwa, Vizianagar, Burdwan, Begum Sahiba of Bhopal and the Prince of Mysore.

A similar durbar was held in honour of the Prince of Wales (later Edward VII) in 1876, which was attended by luminaries from all parts of India. Syed Amir Ali Khan, a leading lawyer of Sadder Dewani Adalat and an adherent of the British sovereign, tried to persuade the King to join the party but failed. Sharar narrated that the fact that the King did not greet him had irked theP. On being enquired the King answered, 'If you consider me to be a King then it is below my status to go to you. But if, in your eyes, I am a homeless beggar then how dare I face you?'[21] The Prince was impressed and went to meet the King in his palace in Metiyaburj. A grand salutation was arranged and the prince was welcomed with an offering of a diamond-studded walking stick.[22] However, no such entry is found in Sir William Howard Russell's official account of the Prince's visit.

Maharaja Ishwari Prasad Narayan Singh of Benaras was a great admirer of Wajid Ali. He came to Calcutta to attend the durbar for the Prince of Wales in 1876. He wished to meet the King and to felicitate him with some precious gems, but the King refused to meet him. Eventually, the King confessed that it was his destitution and inability to reciprocate the Kashi Raj with a more precious Khilat that had prevented him from meeting his visitor.[23]

Indeed the King led an ordinary life besides the pageantry of his palace and durbars. Till the end of his days, he remained overawed by British arrogance. He was inordinately religious, but secular in his thoughts. The king belonged to the Shia sect, but was extremely reverent to the Sunnis. Once, a literary piece published in the name of the King had rankled the Sunnis of Calcutta. When he came to know of it, the King was aggrieved and apologized to the Sunnis. On another occasion, a dispute bubbled up between two persons in his palace on the question of their sects. When they came before the King hoping that he would address their misgivings, he not only reprimanded them but also removed them from service. The King observed, 'Of my two eyes, one is Shia and the other is Sunni.'[24] In the overwhelming Sunni majority in Calcutta, Wajid Ali's confidants were mostly Sunnis. The person in-charge of his zoo was a Sunni Muslim; his Chief Secretary Munshi-ul-Sultan was a Sunni, as was his Vazir—Munsarim-ud-Daula, the chief paymaster. The management of his Sibtainabad Imambara and Baitul Naajat was bestowed in the hands of Sunnis. 'No one ever noticed who was a Sunni and who a Shia,' wrote Sharar.[25]

Legend goes that before the construction of Shahi Masjid in Metiyaburj, the King proclaimed that anyone who had never missed his daily prayers since adulthood could come forward and he would be conferred the honour of laying the foundation stone of the Masjid. A month went by and no one claimed to have the distinction. Finally, the King himself laid the foundation, as he was the only person in Metiyaburj who had never skipped his daily prayers.

The King was an early riser and he would start his day at four in the morning. After saying his morning prayers or Fajr, and reading the Wazaif, he would recite the Holy Quran along with his Mujtahids till eight or nine in the morning.[26] Wajid Ali recited his prayers with utmost devotion and introduced the system of counting Rak'ats by engaging a person sitting in front of him. Wajid Ali was equally benevolent to his Hindu adherents who frequently visited his palace.

The King would go about his daily ablutions after he had said his prayers. He suffered from fistula and would spend a long time sitting on a chowki in the form of a commode that was padded with velvet. His obesity disabled him from even washing himself. Two ladies called Bhistans were engaged to pour water over him and keep him clean. The Bhistans or water carriers were also his mutá wives. The King would not allow any woman to undress him unless she was his wife. He would sit in his durbar to address the petitions and matters connected to his estate in Metiyaburj after morning refreshments. 'The king passed orders with his own hand but sometimes, he gave directions to the members of the Dar-ul-Insha (the Secretaries) for writing the dictated orders. Every paper was put before the king for proper instructions,' narrated a literary source.[27]

The King would have his lunch after the midday prayer or Dhuhr, and then take a nap. After reciting his Asr or evening prayers, he would go for a stroll around his estate. He preferred to ride in a bocha, a modified sedan chair carried by bearers wearing uniforms and enjoyed his menagerie or the picturesque riverside and the lush green Botanical Garden on the opposite bank. Bocha was the only way of transport for the King and often he would prefer one for going around inside his Palace. A literary source elucidates,

> *Every vehicle (Bocha) had a particular name with a poetic tinge in it. The Royal vehicle was preceded by a herald who advances with the cries of 'Be careful' and 'Attention!' The King was surrounded by companions and ministers like*

> *stars. They accompanied him everywhere, except the Zenana Khana.*[28]

His favourite bocha was 'Ganga-Jamni', which was embroidered with gold and silver and covered with velvet cushions.

The King changed his dress every day. His favourite dress was the angrakha (full skirted tunic), which was made of fine sharbati-makhmal that he liked to wear even in winters, and covered himself with a light shawl. Angrakha was popular in Delhi and came to Lucknow later. It had a slit on the left side of chest, and was a trendy style of the time.

After spending the evening in his menagerie, the King would conduct his Maghrib or sunset prayer. His last prayer Isha'a was the time for devotional offerings. His durbar started after Isha'a when he would meet his companions (aide-de-camp) for various administrative issues. It was then that Metiyaburj would plunge into inexpressible liveliness. Dance and music continued till dinner was laid out at one or two in the morning. It was only then that he would retire for the night, but would wake up again at dawn to say his prayers.

Not all, but some Nawabs of Awadh were fond of alcohol. Asaf-ud-Daulla preferred Western liquor and procured bottles from Calcutta. Many of his evenings were frittered away at drunken parties. Saadat Ali Khan relished spirits and was a generous host who would give away valuable presents to his guests when drunk. Nasir-us-Din Haidar was driven by western ideals and was an impenitent drinker. King Amjad Ali was a devout Muslim and would take only tea when invited to the Residency. Wajid Ali Shah, despite all his sensual tastes and love for music and fairs, abstained from drinking.[29]

Wajid Ali Shah reared a flock of twenty-four thousand

pigeons in Metiyaburj and had in his collection almost every variety—shirazi, guli, peshawari, gulvey, laqa, lotan, choya, chandan, yahu and so on. He also bred rare varieties of green pigeons. Hundreds of keepers were engaged to look after his precious birds and Sharar recounts one Ghulam Abbas who was an unrivalled expert. The Badshah was fond of watching the flight of pigeons as they did their acrobatics in the air. The well-trained birds would flutter their wings and settle down around the keeper as he waved a flag over his head.

Quail fighting followed Wajid Ali Shah to Calcutta. The art had its origin in Punjab and thrived amongst the gypsies migrating to Lucknow. In Metiyaburj, quail fighting was typically an indoor event and fought on an ornamental carpet laid in the middle of a hall. Button quails were preferred over bush quail and the beaks of the birds were sharpened with a penknife. The birds were brought to the arena in dainty bamboo cages adorned with strips of ivory. The birds were called by hyperbolical names such as 'Rustom' or 'Sohrab' and so on. Expert quail-fighters from Lucknow were retained in the King's court, and Sharar recounts two adept quail-fighters in Metiyaburj by the names of Darugha Ghulam Abbas Chotey Khan and Ghulam Muhammad Khan Khalispuri. Almost all types of birds, which could be tamed, were made to fight. The list was incredibly long and included partridges, lavwa (a variety of partridge), guldum, lal and pigeons. Sharar witnessed lavwa fighting in Metiyaburj under an expert player. Cockfights were an all time favourite in the Lucknow durbar. In Metiyaburj, cockfighting was held at Ali Naqi Khan's residence, often joined by English aficionados who would field their own birds to challenge the oriental winners. Although cockfighting was synonymous with clandestine betting, the sport had an iconic valour. A special

Arabian breed of rooster called asil was brought from Lucknow for a sure bet.[30]

Animal fights was a popular sport in Lucknow. It had come down the dynasty and reached its peak during the reign of Nasir-ud-Din Haidar. A host of colonial narratives depict the grandeur of wild sports organized by the Nawabs to honour their guests. Some of these sports were too brutal. Wajid Ali had no predilection for such brutal fete, rather the King loved to watch birds fighting each other and sometimes even rams. Ram fights were a crowd-pulling event in the squares of Metiyaburj, as it was in Lucknow, and betting behind the scenes was common. Rams were reared and fed with great care and attention. Two persons, each holding a ram, stood several hundred yards from each other. They would release the rams at the same time and the rams would smash into each other, as their horns would lock. Sharar witnessed one such fight in Metiyaburj, where the skull of a ram was split open by its contender. In Calcutta, Munshi-ul-Sultan, the Badshah's Chief Secretary, would raise several rams in the pen of a butcher for the grand show. Ram fighting turned into an annual fete in Metiyaburj and British guests were specially invited by the King to watch the great show in his menagerie. The grand show was acclaimed by the royal audiences and their 'hurrahs!' prevailed over the noise of butting between the two rams.

Kites of different shapes, sizes and colours dotted the sky of Metiyaburj to the utter delight of mesmerized spectators. Traditionally, the art of kite flying was started by the Nawabs almost a century back. The Nawabs of Lucknow would fly their kites from their palace rooftops. A small purse containing gold or silver coins would be attached to the kite. This served as a prize for those who would run after the kite that had been severed by the opponent. The tradition streamed down to colonial Calcutta and the Bengali elite were quick to catch on. Here also the babus boasted of their opulence by stitching currency notes to the kite or getting their names inscribed on it. Wajid Ali Shah designed his own kite with one-and-a-half bows supported by a stick at the back and a small paper tussle attached to the bottom. The King brought with him to Calcutta one of the best kite fliers from Lucknow, Ilahi Baksh Vilayat Ali.[31] Today, Metiyaburj is the largest producer of kites in the world.

Wajid Ali Shah lost his kingdom but regained his intellectual ecstasy in Calcutta. Moulana Sharar observed:

> *I have seen with my own eyes the King, his Durbar, the grand living of the Mahlats (wives), the interesting society of the Princes, and splendour of desolate Lucknow in Bengal [sic].* [32]

No wonder the reverie of regaining his lost monarchy had ebbed. The King had nothing to lose. A new life was unfurling before him and he looked forward to that.

Seven

The Private Life of the Banished King

Abdul Sharar once wrote,

> *I do not know Wajid Ali Shah of his regal days. But Wajid Ali Shah of Metiyaburj, whom I have seen in my own eyes, personified in himself Itteqa (fear of God), abstemiousness, devotion to God, etc. All the beautiful women in his Mahalsara (Palace) were lawful to him by Mutá (being married to him in the Mutá form). And he was so much strict in this that none, except his Mankuha or Mamtuá wives, could approach him to perform even the lowliest or the most contemptible of the daily chores. Young women, who had to perform the necessary services, were married by Mutá and included in the circle of his harems and the legality (of cohabiting with them) was sanctioned by the Qibla-o-Kaaba (the Head Priest according to the religious law). There maidservants could never have the honour of sleeping with him but they had added to the number of Mumtuá wives. Bhistan (women water carrier) was called Nawab Abrasa Begum, and Mehtrani (one who cleans the toilet pot) was named Nawab Musaffa Begam [sic].*[1]

Wajid Ali Shah's romantic but generous patronage to a large assortment of women ranging from female palanquin bearers to courtesans and from dancers to domestic help has evoked the imagination of Western chroniclers and even led to the creation of luscious tales about the King's personal life. With so many women around him, it was no wonder that the romantic King fell in love with hundreds of beautiful and desolate women in his court, both in Lucknow and in Metiyaburj. Even the most authentic narration by Abdul Halim Sharar is not free from cynicism. The commentator infers, 'The King appears to be one of the most dubious in all the records of history', and yet 'extremely devout, abstinent and a strict observer of Muslim religious law.'[2] The alleged moral laxity, for which the Awadhi King is censured, is indeed permitted in the edicts of Islam. Wajid Ali's 'immoral act' is only a testimony to the religious commandments of his faith. He had never denied the religious edicts endowed on women in Islam. Neither had he tried to hide anything from the public gaze.

What others call 'concubines' were in fact the King's legitimate wives. The only difference was that he engaged himself in temporary contracts called mutá marriages, which were for a fixed period of time. These marriages would terminate ipso facto after the expiry of an agreed period, unless renewed by the King. Mutá ceremony was conducted in the same way as a Nikah marriage.[3] The children born to the mutá wives were legitimate and had equal rights as the children born to nikah wives. However, the mutá wives had no claim over the royal property. Although a Shiite is permitted to have only four nikah marriages, there was no limit to the number of mutá marriages.

Wajid Ali mentions in *Huzn-e-Akhtari* that he had sixty to seventy mutá wives in his harem, but only five or six had come with him to Calcutta. The number of his mutá wives in Calcutta is established only until the time he was detained in Fort William, and does not include the mutá wedlocks that he entered into in the next twenty-eight years of his life in Calcutta. The romantic king dedicated an entire masnavi to his begums, which is indeed a goldmine to discover hitherto unknown aspects of his marital life. *Bahr-e-Mukhtalif*, the masnavi in reference, was probably composed in Fort William. It enumerates both his permanent and temporary wives and his children, along with their names. The list testifies eighty mutá wives and two permanent wives, Khas Mahal and Akhtar Mahal. Both Khas Mahal and Akhtar Mahal came to Metiyaburj with the King. Khas Mahal was the daughter of Nawab Ali Khan and niece of Nawab Ali Naqi Khan. The marriage had taken place during the lifetime of King Nasir-ud-Din Haidar. Akhtar Mahal was the third daughter of Ali Naqi Khan and was known for her charming beauty.

Ali Naqi Khan's family was reputed for its musical inclinations and Akhtar Mahal's talent for music had brought her closer to the King. However, English commentators inferred that this marriage was a strategic agreement between the two families so that Wajid Ali could save himself from an intrigue being hatched by his Prime Minister. Khas Mahal, the King's chief consort, was the first lady and her son was the heir-apparent. She was accorded with the highest monthly allowance of five thousand rupees, while none of his other wives received a monthly allowance that exceeded three thousand rupees.[4]

Sharar, who had seen Wajid Ali Shah closely in Metiyaburj, offers a positive twist to his polygamous tendency: '[The] Nawab was a very religious and cautious person and anxious not to cast a glance on Na-Mahram women (i.e. women who were not legally married to him).'[5] In the royal palace of Metiyaburj a crowd of female attendants were engaged like Pesh-Khidmuts (maidservants), Mahaldars (female palace guard), Mughlanis (female tailors), Madandars (housekeepers), Bhistans (female water carriers) and Khakrobans (sweepers), all of whom were personal attendants to the King. However, only a few of them were married to the King as mutá wives and held a place in the royal harem. Evidently, there were a host of female attendants who were part of the King's private life, but were not recognized as mutá wives. The mutá wives were given the title of 'Begum'. However, on giving birth to a child the status of a begum would be raised to 'Mahal'. The begums were paid a monthly allowance of six to ten rupees like that of an ordinary maidservant, but were provided with royal dresses. However, on being raised to the status of Mahal, the monthly honorarium was increased to one hundred rupees or even two hundred rupees. Moreover, she was then provided with separate living quarters known as a Mahalsara with servants and guards. Most of the king's mutá wives were trained in music and dance and performed for the King. He seldom visited them or wished to see them for any other reason except in his bedchamber.

Sharar wrote that the King never went to see a mujra in Lucknow; nor did he ever visit any prostitute in Calcutta.[6] He was a devout and pious person, and made it a rule not to look at women who were not married to him, either temporarily or permanently. The caveat coerced him to enter into a mutá arrangement with a young water-carrier and she enjoyed the title of Abrasa Begum or Lady Water-Provider in Metiyaburj. A young sweeper's fortunes were transformed when she was picked up by the King as his mutá wife and awarded the title of Musaffa Begum or Lady Purifier. The King's magnanimity did not touch any other maids coming close to him. Indeed, he could not be expected to shower such munificence on hundreds of women in Metiyaburj. Sharar's first-hand narration gives evidence of how the King satisfied his sexual desires in the garb of mutá marriages. Wajid Ali Shah made full use of Shiite laws. His polygamous cupidity unfurled in Metiyaburj in the most crucial period when social reformer Iswar Chandra Vidyasagar was declaring war against the evils of polygamy in Calcutta. He had submitted a petition before the British Government that had been signed by fifty thousand eminent personalities of Calcutta, in 1856.

Wajid Ali Shah had never denied his affinity for women; neither had he tried to hide anything in his literary creations. His autobiographical account, *Tareekh-e-Parikhana* (meaning, Chronicles of Fairy House), is not only an eloquent but also a bold account of his private life, replete with secret anecdotes, which otherwise would have remained obscure. Wajid Ali reveals his first sexual encounter at the tender age of eight, when he was seduced by Rahiman who was one of his female attendants. He was also sexually enticed by a thirty-five-year-old woman named Ameeran who was his mother's help, and that romance continued till he was eleven. When the Prince was eleven years old he was charmed by one Banno Saheb, but since she was married there was no union between them. The Prince then fell in love with Banno's sister Haji Khanam, who was also married. But Haji Khanam surrendered to the Prince and their secret affair continued till he was fourteen years of age. The Prince had his first lawful marriage when he was fifteen years old and the bride was Alam Ara Begum (Khas Mahal). But his lasciviousness did not end after his marriage. He fell in love with one of his maids, Moti Khanam, who was a good dancer. He even composed poetry in admiration of Moti even as it threatened his relationship with Khas Mahal. Eventually, the Begum relented after an irksome altercation. The Prince was attracted to Saheb Khanam, a thirty-two-year-old talented singer and a maid to his father. Thereafter, several women came into his life such as Sarfaraz Begum, Nanni Begum and Umda Begum. The list is exhausting. They were all married to him and became one of the first batches of mutá wives in his harem.

Wajid Ali was obsessed with the royal domestic helps, albeit some of them were talented dancers and singers. Sharar was perhaps right in his assessment:

He would fall in love with female palanquin-bearers, courtesans, domestic servants and women who came in and out of the palace, in short with hundreds of women, and because he was the heir to the throne, he had great success with his love-affairs, the shameful accounts of which can be read in his poems, writings and books. His character appears to be one of the most dubious in all the records of history.[7]

The British authors might well be right in arguing that Wajid Ali's Parikhana was his harem, while his 'paris' or fairies were concubines and courtesans. British historian Michael Edwardes duly analysed the King's escapade, saying:

A girl usually entered as a Khawasin or attendant. If the king liked her, she was promoted to Pari, or dancing-girl. If she was taken into concubinage, she was called a begum. Ultimately, if fortunate enough to have a child by the King, her name was changed and the word 'Mahal' added to it.[8]

In 1875–76, while in Calcutta, the King penned another literary marvel, titled *Banee* (meaning, The Bride), wherein he listed the names and number of his wives. The book elucidates a hundred and twenty-four mutá wives in Metiyaburj, whom he had selected for their innate gift of singing and dancing. The banished king specially mentions the names of forty-seven

Mahals, thirty-two Begums and four mamtúas (mutá wives) who were dear to him. The King lived for eleven years after he wrote this book and the account does not include his marriages thereafter. The edifying account of Shiek Tasaddul Hussain mentions something new. He wrote:

> *At the death of the deposed king in Calcutta, the number of his Mutái wives, besides the Nikahi wives, were two hundred and fifty. They were divided into eight categories and were paid monthly allowance from one hundred and fifty to fifteen rupees only. Some of them were paid a lumpsum and made to leave.* [9]

During his heyday in Lucknow, the King did not have more than seventy wives, and the number swelled to two hundred and fifty while he was in exile, when the circumstances were extremely hostile and he was growing older. Historian Mirza Ali Azhar believes that in total eighty-three women had the honour of sharing the bed with the King. The figure might be even more as the kind-hearted King, perhaps did not have the heart to turn away the hapless ladies after their contracts were over. But the most authentic figure appears in the government pension records of the descendents of Awadh in Calcutta. The record prepared by Lieutenant Colonel W.F. Prideaux, counts two hundred and eighteen mutá wives and thirty-three Mahals who used to get government pension after the King's death. Only one wife named Dulari Begum was discarded by the King, although she was not deprived from her pension.[10] Nevertheless, Wajid Ali Shah tried his best to safeguard his women, no matter what their status, and to protect them from any disappointment.

Eight

Wajid Ali Shah: A Theatrical Genius

The ostentatious and vulgar Nawabi culture, which was visible in Wajid Ali Shah since his adolescence, has a different implication. The heir-apparent of Awadh displayed a profligacy that worried his father and gave a free rein to scandalmongers. The Prince unhesitatingly picked beautiful women who had some talent in music or dance and put them up in a lavishly decorated palace—Parikhana or 'fairy land'. Parikhana was neither the name of a house nor the name of his book or his harem. Wajid Ali used the word poetically to denote his music school where his begums used to take lessons in performing arts.[1] The 'fairies' were put through rigorous training under maestros of music and dance. Female sentries were posted at the gate and no one was allowed inside, except the teachers. Lakhs of rupees were spent to maintain the Parikhana, pay the teachers and in providing costumes and ornaments to the fairies. Many talented performers of art made their debut in Wajid Ali Shah's Parikhana. Some of these fairies were married to him and were elevated to the status of a Begum. Those who attained motherhood were promoted to the status of Mahals, but with that ended their careers in dance and music. A Mahal had to spend the rest of her life behind the purdah. So was the case of Izzat Mahal or Ma'shuq Mahal.[2]

After ascending the throne, Wajid Ali Shah was too engrossed in bringing about administrative reforms and the Parikhana was deprived of all his tender care. The fairies and Begums were now forced to stay behind the curtains for a while. This period did not last for long and soon the King, baffled by British political intrigues, took recourse in love and decided to spend more time with his fairies once again. But before he could fully reorganize the Parikhana, he became seriously ill for a long period.[3] The King, who had been ill since January 1849, recovered from his illness in October 1850, with a reinvigorated love for music and dance. The lights of his Parikhana came on yet again.

Wajid Ali Shah did not allow religious orthodoxy to come in the way of his obsession with oriental music. The King had realized that in order to cherish the essence of Hindustani stagecraft, one must understand the fundamentals of Hindu culture and mythology that had come down the ages. He rediscovered the cult of traditional India that was firmly rooted in ancient thought. Lord Krishna became his role model. Wajid Ali Shah discovered within himself the archetypal romantic image of Krishna with his tenderness and mesmerizing beauty to enflame the desire of the individual soul for union. Krishna's romance with his gopis (female devotees of Lord Krishna) on a full-moon night on the banks of Yamuna was a perennial theme of inspiration to Wajid Ali Shah. The divine sport of Raas Leela that had once been enacted by Krishna, morphed into Rahas in Lucknow. Wajid Ali's Rahas was an opera with a perfect blend of dance from the Braj region depicting the mystic life of Krishna, and his own composition of kathak. The choreography contained thirty-six compositions of group dancing (chhatt s i ad-i rahas-i sulta i) performed by going round in circles and semicircles. The thirty-six Rahas were categorized into two formats, Rahas mubārak-i sultāni comprising seventeen forms and Rahas-i sultānī, which had fifteen forms. The other pieces of Rahas were 'operatic' in nature of which *Radha Kanhaiya ka Kissa,* was from his own composition. The *Kissa* was the first modern Urdu drama and a perfect blend of Indian and Persian conventions. Wajid Ali not only instructed the dancers but also directed their mudras and bhav.[4] The instruments used were jhānjh, pakhāwaj and bansuri.[5] Wajid Ali Shah's book titled *Banee* also describes his thirty-six types of Rahas that were all set in kathak style and had poetic names like 'Mor-Chchatri', 'Ghunghat', 'Salami', 'Mor Pankhi' and 'Mujra'. The literary piece gives exhaustive notes regarding the costumes, jewellery, and stagecraft of the time.[6]

Wajid Ali made full use of his Parikhana to stage Rahas, where he himself played the pivotal role of Krishna and wore the typical costume of a Hindu god. The Rahas dance and Urdu opera was a weeklong spectacular dance-drama festival held in Lucknow, and was popularly known as Jalsa.[7] Historians have often faltered in their assessments of various theatrical performances of Wajid Ali Shah and often drawn wrong conclusions. In Wajid Ali's own lexicon—'nautch' denotes solo dance; whereas in Rahas—nautch signifies circular dance in which he often played the lead character of Lord Krishna. Rahas Dhari was a spectacle of dance and worship whereas Rahas Nataka was a dance drama with a definite storyline, such as his *Radha Kanhaiya ka Kissa. Rahas ka Jalsa* was a dramatic display of the stories of three masnavis.

The first jalsa was performed in 1843, before Wajid Ali Shah ascended the throne. It was an impressive congregation of renowned artists of North Indian gharanas and performers of drama and operas. This is where the heir-apparent staged his first self-composed drama *Radha Kanhaiya ka Kissa*. Historians often extol Wajid Ali Shah as the first playwright of Hindustani theatre. This was the only jalsa organized by the King during his pre-kingship days. Although hard to believe in the wake of British propaganda about the King's indulgence in music and other frivolous pursuits, it is a fact that no jalsa was held for as long as seven years after the first one. The King could not devote much time to music after ascending the throne. Besides, his illness had kept him away from the stage till 1850. The second jalsa was staged after the King recovered from his illness in 1850. Thereafter, the King held two more jalsas in 1851 before he settled in Metiyaburj.

Wajid Ali Shah's fervent appetite for good music, dance and women continued unabated during his stay in Calcutta. His hefty annual income was mostly squandered to nurture his leisurely pursuits in Lucknow after he ascended the throne. But his opulence in Calcutta was limited to twelve lakh rupees, annually. Even then, Metiyaburj emerged as an edifying hub for the music connoisseurs. Many exponents of the Lucknow gharana followed the trail of the King and settled down in Calcutta. Wajid Ali made full use of his womenfolk to marshal nearly twenty dancing troupes in Metiyaburj and gave them dramatic names as— Radhamanjilwali, Jhumurwali, Latkanwali, Sharda Manzilwali, Nathwali, Ghunghatwali, Raswali, and Nakalwali.[8] Music in his life was revived after his release from Fort William on 9 July 1859 and from then the King staged twenty-three jalsas till 1875.[9] The jalsa performers, both male and female, were paid-artists and the King had to cough out a sum of twelve thousand, eight hundred and fifty-nine rupees per month to turn his stage dreams into reality.

From the details available in *Banee* (1875), it is evident that *Radha Kanhaiya ka Kissa* was staged regularly in Metiyaburj from 1861 onwards. However, confusion still remains about its composition. Although Masud Hasan Rizvi[10] finds no difference between the Rahas Natak played in Lucknow and the one played in Calcutta, historians believe that the version played in Calcutta was superior as it had more sequences and more skilled performers. The Lucknow version of the *Kissa* had six characters—Kanhaiya, Radha and four milkmaids—whereas the play enacted in Metiyaburj had twenty-one characters including a new comic character of Rama Chera. The dialogue was more prosaic than poetic.[11] In Metiyaburj, Abbasi Begum played the role of Kanhaiya while Mandar Begum became Radha in the first staging of the *Kissa* in 1861.

Wajid Ali Shah's life is replete with myths and legends. It is said that after his birth the royal astrologers predicted that due to the evil influence of stars, there was a chance that the prince would become a yogi or ascetic. To nullify all ill-effects the child should be dressed like a yogi on his birthdays. The King never faltered in this practice and even after ascending the throne at the age of twenty-four, he would incarnate himself as a yogi on his birthdays. He would step into his court pompously like a yogi wearing a saffron robe and holding a rosary in his hand. His face and body would be smeared with ash of pearls. The King would walk slowly into the court along with two beautiful Paris (fairies) dressed like Yoginis.[12] The auspicious occasion developed into a sacred pageant or mela, popularly known as Jogia Jashan (or Kaiserbagh Mela). The celebration was open to all, irrespective of cast and creed. The only caveat was that the people had to come dressed in saffron like Yogis.[13] Wajid Ali Shah must have introduced the custom in Calcutta as well, but there is no authentic record to support this.

What is praiseworthy is the simplicity of religious beliefs and the secular approach followed by the rulers of Awadh in the state, which was predominantly Hindu. Asaf-ud-Daulla would spend five to six lakh rupees every year to celebrate Holi. He also undertook the task of renovating a Hindu shrine at Suraj Kund. Ghazi-ud-Din Haider initiated the annual Basant Mela or the Spring Festival at Baradari in Hasan Bagh where all visitors to the fair would come in their best saffron coloured garments. Even birds and animals were stained with saffron.

It was during the reign of Wajid Ali Shah that Lucknow became the seat of oriental culture and ethos. The art of dance, drama, poetry, literature and music reached its pinnacle during his time even when his European critics construed the King's passion for music as the root cause for misadministration of the state and oppression of his subjects.

Wajid Ali Shah's experiment with theatre during his nine-year-long reign in Lucknow finds special mention in the history of Hindustani theatre. In 1846, Wajid Ali staged another play based on the love story of Princess Ghazala, titled *Darya-i-Tashsq'*.[14] In 1853, his *Afsane-i-Isbaq* was staged. After that, *Bhahar-i-Ulfat* and several more followed. But the most allegorical presentation of the whole genre of Hindustani theatre in India was the staging of Aga Hasan Amanat's *Inder Sabha* in 1854. Based on Hindu mythology, the play included 'thirty-one ghazals, nine thumris, four holis, fifteen songs and two chaubolas and five chhands with enough scope for dances as well.'[15] In the enactment of this play, neither was there any curtain nor did the stage have any formal setting. Rather, the play was set in the tradition of Indian stagecraft. Strangely, Wajid Ali Shah did not play any role either in *Radha Kanhaiya ka Kissa* or in *Inder Sabha*. He only dressed up in the attire of a Jogi for Jogia Jashan, which was not a drama.

India has an indigenous dramatic tradition, which was not influenced by foreign cultures and emerged as a distinct genre of Sanskrit literature based on Hindu mythology. Urdu theatre came much later to India, and scholars believe that the curtain was raised with the enactment of *Inder Sabha* in Wajid Ali Shah's court. For the first time a drama that had been composed in Urdu, had emerged from the court precincts and made its debut on public stage.

Wajid Ali's penchant for Urdu theatre in Calcutta was not well documented, although many of his performers had followed him to Metiyaburj, where they had finally settled. Even Sharar's account fails to shed light on the staging of Urdu theatre in the King's durbar. The reason for such apathy could be explained by quoting Sharar:

> *But suddenly refined society lost interest in these new plays. Love for music made the elite turn their attention again to troupes of singers and dancers and forms derived from natak were patronized only by the masses and the people of the bazaar.*[16]

Sharar blames the faltering eloquence of Urdu script for the change in the audience profile.[17] Notwithstanding Sharar's elucidation to justify theatre-apathy amongst the elite, Bengali stage-art had generated considerable interest amongst the Bengali intelligentsia even before the banished king came to settle in Calcutta. However, Urdu theatre could not arouse much enthusiasm among the Bengali audience.

Nine

An Exponent of Kathak

The Bengali bhadraloks in Calcutta lived a dual existence under the colonial sky. The fervent espousal of the European ethos did not in any way hinder their increasing passion for classical dance. Besides being the political capital of colonial India, Calcutta was also the country's foremost cultural hub. Indeed, the intellectual and artistic grandeur was fast spreading its wings in the city. The Zamindars of Calcutta, embellished in their best feathers, learned to cherish the kernel of North Indian classical gharanas in early nineteenth century. However, what the Bengali elite were sorely missing in the majlis was provided when the banished king of Awadh came to settle in Calcutta. A classical dance gharana, hitherto unfamiliar to Calcuttans, reached the court of the Bengali gentry. The dance form of kathak had provided the quintessential vigour to the Lucknowi gharana and now whetted the appetite of Bengali intelligentsia.

As kathak found its way from Lucknow to Calcutta, it brought with it a horde of excellent khayal and thumri singers and expert kathak dancers. The rich patrons of Calcutta arranged big musical assemblages or soirees in their mansions where the tawaifs of Lucknow evoked much interest and excitement. Patronage of Lucknow gharana in Calcutta was given a new thrust when Wajid Ali Shah settled in the city with a bevy of baijees brought from Lucknow. The tradition of tawaif culture made a beginning in Calcutta. The Durbar Hall of Metiyaburj became the venue for great musical assemblages of maestros and exponents of classical dance and music. Music lovers of Calcutta gathered to hear Wajid Ali Shah sing his favourite Lucknowi thumris, and to get a marvellous glimpse of his kathak dance. The durbar was lavishly adorned to incite the old memories of Lucknow Baradari.

Although seldom seen or witnessed, the Lucknow gharana was not unknown to the elite of Calcutta before Wajid Ali Shah set foot in the city. Wealthy Bengalis vied with one another in inviting famous dancers, even from faraway Lucknow and Delhi, to entertain their European guests. Dancers from Muslim families, who hailed from North India and were specially acquainted with the Lucknow gharana, were given an exalted position in the courts of the Bengali babus. While the Bengalis called them baijees, the British branded them as nautch girls. Several renowned baijees such as Begum Jan, Hingool, Nanni Jan, Supun Jan, Ushroon and the legendary Nickee graced the dance parties in early nineteenth century Calcutta.[1]

The 'babu–baijee' culture, which was once patronized by the Calcutta elite, alludes to an extravagant pursuit meant more to generate envy rather than to give a fillip and cultivate a performing art. The main characters of this art—the nautch girls— were exploited by their Bengali sponsors and forced to captivate the European guests by their seductive charm. Though Lucknowi classical dance was not unknown to the Calcuttans before Wajid Ali Shah, practising a gharana to ameliorate a classical form of art was never thought of. Wajid Ali Shah, being the greatest proponent of kathak dance in India and an accomplished musician and dancer himself, brought with him the art and culture of kathak to Calcutta.

With the decline of Mughals, the court musicians and dancers of Delhi flocked towards Lucknow in search of greener pastures. The oldest gharana of kathak was practised in Rajasthan, and the performing art had entered the Mughal court perhaps during the reign of Akbar through his Rajput allies[2]. The kathak exponents from Delhi interfaced with the classical dancers of Awadh to develop a new dance form—Lucknow gharana. Direct émigrés from Rajasthan also added lustre to the new dance form. One of the earliest exponents was Pandit Ishwari Prasad Misra, a Brahmin dancer and a devotee of Lord Krishna. His son Arguji continued to bear the torch of his ancestors. Arguji's three sons, Prakashji, Dayaji and Hari Lalji, were also proficient dancers. Prakashji migrated to Lucknow after his father's death and established himself as a court dancer in the durbar of Asaf-ud-Daulla. The Lucknow gharana of kathak was fine-tuned to reach its apex under his three adept sons, Maharaj Thakur Prasad, Maharaj Durga Prasad and Maharaj Maanji.

It was Thakur Prasad who taught kathak to Wajid Ali Shah and was revered as the royal guru. His seat in the durbar was placed next to the King. It is said that Wajid Ali acknowledged his guru with so much wealth that it took six palanquins to carry it. The tradition of kathak was passed on to Bindadin Maharaj and his brother Kalka (Prasad) Maharaj, the sons of Durga Prasad and nephews of Thakur Prasad, who took the art to its highest form. It was during their time that the grandeur of Lucknow gharana of kathak spread across the country. Bindadin Maharaj was also an expert vocalist and composed more than one thousand five hundred thumris. He taught thumris to a large number of female vocalists, including Zohra Bai and Gauhar Jaan. It was he who prompted Wajid Ali Shah to blend thumri in the choreography of kathak.[3]

The Lucknow gharana matured into a distinct and individual style during Wajid Ali Shah's time. The durbar was mesmerized by the performances of the singers and dancers, extolled as the best in the country. Wajid Ali Shah's experiment of blending kathak and thumri was a milestone in the history of Indian music. The quintessence of kathak was expressed in the lyrics of thumri. The expressive movements of the dancers were echoed in the lyricism of the musical style. The King made full use of all the three elements of kathak, that is, Nritya, Nritta and Natya, for his compositions in the choreography of Rahas. On the concluding day of the fete, the King himself would step onto the stage to join the dance. Wajid Ali Shah broke the religious insulation by infusing his school of art with strong secular overtones. It was Maharaj Thakur Prasad and his descendents who instilled in him the elixir of Lord Krishna's credo. Wajid Ali himself gained better credence of being a sincere devotee of Krishna and would often dress up as Krishna himself. The women in colonial days would never even dream of learning kathak, as it was contemptuously looked down upon as a lascivious type of dancing that was suitable only for prostitutes. But it was not so to the last King of Awadh. Wajid Ali Shah himself engaged kathak teachers to instruct his mutá wives living in his Parikhana.

In 1856, after Wajid Ali Shah had settled down in Calcutta, a retinue of dancers who were proficient in classical kathak of Lucknow gharana were brought to Calcutta to embellish the classical culture of the city. Wajid Ali Shah's guru Thakur Prasad passed away that same year. Bindadin and Kalka Maharaj decided to stay back, although Bindadin had to leave Lucknow during the great mutiny. Kalka Prasad preferred to reside in Benaras.[4] The King's departure sounded the death knell of the grandeur of court-dance in Lucknow, but kathak did not lose its glamour.

Whilst in Calcutta, Wajid Ali penned a book titled *Musammi Ba Banee*, which was lithographed at Metiyaburj. The literary piece is a treasure trove of kathak. The book testifies that kathak was no longer a Hindu form of art in Lucknow but was adopted and improved by Muslim exponents under Wajid Ali Shah. Many of his disciples were engaged to train his Begums behind the purdah. Wajid Ali himself taught two to three hundred dance items to his Begums and disciples.[5] The King has described three hundred and sixty dancing gats[6] in another literary marvel named *Sautal Mubarak* compiled in 1852, which he composed and later choreographed to reinvent kathak. He chose only sixteen of them for his court performance, while most of the remaining compositions slipped into oblivion.[7]

Truly speaking, the tradition of the Lucknow gharana was largely preserved and nurtured in the dark alleyways of Lucknow since its heyday. If the exponents of dance and music in the court of Wajid Ali Shah went on to win laurels, it was the tawaifs living in the kothas[8] of obscurity who embellished their creation and fostered the art and saved it from being lost in the sands of time. In the post-Nawabi era, classical kathak continued to live in its purest form amongst the courtesans of Lucknow, embodied as tawaifs. Customarily, tawaifs skilled in singing were called bais and those skilled in both dancing and singing were called Jaans.

Legend has it that during the festival of Holi in 1867, Wajid Ali Shah danced in the attire of a nautch girl. The rare sight was witnessed by connoisseurs of Calcutta's music circle like Aghore

Nath Chakrborty, Sajjad Mohammad and other honoured guests gathered in his Durbar Hall. It was an unforgettable evening. The Badshah also sang and the audience could feel the ecstasy of his Lucknowi thumri. Sometimes Nasir-ud-Din Haidar dressed and talked like a woman, which often encouraged and fed the scandalmongers, but Wajid Ali's masquerade was more of a symbol than disguise and done for the sake of art only.[9]

Ustad Asadullah 'Kaukab' Khan believed that Wajid Ali never danced, but his body swayed to the impulse of 'lai' or time beat. Kaukab heard from his father Ustad Niamatullah Khan (1827–1903) who had been in Badshah's service in Lucknow and also in Metiyaburj that the King moved his toes in sleep with the rhythm of lai, an evidence of his indisputable devotion to dance and music.[10]

Sharar also emphatically believed that Wajid Ali never danced. He wrote: 'It is said that the King danced but it is absolutely wrong and baseless.' According to him it was a British conspiracy supported by some of the accomplices from royal family who wanted to tarnish the King's image. Many contemporary paintings that showed him dancing with his ladies were concocted. Sharar claims,

> *After full investigation I have come to know that all of them [paintings] are fraudulent and false. The truth about the Melas at Qaisar Bagh is that the King did not dance but indulged in the gambols. The fact is that he never danced at Lucknow when he was a King or at Metiyaburj.*

Yet the King was a connoisseur of the art and Sharar avers,

> *Being a master of music and having observed dancing for a long time he had developed a keen insight in the art of*

> *dancing also. And if any dancer committed any mistake, while dancing, he would, sitting on his bedstead, point out the mistake and give the correct direction with his hands.*[11]

Wajid Ali Shah's interest in dance and music evoked much sensation and impression amongst the baijees in Calcutta. The dancers, mostly concubines living blissfully under the patronage of their babus and having slithered through the murky mazes of life, aspired to attract the Badshah and if lucky, hoped to make a fortune as his mutá wives. It goes without saying that none had the merit and excellence, which the Badshah was looking for. Perhaps, Wajid Ali Shah was unaware of the socio-cultural ethos that was prevalent in contemporary Calcutta. In reality, before the King's arrival, dancing in Calcutta was confined to the abodes of women dancers of lower orders called khemtawaalis whose voluptuous movements of hips and flashing of limbs were in complete contrast to the classical dance of Lucknow. The Bengali elite were fond of either khemtas from lower orders or baijees from upper classes, or sometimes even ordinary prostitutes from Calcutta's bordellos.[12] Classical music and dance were among the least of their priorities.

The Radha–Krishna narratives were expressed in lascivious style and with vulgarity that was evident in gestures of the divine pair. Wajid Ali Shah discovered a distorted version of his Rahas dance in the application of khemta in folk dramas organized by leading proponents in mid-nineteenth century Calcutta.[13] Khemta was also found to have been introduced to the Muslim religious entertainments like tazia processions of Muharram, in the pre-Wajid Ali era in Calcutta.[14]

The decline of Delhi and Lucknow after the Sepoy Mutiny led to a decrease in the patronage given by the old aristocrats.

This was one of the reasons for emigration of the nautch girls to Benaras and largely to Calcutta. The emerging Bengali zamindars, traders and dewans of the mid-eighteenth century fostered the nautch girls and their ensembles, who were migrating from the North, in their own country houses. The patronage was given more to flaunt their affluence than to uphold the quintessence of a new gharana. A new breed of courtesans adept in kathak and thumri could be seen mainly on Chitpore Road and adjacent streets and by-lanes. The skills cultivated by them, while they lived in the dark alleys practising their trade, were incredible.

But the influx of North Indian baijees also had a dark side to it. A manifold increase in the flesh trade of Calcutta was witnessed in the mid-eighteenth century. Unlike the tawaifs of Lucknow, the nautch girls of lower classes who had failed to find a babu finally took refuge in the mushrooming brothels of Calcutta. A few of the Calcuttans were acquainted with the culture of tawaifs.[15] Yet, the city's landed gentry were not far removed from the world of temptation. In the durbar of Metiyaburj, the dancers were borne for the sake of art. Prostitution was forbidden. The King had no fascination to keep mistresses, but he had a deep desire to nurture the art of kathak amidst his dancers, many of whom were adored as his mutá wives.

There are reasons to believe that the influx of baijees from the North, especially from Lucknow, produced a ripple effect in Metiyaburj. Dancers of distinction perhaps had tried their fortune in the durbar of the king, but contemporary accounts fail to mention the names of any specific court dancer in Metiyaburj. Even Sharar could not provide this information. Only on one occasion does Sharar recall the mesmerizing performance of

Munsarim Wali Gohar who came to Metiyaburj and staged a kathak performance for three hours. Many talented dancers of the King's durbar and other distinguished guests witnessed her incredible performance.[16] On the contrary, some of the baijees in Calcutta carved out a cultural space for themselves in the Bengali bhadralok society, especially in the purview of dance, drama and music.

It would be simplistic to view the King's success story in only the light of kathak. Critics believe that kathak in the court of Wajid Ali Shah was more a mimicry of the Hindu stage art rather than a perception of the classical form of dance. They wondered how far could the King, a Shiite Muslim, embrace the Hindu philosophy. The Lucknow gharana of kathak reached its excellence under Bindadin and Kalka Maharaj. Bindadin was only twenty-six years old and Kalka was even younger when the lanterns of the Awadh court were blown out and yet they took the gharana to new heights after Wajid Ali Shah left Lucknow to settle in Calcutta. There was no other maestro who could match up to the calibre of Bindadin in Calcutta. Notwithstanding the critical arguments of historical commentators, Wajid Ali Shah is still considered a doyen of the performing arts, who has left an indelible mark on Indian classical music and dance.

Ten

A Prelude to Thumri in Calcutta

The dulcet notes of a song resonated across the long corridor of the Durbar Hall in Metiyaburj. The floor, covered with decorative carpets and enveloped in white linen or chandni, was graced by the assembled musicians. Large mirrors and crystal chandeliers added to the aura and reflected the admirers gathered in the Hall. The sound of ghungrus was reverberating the alleyways of the palace. The ambience was reminiscent of the lost glory of Lucknow. A Bengali bhadralok stepped down from a buggy and sauntered down the hallway of the durbar. He was cordially greeted by Wajid Ali Shah and seated next to him.

Raja Sourindra Mohan Tagore (1840–1914) was one of the greatest connoisseurs of music of the time. Raja Sahib had travelled all the way from Pathuriaghata to Metiyaburj to enjoy the quintessence of Lucknowi thumri. The musical genre was not unknown to him, yet the thumri that was sung in the durbar of Metiyaburj had a unique distinction. Raja Sourindra Mohan Tagore had a perfect understanding of the Hindu musical genre that had won him laurels from all corners of the world. But thumri held a place of pride in his heart, especially when the King's own compositions were sung in the durbar. With this, the story of an exotic and highly mellifluous musical genre started to unfold on the banks of the Hooghly.

Wajid Ali Shah's most popular thumris are those that are the saddest yet sweetest of parting songs. In the durbar of Metiyaburj, the Badshah sang his own songs with great devotion and patriotism. Whilst singing, he would be in a state of joyous ecstasy, transported back to his beloved Lucknow, both in body and soul. He would sit quietly for a moment and tears would trickle down his face. Thus, he lamented,

All this time I was in a dreamland as though transported by unknown hands to my Kaisarbagh Baradari. Ah, what I have left behind! Now, only the sweet memories linger.[1]

The Durbar Hall of Metiyaburj would be brimming with eminent musicians and music personalities of Calcutta who had assembled to cherish the archetypical style of Lucknowi thumri and kathak dance composed by Wajid Ali Shah. The distinguished dhrupad exponents of Bishnupuri gharana—Jadunath Bhattacharya (1834–80) popularly known as Jadu Bhatta, and Aghore Nath Chakravarty, were great admirers of the Badshah's durbari thumri at Metiyaburj. Pandit Jadu Bhatta was also the music-guru of Rabindranath Tagore and a resident of Thakurbari at Jorasanko for some time.[2] He sang dhrupad in the durbar of Metiyaburj and was accompanied by the notable pukhwaji Keshab Chandra Mitra.[3]

Among several other musicians of Calcutta who came to visit Metiyaburj, Murad Ali Khan was one. The renowned North Indian dhrupadiya of Tilwandi gharana was a long time resident of Calcutta. Murad Ali was one of the very few singers who were given the right to sing the Deepak rag in the durbar.[4] It is said that he was a court musician of Wajid Ali Shah's in Metiyaburj for a while and left the durbar during the Badshah's lifetime. He was also the music guru of Aghore Nath Chakravarty.

The Badshah continued his Bhairavi thumri in *bol banao* style:

Babul mora naihar chuuto hi jaaye
chaar kahaar mil, mori doliiyaa uthaaye
more apanaa begana chhuto hi jaaye
anganaa to parbat bhaye, dehlii bhayi bides
je baabul ghar aapano, mai chali piya ke des

Meaning—

O father, I depart forcibly from my home
Four men gathered to lift my palanquin
my loved ones will become strangers
the innermost portals of my home will be unreachable
as I leave my father's home and go to my husband's
country.

This immortal piece enthralled not only the honourable guests of Metiyaburj, but continues to enliven the hearts of millions of listeners even today. Hidden in these lines is an esoteric allegory of a desolate heart after he is separated from his homeland and banished from his kingdom. The four bearers of the palanquin (*'chaar kahaar mil, mori doliiyaa uthaaye'*) are symbolic of the four bearers of his coffin. The Badshah might have been contemplating to end his life in self-exile and thus his song had taken him away from all mores of life. However, it was his passion for music that incited him to keep his sweet memories of Lucknow alive. Soon, Metiyaburj, his kingdom-in-exile, blossomed as a centre of classical vocal and instrumental music, where a large number of musicians from northern India would congregate.

Initially referred to as a raga rather than a genre, thumri

in the latter form is believed to have originated in the court of Lucknow under Wajid Ali Shah.[5] The common theme that runs through most of his durbari thumri is 'separation'. Although some texts epitomized the heavenly joy of lovemaking, it was eclipsed by the pangs of departure. While the throne of Delhi was losing its lustre by middle of the eighteenth century, Lucknow was emerging as a political, economic and cultural centre of northern India. Lucknow was gifted with an elite class that had both the taste and wealth to patronize innumerable courtesans and musicians that had migrated from Delhi. The Lucknow tawaifs were diligently trained in classical music and were exalted as eminent exponents of classical art. But unlike the Mughal penchant for classical music, the Lucknowi durbar tended to renounce the demanding dhrupads and kheyal for the lighter and more adaptable thumri and ghazal.[6]

In the two decades preceding the great revolt of 1857, thumri reached its apogee of popularity in Lucknow court. Thumri in combination with kathak made its debut in the court of Wajid Ali Shah and remained enmeshed in the kothas of the Lucknowi tawaifs till mid-nineteenth century. While Wajid Ali Shah is ascribed as the father of present-day genre of thumri, it was his courtier Sadiq Ali Khan who was the single most important figure to develop Lucknow gharana of thumri. Sadiq Ali Khan was trained in kheyal and was one of the very few masters whose name is associated with the transformation of thumri from kheyal. Chroniclers believe that it was he who refined and introduced the bandish thumri in Lucknow. Believed to be a centenarian, Sadiq Ali Khan had many renowned disciples including the Badshah himself as well as Bindadin Maharaj, Qadr Piya and some distinguished tawaifs like Haidar Jan and Najma.[7]

Thumris were traditionally composed in Braj Bhasa, or the

dialect of Agra–Mathura region of North India, which was closely associated with the devotion of Lord Krishna. Some were composed in Khari Boli and a few in Urdu. Incorporating Urdu vocabulary in some of the compositions is indicative of the region's desire to adapt to Muslim taste. Wajid Ali Shah was an adept composer of light classical thumri under his pen name, Äkhtar Piya. The King composed his thumris in Braj Bhasha and some in Urdu as well. Together with Bindadin Maharaj, Wajid Ali composed melodies of light classical thumris to blend with kathak. Dadra also emerged along with thumri in the court of Wajid Ali Shah. Dadra, a genre of light classical Hindustani music, resembles thumri in many aspects and gave much more freedom to the artists. The text that dealt with love and passion was originally sung in Dadra tal (rhythm) in the King's court.[8] Another important thematic form of thumri was one that was composed to celebrate the vernal festival of Holi. The deposed king was a secularist and his compositions of thumri crossed the narrow boundaries of religious chauvinism. Based on the sensuality of Krishna-cult, Wajid Ali's lyrics comprised several names of Hindu avatars such as Hari, Radha and Jugal Kishore.

A much lighter classical music-genre called ghazal had flourished in the court of Lucknow during the heyday of Wajid Ali Shah. The Badshah was passionate about Urdu poetry and composed some immortal ghazals, which are sung even today. Ghazal, a Muslim oriented semi-classical genre, lay outside the tradition of Sanskrit-based musical themes. The efflorescence of Lucknow culture played an important role in bolstering the more adaptable ghazals and thumris than the austere dhrupad and kheyal. The famous Urdu poet and composer of some evergreen ghazals—Amir Meenai (1826–1900) served in the court of Wajid Ali Shah for five years till the mutiny broke out.[9]

Chroniclers narrate that Wajid Ali Shah brought with him a bevy of gifted musicians in his mimic capital of Metiyaburj. However, no authentic record is available to testify that the great maestros of Awadh had settled in Calcutta along with the deposed king. The connoisseurs either stayed back in Lucknow or migrated to enrich the durbars of other princely states. Calcutta was never considered productive by the genius players before the beginning of the Nawabi era.

Unlike classical dance, Bengal had perceived the taste of classical music long before Wajid Ali Shah's arrival. A dhrupad style of Bengali classical music made its debut in the court of Malla King Raghunath Singha II of Bishnupur in Bankura district between 1702 to 1712, after he brought in Ustad Bahadur Khan Se`nia and his pukhwaj player Peer Baux, from Delhi on a very high remuneration.Bahadur Khan, a descendent of Tansen's lineage developed the famous and the only classical genre in Bengal, the Bishnupur gharana.

Pandit Jadhunath Bhattacharya (alias Jadu Bhatta) the distinguished musician who also attended the court of Metiyaburj, was a dhrupadiya of Bishnupur Gharana.[10] Although dhrupad started losing ground to kheyal in North India from eighteenth century onwards, the metamorphosis happened much later in Bishnupur. Aghore Nath Chakravarty of Bishnupur gharana and a celebrity in Metiyaburj durbar experimented with Bishnupuri kheyal. Wajid Ali Shah got a flavour of Bishnupuri gharana when these guests visited his durbar in Metiyaburj and sung in their own style.

Wajid Ali Shah's presence led to the decision of innumerable musicians to migrate to Calcutta. It was then that Bengal got the taste of a distinguished North Indian semi-classical gharana. The Badshah brought with him to Calcutta his thumri along with his nautch girls and musicians who could create magic on their instruments. Thumri as a genre soon percolated down from the zamindars to the womenfolk of the city's bordellos. Chitpore was one such area where the courtesans followed the lifestyle of Lucknowi tawaifs. A new generation of talented musicians was born who further refined the thumris. Lucknow never encouraged pure classical music; rather it bolstered a variety of light classical styles and made them popular throughout the country. The musical culture of Bengal preferred the lighter style of thumri to the abstruse kheyal and dhrupad. In Calcutta, similar to Lucknow, thumri went concurrently with kathak.

When Wajid Ali Shah came from Lucknow to settle in Calcutta, the babu culture was already tuned to accept the brilliance of his thumris. Wajid Ali Shah aroused much interest amongst the elite in Calcutta to whom the grandeur of Lucknowi thumri was not unknown. Rather, the influence of Lucknowi thumri was so strong in Calcutta that classical music was completely swamped and replaced by light classical style after 1860.[11] The King composed several raginis under his pseudonym Äkhtar Piya and named them Jogi, Juhi and Shah pasand, the last meaning 'favourite of the king'[12] and charmed his audiences who were hitherto alien to him.

Although some of the most mellifluous ghazals were composed by the King for his books *Diwani-Akhtar* and *Huzn-e-Akhtari* in Calcutta, the Muslim oriented genre of music was not enjoyed by the Hindu-dominated Bengali bhadralok society. The amicable cultural interaction between the two religions, which was a distinctive feature in Lucknow was somewhat missing in Calcutta. Calcutta which was greatly swayed by the egos of Hinduism, unlike Lucknow, looked down on ghazals as a product of Islamic culture. The new style of North Indian majlishi music found no place in the heart of Bengali elite. Traditionally, ghazals are poetic expressions of the pangs of separation and loss. Wajid Ali's own ghazals were full of pain and pathos reflecting his grief-laden heart. But Urdu and Persian lyrics baffled the people of Calcutta's music circle and in the durbar of Metiyaburj too.

Before the advent of thumri in Calcutta, another semi-classical form of North Indian music called tappa found its way from Lucknow into the heart of Bengali music lovers. Tappa is said to have developed in the court of Asaf-ud-Daulla from popular folk songs of camel riders in Punjab and Sindh and the credit for it goes to Asaf-ud-Daulla's court singer Shori Mian (1742–92). Wajid Ali Shah's penchant for tappa is not very evident, although scholars believe that during his time kheyal was sung in tappa style and a new sub genre called tappa-kheyal was developed by him.[13]

According to some authors, Imam Bandi, the famous tappa singer of Benaras, spent many years in Metiyaburj. She trained a number of students including her son Ramzan Khan and Nagendra Nath Bhattacharya. Ramzan Khan became a famous singer of tappa-kheyal style,[14] who stayed in Calcutta till his death.[15]

A large number of composers from Delhi and Lucknow had dissociated themselves from their erstwhile Muslim supporters and migrated to Calcutta in early nineteenth century. Now they thrived under the lavish tutelage of Hindu bhadraloks despite the presence of a decent Muslim population in Calcutta. The deposed king was poised to be the leader who prodded the budding Muslim gentry of Calcutta to patronize great performers of music.

Though the King was accompanied by a bevy of adept

musicians, his hunt for talent never stopped in Calcutta. Sharar once narrated an incident when Wajid Ali became restless to meet one Dhunni Khan, a famous singer in Calcutta. Dhunni was performing in a majlis at Metiyaburj in the house of a noble and his melodious voice reached the ears of the banished King. Dhunni Khan obliged to sing before the court, but after hearing his songs the King commented, 'He has a good voice but does not know music.'[16] The King therefore rejected him and Dhunni Khan found no place in his court.

The quest for talent went on till his last days. Near the end of his life the King gave refuge to a twenty-six-year-old Jewish Armenian lady, who had come to seek fortune in Calcutta from Benaras. Malka Jaan, as she was called, had her training in music under Kalloo Ustad and had learnt dance from Ali Baksh of Lucknow.[17] Her original name was Victoria Hemmings who later embraced Islam and renamed herself as Malka Jaan. Malka was known for her stunning beauty cloaked in white skin, personal appeal and excellent skill in Hindustani classical music. When she was invited to perform at Qasr ul Baiza in Metiyaburj, the tawaif enthralled the Badshah by singing two of his own thumris. A wave of emotion rippled through the court and an overwhelmed King was struck with nostalgia. The long-cherished dream of Malka Jaan of Azamgar to establish herself in the court of Wajid Ali Shah was realized. She was appointed the court singer and her illustrious musical career started to bloom. Malka Jaan settled in Calcutta in 1883 with her ten-year-old-daughter, Angelina Yeoward alias Gauhar. Malka Jaan was a gifted poetess. Her Urdu verses were complied as *Makhzan-e-ulfat-e-Mallika* and published in Calcutta in 1886. Malka bought a house at Chitpore where she lived for the rest of her life. Gauhar was brought up in the cultural milieu of Chitpore.

She would often lurk in a corner of Wajid Ali Shah's durbar to watch her mother perform. Gauhar was exposed to North Indian classical gharanas in Metiyaburj. Gauhar blossomed as the iconic Gauhar Jaan and became the first Indian artist to press a gramophone record in 1902.

The kheyal exponent Ali Baksh was employed in the durbar of Metiyaburj, but the exact year of his arrival in Calcutta is not known. Ali Baksh stayed in Metiyaburj while the King was alive and afterwards he spent some years in the Barabazaar area of Calcutta and finally went back to Gwalior. The only Bengali student he had in Metiyaburj was Pandit Bamacharan Bandhopadhyay who eventually became a legendary kheyal singer in Bengal. Ali Baksh's blessings on his favourite student gave him an opportunity to sing kheyal raag Bhopali before Wajid Ali Shah. The King's commendation in the durbar was indeed the lifetime recognition for Bamacharan in his music career.

Abdul Halim Sharar in his commentary mentions the names of Ahmed Khan, Taj Khan and Ghulam Hussain Khan as distinguished singers in the court of Metiyaburj. Ahmed Khan was an exponent of kheyal and tappa in Lucknow who came to Calcutta after the King was deposed. But how long he stayed in Metiyaburj is not known. Ahmed Khan had many Bengali students of whom Benimadhab Adhikari, alias *Beni Ustad*, was the most eminent. Pandit Bamacharan Bandhopadhyay also took training under Ahmed Khan for some days in Metiyaburj.[18]

Little is known about Ustad Taj Khan, except that he was a dhrupad and kheyal singer of Senia lineage in the court of Lucknow and came to Metiyaburj with the King. Afterwards, he left Calcutta and joined the royal court of Nepal.[19] Bamacharan Bandhopadhyay came in contact with Taj Khan during his stay in

Calcutta. There is hardly any information available on Ghulam Hussain in the music circle of Bengal.

A host of North Indian musicians were engaged in the durbar of Metiyaburj though their names are not known. However, some of them can be traced from the oral tradition of Bengal and the memoirs of many distinguished Bengali musicians who spent their student years in Metiyaburj.

The debut of Lucknowi thumri in Calcutta by Wajid Ali Shah triggered a spurt of creativity in the sphere of Hindustani classical music of Bengal. Soon Calcutta emerged as an edifying hub of classical music in India and for this the credit goes to the King. Wajid Ali was not only a benevolent patron of music but was himself a gifted composer. His experiment with Hindustani music opened a new horizon in the history of semi-classical genre. But his reputation did not remain unblemished. While the popularity of thumri was widely attributed to the munificent support of Wajid Ali Shah, his ardent generosity could not escape the criticism of one of his contemporary writers Ustad Asadullah Kaukab. Kaukab, a renowned Sarodia[20] and musicologist of his age who stayed in Metiyaburj wrote:

Wajid Ali was a master at the art and possessed the knowledge of an expert but cannot escape the criticism that it was his conventional and cheap tastes that made the music of Lucknow frivolous and easily understood by all. In accordance with popular tastes even the most discriminating singers omitted difficult techniques and based their music on light, simple and attractive tunes which could be appreciated by everyone... During the reign of Wajid Ali Shah there was a large number of musical experts in Lucknow, but the singers which had influence at court and received royal titles, were

> not among the most adept... There was much talk of music
> at the time of Wajid Ali Shah, but the art had fallen from
> favour and only the commonplace aspects were in vogue. In
> Lucknow, Kadar Piya[21] (one of the pseudonyms of Wajid Ali)
> composed Thumris, which became popular with the masses
> with the result that music was cheapened. Most music lovers
> lost interest in the classical forms of ragas and raginis and
> began to enjoy Kadar Piya's Thumris.[22]

The criticism was undoubtedly idiosyncratic and unfortunate. Asadullah Kaukab, a keen observer of Hindustani gharanas of fine arts since the beginning of his career, was puritanical in his views. The King's innovation was therefore frowned upon. Probably he was right in his own wisdom. Yet, the King's generosity in developing a variety of light classical styles explicitly whetted the appetite of the Bengali intelligentsia.

Eleven

Wajid Ali Shah and the Dulcet Symphony of Metiyaburj

In the middle of the nineteenth century, Calcutta blossomed as an epicentre of Hindustani classical music following the trail of Bengal Renaissance. The window was opened to let in fresh air from the North to sweep away the smugness of the Bengali bhadhraloks. Music maestros migrated to Calcutta irrespective of their place of origin and embraced the city as their second home. And so did the deposed King of Awadh. His entourage of musical performers got deeply entwined in the social and artistic identities of the Bengali intelligentsia. Bengal witnessed a second resurgence after 1857, a renaissance in performing art that was stimulated by Wajid Ali Shah and his aficionados. The King brought with him a team of instrumentalists to Calcutta to embellish his thumris and kathak. These musicians made their debut in composing a new genre of background music hitherto unknown to the Bengali music lovers.

The impressive durbar of Metiyaburj that stemmed from the remembrance of Kaiserbagh baradari was enlivened in 1858. The year marks a watershed moment in the musical history of Bengal. The Badshah built a huge oval-shaped building known as Qasr ul Baiza on the banks of the Hooghly where the music ensembles would meet. A large circular durbar hall was located on the upper floor. The room was devoid of corners so that musicians could be seated along the wall and the centre could be kept free for the performers. The mellifluous flow of music ceaselessly filled the air of Qasr ul Baiza day and night. When the mehfils were over, the musicians would continue their practice well into the day. The Badshah desired to have an uninterrupted musical milieu in his durbar, so that whenever he wished to listen to some renditions all he needed to do was to enter the circular hall.

With the decline of the dhrupad in late eighteenth century, the traditional musical instruments associated with dhrupad style such as the bin, rabab, sursingar and the pukhwaj[1] gradually yielded to the rising popularity of the sitar, sarod, sarangi and tabla. Tabla replaced traditional pukhwaj and became the most important accompaniment for kathak and thumri. Many traditional musicians moved their domain to the new genre of musical instruments.[2]

Although oral tradition accredits Amir Khusrau, the progenitor of North Indian classical music of the thirteenth century, as the inventor of the modern sitar in India, the story fails to impress modern chroniclers. Probably Amir Khusrau is mistaken with another eighteenth century musician named Khusrau Khan of Delhi.[3] The latter was the younger brother of Nyamat Khan (Sadarang)—the famous kheyal exponent of Muhammad Shah Rangeela's durbar. Khusrau Khan's son Firoz Khan (Adarang) was a distinguished court singer of Muhammad Shah Rangeela. The two maestros Nyamat Khan (Sadarang) and his nephew Firoz Khan (Adarang) mastered the art of playing a variety of musical instruments. Firoz Khan's son Masit Khan established a new style in the history of sitar by inventing a new dhrupad style called Masitkhani Gat.[4] Notwithstanding the soaring popularity of Masitkhani Gat in Delhi, a lighter and faster gat of sitar, believed to have been designed on the principles of thumri, tarana and to some extent kheyal, evolved in the court of Wajid Ali Shah and soon prevailed over the Masit Khan's style. The gat was created by Wajid Ali Shah's most trusted confidant Ghulam Raja Khan and his immortal creation was famed as Razakhani Gat.

During the reign of Wajid Ali Shah, Lucknow witnessed some of the best instrumentalists ever born in India. The Badshah himself was a sitarist and had learnt to play the sitar at the age of nineteen.[5] In *Tareekh-e-Parikhana* the King mentioned that he learnt sitar from the famous sitarist Kutub Ali Khan. Sitarist Payree Khan also eulogized Wajid Ali's skill in playing sitar. Evidently, the stylistic thumri and kathak would not have triumphed if they were not complemented by an assembly of talented instrumentalists, both in Lucknow and in Metiyaburj. Ghulam Raza Khan is believed to be one of the favourite students of Masit Khan, although he had no explicit musical lineage. His father Ghulam Ali Khan was a musician in the court of Rampur.[6] Raza Khan's years in Lucknow saw him at the apogee of power and influence. Colonel Sleeman believed that it was the infidelity of his musicians particularly the dharis[7] and their ascendancy in state administration, was the root cause of Wajid Ali Shah's downfall. The King's close association with the musicians incurred the displeasure of the British representatives in Lucknow. Wajid Ali Shah's prime minister—Ali Naqi Khan— was also a sitarist, a binkar and a singer, and Sleeman's suspicion that he was an arch conspirator against the King, perhaps had some grain of truth.[8] Ali Naqi Khan too was a performer in Metiyaburj.

The court of Metiyaburj nurtured an assembly of adept

musicians who had migrated from Lucknow. Although there is no authentic record to testify the arrival of a star dancer or a star vocalist in Calcutta, the gap in the durbar of Qasr ul Baiza was bridged by the brilliance of a handful of adroit instrumental performers from Awadh. Ustad Basat Khan (1787–1887) of Senia lineage came and settled in Metiyaburj in 1858 He introduced rabab in Metiyaburj. Basat Khan and his brothers were the last prodigies of dhrupadi rabab that had been developed by their ancestor Mian Tansen (1506–89) and had descended through his son's lineage. The genealogy is famed as 'Vilas Khan rababiya' line. The rabab that was introduced in Metiyaburj had its origin in Akbar's court, although sarod maestro Karamatullah Khan and the Calcutta oral tradition trace its origin from Afghan rabab, which entered the court of Lucknow via Rampur and eventually came down to Calcutta along with the deposed king.

Basat Khan also introduced sursingar in Metiyaburj, which was well received by some of his pupils in Calcutta. Wajid Ali Shah took keen interest in popularizing the instrument in his court. Sursingar was invented by his brother Jafar Khan and possibly acquired its new feature of metallic fingerboard in Calcutta.[9]

Ustad Basat Khan came to Metiyaburj probably in 1858, when he was 71 years old.[10] He was accompanied by his sons Ali Muhammad and Muhammad Ali Khan, and Jafar Khan's grandson, Kasim Ali Khan. Basat Khan stayed with the King only for two years and finally settled in Gaya. His second son Muhammad Ali Khan is remembered as the last exponent of rabab in Calcutta.[11] Despite his brief stay in Calcutta, Ustad Basat Khan left a legacy through his immortal creations and his accomplished disciples such as his sons Ali Muhammad and

Muhammad Ali Khan, Kasim Ali Khan, and the great sarodia, Niamutallah Khan.

Jafar Khan's grandson Kasim Ali Khan was one of the greatest binkars and rababiyas of Senia family who played in Metiyaburj. He was trained in rabab, sursringar and dhrupad by Basat Khan in Metiyaburj under the patronage of Wajid Ali Shah. His music had an enduring quality and resonated through the decades and across the entire northern part of the country. Kasim Ali Khan left Metiyaburj sometime after Basat Khan, and went to Nepal.[12] But Kasim Ali did return to Calcutta once and blessed a band of instrumental geniuses in greater Bengal. Eventhe legendary musician Ustad Alauddin Khan's father Sabdar Hossain Khan was Kasim Ali Khan's student.

The culturally rich Tagores of Pathuriaghata became closely associated with the banished king of Metiyaburj in Calcutta. Ustad Basat Khan performed in the sabha of Babu Harakumar Tagore (1798–1858), father of Raja Sourindra Mohan Tagore of Pathuriaghata. Sourindra Mohan Tagore and his elder brother Jyotindra Mohan Tagore patronized a host of talented musicians who came to Calcutta from the North. The parlour in Pathuriaghata was often adorned by notable musicians from Wajid Ali's durbar in Metiyaburj such as the dhrupadiya Murad Ali, the Senia-rababiya Basat Khan, tappa and kheyal singer Ahmed Khan, sitarist Sajjad Mohammad and the famous binkar and rababiya Kasim Ali Khan.[13] Sajjad Mohammad came to Metiyaburj from the Lucknow durbar, before he joined the Tagores of Pathuriaghata. Asadullah Kaukab Khan, the famous sarodiya, received his lessons in sitar and surbahar from Sajjad Mohammad.[14]

Kaliprasanna Bandopadhyay (1842–1900), a follower of Raja Sourindra Mohan Tagore, was a leading performer of sitar and surbahar and once played surbahar in the durbar of Metiyaburj.[15] None of his contemporaries, other than Raja Sourindra Mohan Tagore, had received as many international accolades as he had. Even so, Bandopadhyay was elated to receive an invitation from Wajid Ali Shah to perform at his durbar in Metiyaburj. On that memorable occasion, Kaliprasanna Bandopadhyay's ragas resonated from his surbahar and enthralled the music connoisseurs present in the durbar.[16]

Sarod developed almost contemporaneously and under the influence of sursringar in early nineteenth century. Contemporary virtuoso, Amjad Ali Khan often accredits the present form of sarod to his ancestor Ghulam Ali Khan Bangash, who was Wajid Ali's court musician in Lucknow for a while.[17]

Ustad Niamatullah Khan (1827–1903), the sarod maestro of Wajid Ali's durbar in Lucknow, perhaps came and settled in Metiyaburj two years after the King was deposed. Niamatullah Khan came to Lucknow from Shahjahanpur in the middle of nineteenth century.[18] His descendants firmly believe that it was during his service in the durbar of Wajid Ali Shah that Niamatullah developed the modern form of sarod and that happened in Metiyaburj. He learnt sarod from senia Basat Khan and became the founder of Lucknow gharana.[19]

Ustad Niamatullah Khan lived in Metiyaburj for eleven years and played the sarod in Wajid Ali's durbar. Sarod was performed solo and its use to complement other forms of performing art was unlikely. Niamatullah's son Karamatullah Khan, a distinguished sarodiya who followed his father's trail, claims that during his stay in Metiyaburj from 1858 to 1869, his father instituted three major changes in sarod.[20] He covered the fingerboard with a brass plate, replaced the catgut strings with metallic substitutes and removed two gut frets that had been on the rabab. While the true contributors of such modifications remain debatable, the introduction of brass plate by which the sarod is identified today is accredited to Niamatullah in Metiyaburj. Sourindra Mohan Tagore also testifies the fact. In Calcutta, Niamatullah Khan continued his training under Basat Khan, who had been with Wajid Ali Shah in Lucknow too. It is said that while in Metiyaburj, Basat Khan suggested to his student Niamatullah to change the wooden plate of the sarod to a metal one and to replace the gut strings also with metal substitutes.[21]

Gulfam Ahmad Khan, a contemporary descendant of Niamatullah Khan, narrates an interesting account of how the sarod was modified by his predecessor. The incident took place in Metiyaburj.

> *He (Niamatullah Khan) joined the court of Nawab Wajid Ali Shah and became a disciple of Basat Khan who was a descendant of Tansen. Niyamatullah Khan offered one lakh silver coins to his Guru and started learning Hindustani rāgas. He was an ardent and devoted disciple. During his training he took his guru's permission to alter the design of Sarod. His guru Basat Khan gave him permission to change the existing form of sarod. Niyamatullah Khan took his sarod to an ironsmith and asked him to change the center wooden main body and put iron plate in its place. He got iron, brass and bronze strings attached to his sarod. This fully changed the sound and lent depth to the music. He intensively practiced on the new sarod. His guru was greatly pleased and asked Niyamatullah Khan to play sarod in a function organized in the court of Wajid Ali Shah. Nawab was extremely impressed by his sarod playing and conferred upon him the title of 'Sarkar'.[22]*

Niamatullah did not live on the benevolence of Basat Khan in the durbar of Metiyaburj for too long. Historian D.K. Mukhopadhyay informs that as the Senia left Calcutta after about two years and Niamatullah Khan came in close contact with Ustad Kasim Ali Khan in Metiyaburj, the duo spent hours in practising ragas. Eventually, Niamatullah Khan left Metiyaburj and went to Nepal in 1873. Niamatullah successfully established himself as one of the finest sarodiyas in Metiyaburj. During his stay he introduced some beautiful bandsihes, taans and todas into the sarod playing style.[23]

Niamatullah's sons Karamatullah (1848–1933) and Asadullah (1858–1915) both became illustrious sarodiyas in their own right. They were stepbrothers, as Niamatullah Khan had married twice. Karamatullah was born from his first wife and Asadullah from his second. The brothers started their career in Metiyaburj and learnt sarod from their father. They successfully represented the Lucknow gharana of sarod, also known as Bulandshahr gharana in the history of music. The accounts of the Khan Brothers' childhood and their stay in Metiyaburj are not very clear and lack transparency. Timeline of history reveals that when Niamatullah came to Metiyaburj (circa 1858), Karamatullah Khan was ten years old and Asadullah was just born. It is therefore presumed that the Khan Brothers spent their childhood in the milieu of Hindustani classical music in Metiyaburj amidst legendary virtuosos such as Basat Khan, Kasim Ali Khan, Sajjad Mohammad and above all Wajid Ali Shah himself.[24]

The name of Asadullah Khan, commonly referred to as Asadullah 'Kaukab' Khan, resonates more in the ears of nostalgia-gripped Bengalis and has left an indelible mark on the music history of Calcutta. Kaukab Khan's critical comments on Wajid Ali Shah's court music indicate the profundity of his observation during his stay in Metiyaburj. However, there is a dearth of authentic account to testify Kaukab Khan's period of stay in Metiyaburj and his maturity to understand the quintessence of classical music at that age. However, on his return to Calcutta after the King's death, Kaukab Khan joined the service of the Tagores of Pathuriaghata. In Calcutta, he also wrote a book in Bengali on music called *Sangeet Parichay* with the help of his students.[25]

Enayat Ali Khan (1790–1883) the great grandson of Najaf Ali Khan and a descendant of Afghan rababiya lineage spent a substantial part of his career in Metiyaburj. Enayat was a sarodiya in the court of Wajid Ali Shah but there are no clear indications of how and when he migrated to Calcutta. However, historian D.K. Mukhopadhyay testifies that Enayat Ali Khan was employed in Metiyaburj during 1860s and came into close contact with senia Kasim Ali Khan.[26] He left Metiyaburj towards the end of 1860s but stayed in Bengal till his death.

Wajid Ali Shah's exile in Calcutta contributed to the popularity of tabla in the musical assemblages of Metiyaburj and eventually in greater Bengal. Earlier, dhol and pukhawaj were the two instruments that were widely used as accompaniments for various forms of court music and dance performance. A pukhawaj artist named Nisar Khan was a famous court musician in Metiyaburj.[27] In the King's durbar, both in Lucknow and in Metiyaburj, the tabla was generally played by musicians in a standing position with two drums tied with a sash around the player's waist, probably to facilitate the mobility of the players on the floor.[28]

It is widely believed that Mian Bakshu Khan was the founder of the Lucknowi tabla gharana, which was passed on to Calcutta through his descendant Chote Mian who came to settle in Metiyaburj with his wife Chote Bibi and son Babu Khan. But despite being a descendant of Mian Bakshu Khan, Chote Mian preferred to become a singer rather than a percussionist. He was a kheyal exponent in Wajid Ali Shah's court in Lucknow and settled in Metiyaburj as a kheyal singer. He also composed songs during his stay in Calcutta.[29] Chote Mian's wife, who went by the name of Chote Bibi, was a talented tabla player and the bearer of the Lucknow tabla gharana once established by her in-laws in Lucknow. Under her, Lucknow tabla gharana reached its epitome in Calcutta. She came into prominence as the first female tabla player in Metiyaburj, who would perform in the durbar from behind a curtain. Chote Bibi tutored her son Babu Khan in her in-laws' gharana. Babu Khan played tabla in Metiyaburj durbar as long as Wajid Ali Shah was alive and after his death Babu Khan left Metiyaburj and relocated to Rajabazaar in Calcutta where he died in 1899. His legacy continued through his illustrious students. Prominent among them were Bidhu Bhushan Datta, Bhuteshwar Dey, Govardhan Pal, Jnanendra Nath Banerji, Laxmi Narayan Babaji, Manilal Mitra, Manmatha Nath Ganguli and Nagendra Nath Bose.[30]

The Lucknow tabla gharana was further ameliorated in Calcutta by Ustad Amman Khan and Ustad Anis-ud-Daulla. Both learnt the gharana from Mammad Khan, who was the grandson of Mian Bakshu Khan. Amman Khan and Anis-ud-Daulla came to Metiyaburj and gained prominence as proponents of Lucknow gharana of tabla in Wajid Ali Shah's durbar.[31] The Lucknow gharana perfectly blended with the combination of kathak dance beats and thumri tunes that had originated in Lucknow.

Lucknow gharana is one of the six main gharanas in

tabla. Farrukhabad and Banaras gharanas, which were highly recognized and equally enjoyed in the durbar of Metiyaburj, were offshoots of Lucknow gharana. Farrukhabad gharana was founded by Vilayet Ali Khan whose great grandson Nanne Khan (1863–1937) came to Metiyaburj as a court musician of Wajid Ali Shah's. He was the forbearer of Farrukhabad tabla gharana in Calcutta and passed on the gharana through his adept son and an inimitable tabla maestro Ustad Masit Khan (1892–1974).[32] Descendants of the pupils and protégés of Masit Khan are well known in Calcutta even today. Gyan Prakash Ghosh and Rai Chand Boral were two such disciples of Ustad Masit Khan.

Shehnai or the Indian flute was an integral instrument in the Naubatkhana of Metiyaburj that was played during various intervals of the day. Of all the shehnai players in Metiyaburj, Ustad Pyare Khan was the most adored. He was the teacher of Shyamlal Goswami, an honoured visitor to the Badshah's durbar, but Shyamlal played the same tunes in esraj.[33] Although sarangi still held a high position in the durbar of Metiyaburj, the then newly introduced esraj was gaining ground. The legendary sarangi player Ustad Badal Khan (1834–1937) of Panipat spent his early life in Metiyaburj as a court musician. Yet, the Bengali elite could never get around to embrace sarangi. It continued to carry a social stigma for its close association with the tawaifs-courtesan tradition and culture.

Esraj was fast becoming popular as an accompanying instrument in the musical assemblages of Calcutta. Musicologist Swami Prajnanananda believed that the esraj was invented 'perhaps by a Bengali artist' in the court of Wajid Ali Shah in Metiyaburj. However, he could not name the creator.[34]

After Wajid Ali Shah left Lucknow, the musicians lost their dominance in the court of Lucknow and dissipated in various directions in search of new patrons. Lucknow fell on evil days and lost its grandeur. While some virtuosos held on to their bastions in the lacklustre kingdom of Awadh, a galaxy of musicians faithful to the deposed king followed him to Metiyaburj. However, the milieu of Calcutta was not found amiable to most of the exponents of art. Soon they started flocking towards the upcoming havens of culture. Senia-rababiya Basat Khan left Metiyaburj within a couple of years and finally settled in Gaya. His sons Ali Muhammad Khan went to Nepal and Muhammad Ali Khan moved to the court of Gidhar. Murad Ali, the dhrupadiya of Tilwandi gharana relinquished the durbar during the Badshah's lifetime. Ustad Kasim Ali Khan went on to seek his fortune in other parts of Bengal, while dhrupadiya Taj Khan settled in Nepal. Sitarist Sajjad Mohammad joined the court of Pathuriaghata; Niamatullah Khan lived in Metiyaburj for eleven years but finally migrated to Nepal as did his sons Karamatullah Khan and Asadullah Khan. Sarangi player Badal Khan spent only few years of his early life in Metiyaburj. Sarodia Enayat Ali Khan left Metiyaburj in the late 1860s and moved to other places in Bengal. The list is endless!

These maestros never considered Calcutta as a traditional centre of Hindustani classical art. Perhaps the memory of the glorious days in Lucknow, which they thought about day and night, deterred them from bringing about a passion that was needed. However, the pronounced effort of Wajid Ali Shah to rekindle the burnt-out dream of his musicians attracted some of them, at least for a while. Nevertheless, some wondered whether the metaphorical dead elephant was still worth a fortune.

Twelve

'Nawabi-yana' in Metiyaburj

Lucknow was exalted for its tradition of courteous conversation and the felicity of the people who lived there. The citizenry had grown up in a milieu of refinement and subtlety during the grandeur of the Nawabi days. It was called the 'City of Adab' or courtesy—a synonym for 'the city of Pehle Aap', literally meaning after you. For centuries the city had enjoyed civility and happiness and had never faced the ire of bloodshed in the annals of history. There was no militancy, no invasion, no insurgency and no bloodbath for ascendancy to the throne. The British slowly assimilated Awadh but did it through a bloodless path and were never frontal. Perhaps, the surge of unbridled bliss and merrymaking diverted the attention of the citizens from the clouds of incertitude that were looming large over the horizons of Awadh.

The same wit and wisdom rippled down the Ganges into the mimic kingdom of Awadh that lay on the outskirts of Calcutta. The wrath of mutineers was over and the King had made a conciliatory settlement with the government. Harmony and tranquillity prevailed yet again and the doves of peace fluttered over the kingdom of Metiyaburj. The followers of the banished King turned the place into a haven, where the aura of Lucknow was imitated in every bend.

The eloquent flow of Urdu and Persian poetries in the alleyways of Metiyaburj was a noteworthy testimony of the archetypical Lucknowi culture being imbibed in Calcutta. Sharar wrote that there was not a single educated person in Metiyaburj who did not know Persian and even the women used to compose Persian verses.[1] The dialect of the commons was rich and adorned with poetic metaphors and similes. The beauty of masnavis, soz, ghazals, quasidas, rubais, salaams and marsiyas were springing out from the pens of lyricists and poets in Chota Lucknow. While Urdu was the mother tongue of the Mughals in Delhi, Lucknow was well acquainted with the Persian language owing to the Persian origin of the Nawabs. The official court language was Persian during the British rule till 1832 and was then replaced by Urdu. In Calcutta, Persian and Urdu were cultivated among many Hindu elite. Ram Mohan Roy, himself an accomplished Persian scholar, brought out the first Persian newspaper in 1822.

Wajid Ali Shah himself was a prodigy of Persian and Urdu literature, a poet, a lyricist and a literary genius. He started writing poetry at the age of eighteen. During his visit to Metiyaburj in 1874, Garcin de Tassy, the French Orientalist and a professor of Indology, applauded the King's literary pursuits by saying:

> *I do not have to appreciate here this very political resolution, neither do I have to appreciate the qualities or defects of Wajid Ali Shah, as a sovereign, but I am interested in him as a distinguished scholar and as eminent poet in Hindustani (translation from original French).*[2]

Tassy made his compliment perhaps before going through the King's last and the lengthiest literary work *Masnavi Sabatul Quloob*, which was left incomplete upon his death in 1887.

The masnavi contains 44,562 couplets, running into 1,061 pages, which largely supersedes any other masnavi composed in Urdu according to some authorities.[3] Wajid Ali Shah started his literary career when he was a prince and blossomed into a proficient composer in Urdu and Persian under the nom-de-plume of 'Akhtar' meaning 'star'. Most of his literary works were composed in Urdu and were penned after he lost his crown. His lyrics were collected in six diwans apart from his compositions of some eighty marsiyas and qasidas in Urdu and Persian.[4] Indeed, he tried almost all the species of literary compositions and wrote qasidas, ghazals, marsiyas, salaam, qita, rubai and masnavis. Wajid Ali Shah translated Persian religious verses to Urdu and the books were published in Metiyaburj.[5] But of all his works of literature, the ones most revered are his masnavis. Written in Urdu and mostly in Metiyaburj, his masnavis are truly treasure troves of historical evidences, which beckon an analytical interpretation of his tastes and preferences.

His masnavi, *Huzn-e-Akhtari*, meaning 'sorrows of Akhtar' was one of the best pieces of literature and can be embodied as his versified autobiography. His 'sorrows' were genuine and not stimulated for the sake of writing. The book, which was printed at his private press at Metiyaburj six years after its composition, was penned entirely during his detention in Fort William and captures the period from his journey to Calcutta to his dolorous life in captivity. The masnavi *Khitabat-i-Mahallat* or 'Titles of the Ladies of His Harem' was a source of valuable information about his ladies and wives, both nikahs (married) and mutás (temporary) and their lives in the harem. This book was also written during his time in Fort William.[6] *Banee* (meaning bride), another expounding literary work of four hundred pages, composed in 1875 in Metiyaburj is a treatise on music and dance and also details his life in his mimic kingdom including a description of the buildings in Metiyaburj, the mushairas held there, the animals in his menagerie and a vivid sketch of life and time of his people.[7] The book was published in Metiyaburj in 1878.[8]

The most detailed account about his wives was the *Masnavi Bahr-e-Mukhtalif,* which the banished king wrote during his stay in Fort William. The book is a valuable document where the names of his wives, sons and daughters from different Mahals living in Metiyaburj and also the wives who left him for some reason or the other are mentioned.[9] His another masnavi *Dulhan* (also meaning bride) was dedicated to newly married couples and contains a collection of songs in dhrupad, kheyal, tappa, thumri and dadra. The preface of the book and the narrations are in Persian, while the songs are composed mostly in Braj Bhasa, the language spoken by the common people in the Agra-Mathura region, mixed with local dialects and Urdu lexemes. The lyrics were strongly influenced by the sensualities of Vaishnavism and romantic myths of Lord Krishna.[10] In one place Wajid Ali introduced himself as *Akhtar Gosai*.[11] This literary piece runs through eighteen pages and was published in Metiyaburj in 1873. Another masnavi named *Najo,* which was published in 1870 at his Metiyaburj press, contains many of his thumris most of which are based on various anecdotes from the life of Lord Krishna.

Wajid Ali Shah has mentioned a list of forty-six books in *Banee*, which he authored mostly during his stay in Metiyaburj. The list obviously does not include the books which he had written after *Banee* was published. Almost all his books were published in Metiyaburj at his private press known as Matbua-i-Sultani, meaning the royal press, under his personal supervision. One can easily ascertain from the volume of literature he had produced after his arrest that the ill-fated king spent most of his time in custody writing masnavis and marsiyas. His emotional expressions of desolation and terrible loneliness are perceptibly captured in his works. Yet, there is no dearth of fluency and spontaneity in his poetic diction. His *Tareeh-i-Mumtaz* is a collection of twenty-nine love letters written to Iklil Mahal from Calcutta. The writings span a period of three years and two months. The first letter was written on 9 July 1856 and the last one is dated 5 September 1859. However, there was a gap during the period of mutiny. There could have been a possibility of dislocation of the mail delivery system or the British Government must have imposed restrictions on his mails. Many of the letters were written in the Fort between 15 June 1857 and 9 July 1859. The subject called for deep emotional expressions, his grief for not being able to meet his Queen, his love, lust and passion. The original manuscript, which is currently preserved in the British Museum, does not bear his own handwriting. Perhaps, his transcriber wrote the letters. Likewise, Iklil Mahal took the help of one Munshi Akbar Ali to transcribe letters on her behalf. Munshi's literary talent was admired by the Badshah in one of his mails.[12]

Another one of Wajid Ali's autobiographical masnavis, *Tareekh-e-Parikhana (Isshqnama)*, was written in Lucknow in 1848 when he was twenty-six years old and crowned as the King. The book is another repository of information about his personal life, his craving for sex, his first physical relation at the age of eight, his pre-marital and extra-marital affairs, about his 'fairies' and musical ensembles and every minutia of his private life, which he confessed in his own poetic diction.[13]

The Badshah would never write on a table; instead, he would recline and dictate his verses to a transcriber. Seldom did he hold the pen, except for the Quran which he wrote in his own hand. He was a prolific writer and had an incredible aptitude to dictate more than one poem simultaneously to different transcribers. His Urdu and Persian skills were strong but he was weak in Arabic.[14] He started his literary career by composing poetry at the age of eighteen[15] and continued to write till the end. He was so passionate about poetry that he gave poetic names to his cavalry regiments such as Banka, Dandy, Tircha, Fop, Ghanghur, Darknand and named his infantry battalions as Akhtari, Lucky, Nadiri and so on.[16] Most of his time in Metiyaburj was spent in writing books. Raja Durga Prasad who was a talukdar of Sandila near Lucknow and had witnessed the last days of the King in Calcutta, had mentioned in his narratives:

> *In these days after deposition, in spite of meagre resources and increase of expenditure, he (Wajid Ali) spends more of his precious time in literary pursuits and benefits his advisers with his latest production[sic].*[17]

The impoverishment of Delhi was the gain of Lucknow and a new era beckoned the literary horizon of Awadh during the reign of Asaf-ud-Daulla. Literature and poetry reached their pinnacle during the reign of the last ruling descendant of Burhan-ul-Mulk's dynasty. Wajid Ali Shah Akhtar was a prolific writer but 'not highly gifted' as once commented by a scholar.[18] However, his mushairas (poetic assemblages) in Lucknow further enriched and diversified the cultural landscape of Awadh. His court in Lucknow saw such glittering gems as Muzaffer Ali Aseer and Fateh-ud-Daulla Barq and eminent Urdu poets like Amanat, Bahr, Tasleem, Zaki, Sahar, Darakshan, Ameer, Qabul, Shafaq, Hunar, Bekhood, Uttarad, Hilal Rind, Khalil, Daya Shankar 'Naseem' and Sarur. His son Birjis Qadr was also a gifted poet in his durbar.

Mirza Salamat Ali 'Dabir'(1803—75) was a famous marsiya-writer in Lucknow durbar since the days of Nasir-ud-Din Haidar. Wajid Ali Shah was also fond of Dabir's marsiyas and deeply revered him in his court. His respect for the poet was so high that once in 1874 Wajid Ali Shah personally made special arrangements for Dabir, who was suffering from an eye problem, to be brought to Calcutta for treatment. Dabir had an eye operation in Calcutta and the surgery was performed by a famous German eye-specialist who came to Metiyaburj as the King's guest.[19]

The tradition of poetic hegemony continued in Metiyaburj with the same lust, love and passion. Akhtar patronized a court of seven poets in his durbar in Metiyaburj and called them Saba Saiyara (Seven Stars). Of his two principal court poets in Lucknow, Barq and Aseer, only Barq came to Calcutta with the King and died in voluntary exile in 1857. Barq was a pupil of Imam Baksh 'Nashik' (d.1838) who was known as one of the two founders of the Lucknow school of poetry. Barq was a close companion of the King since his boyhood.[20] Critics believe that Aseer and Barq ameliorated Wajid Ali's literary deficiency and emended his poems, but the fact is not conclusive. Barq died in Calcutta in 1857 when Wajid Ali Shah was in the Fort. Aseer stayed back in Lucknow and later joined the court of Rampur after the tumult. Therefore, both Barq and Aseer had no scope to touch up the works of Wajid Ali Shah, at least in Calcutta. On the contrary, in his masnavi *Dariya–Tasshuq* the Badshah modestly called himself a self-taught literate. Yet, critics believe that many of Wajid Ali's ghazals composed in Lucknow were retouched and refined by Barq and Aseer.

The famous seven poets of the Saba Saiyara in Metiyaburj

were Barq, Darakshan (a pupil of Aseer), Bahr (a pupil of Nasikh),[21] Hunar, Aish, Saulat and Akhgar, of which the first four poets migrated to Calcutta from Lucknow durbar. Regular mushairas were held in Metiyaburj to revive the lost glory of Lucknow. Eminent Urdu poets such as Mirza Khan Dagh Dehlvi and Nazm Tabatabai sometimes attended the mushairas in Metiyaburj and provided much impetus to develop Urdu poetry in Bengal. Tabatabai (1854–1933) was a Persian descendant from Awadh and was only two years old when Wajid Ali was dethroned. He came to Calcutta during his adulthood and was appointed in the court of the deposed king as Shahi Attaleeq or Royal Teacher of Wajid Ali Shah's grandsons. He stayed in Metiyaburj for few years and left after the King's death. He was a scholar in Persian and Urdu languages and learnt English from the colonial masters in Bengal.

Dagh Dehlvi (1831–1905) was an Urdu poet from Delhi. He was the stepson of the son and heir-apparent of Mughal King Bahadur Shah Zafar and spent his younger days in Red Fort. His literary talent was acclaimed by the poetic King Bahadur Shah Zafar. After the Mutiny, Dagh left Delhi and joined the court of Rampur and stayed there for twenty-four years. During that time he came to Calcutta and attended mushairas in Metiyaburj. Glimpses of his pleasant memories in Calcutta can be seen in his masnavi—*Faryad Dagh*. Among the local poets of Calcutta who visited Metiyaburj, the most prominent was Moulavi Abdul Ghaffor Khan Khaldi, known by his pseudonym 'Nassakh'. He was the deputy collector of Rajsahi and a proud author of many books.[22]

The distinguished Arabic and Persian scholar Moulana Abdul Halim (1860–1926) was born in Lucknow four years after Wajid Ali Shah left for Calcutta. His father joined the court of Metiyaburj in 1862 and Abdul Halim came to Calcutta in 1869, when he was nine years old. He grew to become a scholar in Urdu, Persian and Arabic and adopted the pen name of Sharar (meaning spark). Abdul Halim spent ten years closely with the King in Metiyaburj and produced his labour of love, a social commentary titled *Guzishta Lucknow*. During his stay in Metiyaburj he served a Lucknow newspaper *Avadh Akhbar* as its Metiyaburj correspondent. Sharar never met Wajid Ali Shah in Lucknow, since the Badshah had already settled in Calcutta when he was born. Sharar's account of Wajid Ali Shah's life in Lucknow was thus not a first-hand eyewitness report.

Khawaja Zain-ul-Abedin, who joined the service of the King in 1876 and remained in Metiyaburj till the King's death, witnessed his literary pursuit in the last lap of his life. It appears from Khawaja's account that in his old age, the King would write on his own. Given below is a first hand account of Khawaja, which is quite noteworthy.

The King's usual programme was that he was busy in compiling and writing books from morning till ten or eleven, in the summer season, and from dusk till nine or ten during the winter.

When I was appointed Darogha of the Library it was my duty to attend the King when he was writing. He used to sit folding his legs underneath on a silver-pedestalled Palang and incline, while writing... I remained on this duty till the end. When I used to attend the King, for performing my duty, (then I found) a few Juz (about 10 pages) of lined Foolscap papers with a few reed-pens on a piece of black velvet and inkpot were arranged on the Palang.

He used to write only Marsiyas and Salams during

> *Mohurrum. His last book was a translation of the Persian book, probably, Hayat-ul-Qulub. He used to translate the Persian prose of his book into Urdu poetry with such speed as if he was copying it. He was engaged in this work till a few days before his death.*

The King experimented with the art of calligraphy and often embellished the cross-outs and layouts in his manuscripts with simple artistic leitmotifs (the art that was flourished, later by Tagore). He loved to draw various pictograms in his manuscript, which he called Sanait. For example, the motif of a crown was depicted by writing the word Sallamahu in different planes and then joining the outlines of the letters. Sallamahu means God save him. He wrote Sallamahu on a piece of paper and then rotated the paper ninety degree and again wrote Sallamahu. He then joined the lines and made it look like a crown. Every pictogram has got a meaning. When he drew a bowing flowering plant, he wrote,

> *I am about to explain a good news,*
> *The tree of my life is about to blossom.*[23]

The presence of Wajid Ali Shah in the fields of painting and architecture in Calcutta was not as ubiquitous as it was in other cultural spheres. Though he brought some of his court painters from Lucknow, the artists failed to imprint their identity on the art history of Bengal. The King patronized eminent painters like Gajraj Singh, Asaf Ali, Ghulam Mustafa, Muhammad Masud, Muhammad Wazir, Hassan Ali, Jahan Ali Khan in Lucknow, but no authentic record testifies their presence in Metiyaburj.

Wajid Ali, unlike his forefathers Suja-ud-Daulla and Asaf-ud-Daulla, was never a connoisseur of art, but had his portraits drawn by artists both in Lucknow and in Calcutta. Canvasses were displayed on the walls of Zurd Kothee and other palaces of Lucknow. A few years before his deposition, the King appointed one Muhammad Jan, alias 'Mummoo Jan', who appears to have worked with Beechey and earned his reputation as a portrait painter and in reproducing animal images. After Wajid Ali left Lucknow, Mummoo stayed back to draw portraits of the British officers and their pets.[24] Mummoo Jan finally settled in Metiyaburj and served the King as his court painter.[25] A portrait of the deposed King painted by Mummoo Jan is preserved in the British Museum. The watercolour composition depicts Wajid Ali Shah wearing an embroidered white muslin 'jama', 'paijamas' and slippers with curved toes. He is seated in a European-style armchair with his feet on a blue footstool, set on a patterned red carpet. His left hand is resting on his knee and his right on the hilt of a sword; in the background is a green draped curtain and a picture of a river scene.[26] Few exotic paintings adorned the walls of the Badshah's mausoleum at Metiyaburj, including a rare portrait depicting him in grey hair and moustache. Unfortunately, the paintings are anonymous. Another anonymous painting of Wajid Ali Shah riding a horse on the banks of the Hooghly was in the possession of a private enthusiast, which is now lost.[27]

Wajid Ali Shah's subtle sensibilities logically flowed into the art of gastronomy. When the King came to Calcutta, he brought with him his own chefs, who sought to keep the deposed King in good humour by cooking Awadhi delicacies. The khansamas[28] introduced the art of 'slow cooking' in Calcutta. The wonderful potpourri of ingredients and methodology of Awadhi recipes blended intimately with the Bengali taste. The taste of biryani was brought to Calcutta by him. Culinary specialists hold that the deposed king's entourage was in penury and found the potatoes to be a cheaper substitute for meat in biryani. Potatoes were added to the biryani along with small quantities of meat to feed his train of companions in Calcutta. Since then potato has become a veritable ingredient of the recipe of the biryani made in Calcutta. The King brought with him a huge retinue of staff, including rakabdars (chefs) and masalchis (spice experts), who held high positions in his durbar. Wajid Ali had great culinary senses and the dishes were suitably modified to meet the demands of a new age and a new place. In the culinary history of Calcutta, Wajid Ali Shah's sojourn in Metiyaburj was indeed a milestone. After the death of the King, the chefs of Metiyaburj and their descendents dissipated into the population, opening eateries all over Bengal and propagating the Awadhi culinary legacy.

The traditional Awadhi style of cooking was popularly known as Dum Puhkt, meaning slow and prolonged cooking in low flamed chullahs (clay burners of charcoal). The ingredients were sealed in a large pot called handi, which was put on a slow fire to allow the ingredients to cook in their own juices. The tradition that streamed down the Hooghly and found its way into the royal kitchen of Metiyaburj eventually hit the taste buds of a myriad of gastronomes in Calcutta. After the King was released from his detention Metiyaburj started to revive the lost sensibilities of Awadh. Dum Puhkt style was followed in the royal kitchen of Metiyaburj to cook different varieties of pulaos, dum biryani, dum mutton, dum chicken and even dum potatoes. The table spread used for the Badshah was called Dastarkhwan, literally meaning tablecloth. Sharar witnessed the culinary extravagance of Metiyaburj. The King was an epicure of Awadhi delicacies, though he himself was not a big eater.

His dastarkhwan was sumptuously spread with thirty to forty different pulaos and scores of curries in Metiyaburj. He was fond of halva sohan, a sweet dish prepared with clarified butter and dried fruits. Munshi-ul-Sultan, the King's Chief Secretary in Metiyaburj, was not only a gourmet but also a good chef and loved to prepare delicious dishes himself.

The royal dinner was spread at midnight after the durbar of Metiyaburj was over. A variety of items were laid out on the dastarkhwan, but the Badshah only took a spoonful or a morsel from each dish of pulao. The royal pulao in Metiyaburj was cooked with one asrafi (gold coin) put into the pot of boiling rice and left for cooking. Only the Badshah could digest such heavy dishes. He was also fond of vegetable bhujias.[29] After the meals he would drink ice-cold water.[30] The royal chefs of Metiyaburj followed the same cooking principles as followed in Lucknow by preparing many items like noor pullao, chameli pullao, mazafar, khat-mithe pullao, roomali roti, and sheermal, the melt-in-mouth kakori kebab, tunday kebab, chapli kebab and the incredible moti pulao. The last dish was prepared by grinding edible quality of silver and gold foils mixed with fine quality of rice and other ingredients. The mass was stuffed into the gullet of a fowl, sewed tightly and steamed. After cooking, the chicken was cut open to take out the rice, which looked like shining pearls. The dishes were less spicy but rich in cream, ghee and variety of nuts. Often saffron pills were fed to the chicken to infuse aroma and colour into the flesh. The dishes were much lighter on the palate but retained the quintessential flavour of Awadhi cuisine. Munshi-ul-Sultan of Metiyaburj would often add two-and-a half sheers of ghee and other ingredients to prepare halva sohan.[31]

Food garnishing and table spreads were archetypal Lucknowi

arts, which were imbibed in Calcutta from Lucknow by Wajid Ali Shah. The presentation of various exquisite dishes, the colour and aroma juxtaposed with etiquettes and manners of serving food with an exchange of polite words, rekindled the burnt-out dreams of the people in exile. White pulao was served on crisp-white dastarkhwan, where all other items—from bread to salads and quorma to desserts, were white. The items were served in white or silver crockery. Bitterness could not be tasted in bitter gourd, although it looked garden-fresh and green. Sometimes dishes were subtly prepared to disguise luscious ingredients in such a way that even a culinary connoisseur would find it impossible to distinguish the items from genuine ones.[32]

A delectable Awadhi cuisine would not go down well if it was not suffixed with a piece of aromatic paan (betel leaf) at the end. A betel leaf with a mouthful of refreshing and aromatic spices was a cultural tradition since the ancient days in India and the custom became etiquette of the highest order in the court of Lucknow's Nawabs. Offering a paan full of mouth-watering aromatic mixture and of high quality fragranced tobacco to a guest was a gesture of social amenity in Lucknow and, thereafter, in Metiyaburj.

Harit Krishna Deb, a historian and a descendent of the famous Sobhabazar Raj family of Calcutta, recounts an interesting story to elucidate the incredible power of the shahi paan savoured by Wajid Ali Shah in Metiyaburj. His predecessor, Raja Rupendra Krishna Deb, a contemporary of the banished king, was an honoured guest of Metiyaburj. One day, Raja Rupendra Krishna Deb came to see the Badshah in his palace and was greeted warmly to his manzil. A waft of fragrance in the room was the perfect welcome to the guest. It was a cold night but to his surprise the Raja found his host wearing a light embroidered cloak. The Raja could see his bare chest through the fine woven attire as the Badshah had not worn any warm clothing underneath.

'Aren't you feeling cold?' the Raja asked.

The Badshah smiled and replied, 'Not really, because I am chewing a paan! Would you like to taste one?'

The Badshah offered a paan to his guest and the Raja relished the luscious taste and aroma of the shahi betel-spice. There was no tobacco in it. Perhaps the charm of best Awadhi masala had an edge over the kinds he had tasted earlier. The gentlemen had a good time conversing with each other. When the Raja was about to take leave he once again appreciated the shahi paan and expressed his desire to have another one.

The Badshah was a bit hesitant and cautioned, 'Perhaps, it is better for you to avoid a second one—it is difficult to tolerate.'

However, he was courteous and offered him his paandan. It was a beautifully decorated box embellished with precious metals and jewels. The Raja picked up a second one and started chewing. The Raja left Metiyaburj in his phaeton in the cold winter night. As he was going past the maidan, he started feeling hot and opened the windows of the coach. He removed his woollen shawl and one by one all his warm clothes. It was intolerable and the Raja had to stop his carriage. He got down from the phaeton, climbed up the steps and sat beside the coachman under the open sky. The carriage was moving fast in the chilly night and the Raja with his light clothes was finally relieved. He had realized the strength of the Lucknowi paan![33]

Paan could be a token of love and a remembrance of the past ecstasy. When the Badshah was detained in the fort, Khas Mahal remained with him by sending five pieces of paan everyday. Zafri Begum also expressed her devotion by sending paan to his cell. The Badshahi paan was prepared with specially treated betel leaves called begami. The leaves were buried under the soil for months to remove the rawness and to dissolve the fibres. Exquisite ingredients were procured for the Badshah to prepare aromatic paans called 'gilauri' with conically folded betel leaves wrapped with edible silver foils. The fragrance would remain in the mouth for the whole day. The betel nuts were boiled in milk and moulded to a form called chikni dali. The gilauris are suspended in tiny pegs attached to fine small chains and placed in the paandan. The suspended gilauris were covered by a dome-shaped lid, adorned with precious jewels, gold and silver streaks. The paandan was typically made of brass embossed with jewels depicting conventional flowers and buds set in foliage of ornamental work.

The reminiscence of the King's penchant towards a delectable paan is still enlivened by Motilal Srimali, a descendent of the Shahi Paanwalas who prepared paan for the Badshah in Metiyaburj.

Wajid Ali was fond of smoking and placidly puffed hookah during his leisure. Hookah was connected with an ornamental stem attached to a tobacco bowl called chilam and a pot holding the fire called chambar. The chambar and chilam were carried by an assistant called hookaburdar, who moved along with the King. The best quality of aromatic tobacco was procured for the Badshah in Metiyaburj and were given poetic names by the Badshah as Har-dum-tazah (always fresh), Lab-e-Maashuq (beyond lip) and so on.[34] Hookah was trendy amongst the elite womenfolk of Awadh. Wajid Ali Shah's mother Malka Kishwar was addicted to hookah and would smoke after every meal. Elihu Jaan, the hookah-bearer of the queen recounts that ice was mixed to her hookah-water to make it soothing. Elihu Jaan also accompanied the Queen Mother to Calcutta, but returned to Lucknow with her husband after the Begum sailed off to England.[35] However, hookah was forbidden for thirty days during Ramzaan.[36] The portraits of Hazrat Mahal too, depict the Begum holding the pipe of a bejewelled hookah. Contrary to common belief and attempts to vilify the King's character by some English narrators, Wajid Ali Shah never touched wine or inhaled opium in his life. Little is known about Wajid Ali Shah's social life outside the realm of Metiyaburj. Very few eyewitness accounts are available to testify the King's socialization with the elite of Calcutta. The city's pulsating cultural life must have fascinated him beyond the social grandeur of Metiyaburj. But, the Badshah seldom moved outside his kingdom to socialize with his noble friends in Calcutta. He was fond of watching the spectacular immersion ceremony of Durga Puja on the banks of Hooghly. The distinguished journalist and columnist Nagendranath Gupta (1862–1940) had a momentary glimpse of the King watching the flamboyant Hindu ceremony.

It is said that once Wajid Ali Shah was specially invited by Nanda Lal Basu and his brother Pashupati Basu to their famous ancestral house at Baghbazar, where a grand musical evening was arranged on the occasion of Holi. At the end, there was an ardent request to the Badshah by the respectable audience to show a glimpse of his Lucknowi kathak. He could not deny the request and danced on the floor, which had been sprinkled with *aabir* (pigmented powder).[37] The same ancestral mansion of the Basus in Baghbazar was blessed in 1885 by the footfall of Thakur Ramkrishna Paramhansha.

Wajid Ali Shah celebrated Holi with equal pomp and show, both in Lucknow and in Metiyaburj. Many a time the Badshah was invited with great honour by Babu Roopchand

Mukhopadhyay at his residence in Kalighat during the festival of Holi. Mukhopadhyay was an opulent Bengali and a senior officer in Government Collectorate Office at Alipore. The Badshah knew him for a long time since his pension was disbursed through Roopchand Mukhopadhyay. He was a man of great taste in music and arranged musical assemblages during Holi to honour the King. Wajid Ali Shah also took great pleasure in playing Holi in his Kalighat mansion. The sweet fragrance of the pigmented powders rekindled his lost memories of Lucknow. The evening was celebrated with rich musical concerts, the Badshah being the main focus of attraction. Only for that day he would give permission to his own musicians to perform outside his court.[38]

Thirteen

His Majesty's Incredible Menagerie

Perhaps the only area where the banished king would not have vacillated even for a moment to spend the lion's share of his 'meagre' income was in the upkeep of his garden for animals. The King took great interest in zoological pursuits and in maintaining a large collection of exotic and rare animals. His menagerie in Metiyaburj was a paradise for the people of Calcutta as well as for the visitors and painters who came from abroad. When the Siamese regent, King Rama V. Chulalongkorn was taken to visit the menagerie in January 1872 by his imperial host, he was astounded to see the incredible collection of animals.[1] Prof. Garcin de Tassy of the French Institute recounted his fascinating experience of the menagerie in 1874:

> *The most wonderful aspect of this small estate is its Zoo, which is unique in the whole world. It contains twenty thousand animals. Some of them are very rare. Such a collection of pigeons cannot be found anywhere. (Similarly), so many varieties of snakes and other reptiles have not been seen anywhere else.*[2]

In an edifying article published on 11 November 1874, in *The New York Times*, a correspondent wrote:

> *The King has three principal houses in his little kingdom and*

> has named them respectively, 'Sultan Khana', 'Azad Munzil' and 'Zurd Kootee'. Round the second of these is the Royal Menagerie, unquestionably one of the finest in the world.

Sharar also reported:

> Apart from architecture the King took an interest in animal and he developed this interest to an extraordinary and unsurpassed extent. I do not suppose that any other individual has ever made half the efforts in this direction that he did.[3]

English chronicler James Routledge visited the King's domain in 1874 with his English escort Colonel Mowbray Thompson to delve into the King's style of living and 'to see how the ex-king could spend his allowance of ten thousand pounds a month, and an additional sum which he received as rent from a bazaar outside, and still run into debt.' The visitor got his answer as soon as he entered the King's estate. He was living a life of extravagance with 'two married and thirty-nine unmarried wives, thirty-one sons, twenty-five daughters, six thousand subjects, three or four palaces and a kingdom of incredible animals'.

He wrote:

> ...and amid and around all was a menagerie said to be among the finest of the world. The reader may judge. There were 20,000 birds beast and snakes... around a tank or lake 300 feet long by 240 wide, and alive with every kind of fish that money could procure or attempt to live on the banks of the Hooghly; 18,000 choice pigeons; pelicans and ostriches, swans, geese and birds of many names.[4]

Frank Vincent was one of the very few foreign nationalities to have documented an eyewitness account of the King's life in Metiyaburj and his ardour for animals. Vincent was an American globetrotter who had set a record by travelling 3,55,000 miles across the world. He dropped anchor on the banks of the Hooghly in October 1870 and was taken to Metiyaburj by Munshi Ameer Ali (referred to as the Prince). He wrote:

The King of Oudh owns or leases a square mile of land on the banks of the Hooghly below the city, besides a dozen large palaces. These I was not permitted to enter; but glimpses here and there showed magnificent marble pillars and floors, the marble being imported from France, and gorgeously ornamented furniture. After passing through several of the compounds, the prince led the way to the menagerie, preceded by two or three officials. In the menagerie the most imposing specimens of animal life were an African lion and a Bengal tiger, both very large. Within an immense enclosure, protected by a wire fence, were several thousand birds, mostly waterfowl, and of every conceivable variety, colour, and size. Near the centre of this enclosure was a large pond flanked with a summerhouse. Upon the menagerie he is reported to have spent half a million dollars. So fond was he of the animals and birds that at that time he was absolutely living in the midst of them, and superintending the arrangements for their comfort during the approaching cold season. It was owing to this latter circumstance that I was favoured with a sight of His Majesty before leaving the grounds.

We were standing directly in front of the main palace, looking at a magnificent marble fountain basin, when one of our attendants suddenly cried, 'The king! the king!' I turned and saw before me Wajid Allie, sitting cross-legged in a large

> *palankeen borne by eight servants. Immediately raising my sun-helmet and bowing low, His Majesty was gracious enough to bow twice in return, lifting his cap, made of the finest white linen and threaded with silver embroidery. While the King conversed with his officers a good opportunity was offered to study his development of brawn and brain.*
>
> *He had a large, powerful frame, and a not unpleasant though somewhat sinister countenance, with bright black eyes and regular features. He appeared to be about sixty years of age, wore an iron-grey moustache much turned up at the ends, and his lips were stained a cherry colour from chewing the pawn or betel nut. He was very plainly dressed in white linen, with one half of his olive-brown chest bared. The King inquired who the foreigner was, and the prince's reply, 'A friend of mine,' seemed to be satisfactory. His Majesty certainly did not look the spendthrift and debauchee he is represented to be.*[5]

Indeed, Wajid Ali Shah had to pay the price to keep his passion alive and to nurture his menagerie at Metiyaburj. He spent without restraint to procure animals he was looking for and was ready to meet the demand, whatsoever, to obtain a new species. Once he paid twenty-four thousand rupees for a pair of silk-winged pigeons and eleven thousand rupees for a pair of white peacocks.[6] In his state of penury at Metiyaburj, he ordered to sell a golden bedstead made during the reign of Saadat Ali Khan, to pay for a pair of vultures worth fifty thousand rupees![7]

Sharar gives a glimpse of the enormous sum he spent to maintain his zoo in those days. There were eight hundred attendants and three hundred fanciers for his pigeons, about the same number of people for his fishes and thirty to forty attendants for his snakes. Most of his attendants came from Lucknow. The attendants and keepers were paid six to ten rupees a month, while the zoo officers received a monthly salary of twenty to thirty rupees. The entire management of his menagerie was entrusted upon Munis-ud-Daulla and Raihan-ud-Daulla to whom he paid an extravagant sum of 25,000 rupees per month! Over and above, the King spent around 9,000 rupees on food for his animals.[8] Sharar's account reveals that the King depleted more than one-third of his monthly pension on the upkeep of his zoo!

Nevertheless, the menagerie of Metiyaburj was a fascinating Eden. It sprawled over a large area in front of Nur Mahal, where roamed innumerable spotted deer, bucks, goats, sheep, donkeys, two-humped camels from Baghdad, a pair of giraffes from Africa and other wild herbivores inside vast iron enclosures. Every animal had a particular name and whenever the King talked to his pet, he called it by its name. Stables were packed with rare breeds of horses.[9] A marble pool was built in the centre around which flocked the partridges, ostriches, turkeys, sarus cranes, geese, herons, demoiselle cranes, ducks, peacocks, flamingos and hundreds of other birds, and tortoises. Cages were immaculately maintained and every bit of dropping or shredded feathers of the birds was immediately removed. Visitors could get a glimpse of tigers, leopards, lions, cheetah, lynxes, hyenas, wolves and a variety of wild carnivores as they walked around inside large iron enclosures on the other side of the pool. On the opposite side of the vast meadow, was a row of large wooden cages where exotic species of monkeys collected from different parts of the world romped around. Water pools filled with fishes dotted his garden. Fishes were most auspicious to the King and every morning he would spend time feeding them with his own hands.

The King had a magnificent aviary of eighteen thousand pigeons, which Sharar eulogized as 'the finest existing variety of pigeons'. A large number of exotic birds were let lose in gigantic cages of wire-mesh, called Kunj. The King himself took keen interest to breed them in captivity. Shining brass cages containing a variety of birds were also reared in the Sultan Khana.[10] Photographic evidences of his magnificent menagerie and his township in Metiyaburj are still available. Prof. Meerza Kaukub, a descendent of the King's khandaan, is a proud possessor of some of the rare photographs taken by F. Kapp & Company, Calcutta.

But the most commendable collection of the King's menagerie was his reptile-house. Sharar claims, 'It is unlikely that arrangements for keeping snakes in captivity had ever been made anywhere before and Wajid Ali Shah was the first person to think of it.'[11] Indeed such a concept to display snakes in the open had never been thought of. A large square shaped tank was dug in front of Shahinshah Manzil. It had steep and slippery sides. An artificial mountain in the shape of a dome with sloping sides not more than thirty feet high with equal diameter at the base was built in the centre of the tank. The mountain was perforated and had innumerable holes for the reptiles to crawl inside. Water pipes opened at the top to give the effect of fountains. 'Thousands of large snakes' were reared in an annular moat where the reptiles ruled supreme. Frogs were released into the tank and snakes attacked their prey or basked in the sun. This offered an interesting sight to the visitors and painters. Two large pythons were reared in separate cages and were placed below the artificial mountain. The monsters would grab and gobble up live chickens when given to feed. He had a fine collection of cobras and proficient charmers as well, who could hold and show the reptiles with their bare hands. James Routledge recounts that once a large number of poisonous snakes were seized on their way to the King's menagerie as 'dangerous' by an order of the British Government.[12]

Wajid Ali inherited his passion for animals and birds from his ancestors Suja-ud-Daulla and his son Asaf-ud-Daulla, the latter was the founder of royal menagerie in Lucknow.[13] On the other hand, the concept of private menagerie was not new in the snooty circles of Calcutta. Incidentally, the first zoo was established in Calcutta in 1854 by Raja Rajendra Mallick Bahadur inside his Marble Palace of Chorabagan. The menagerie held a collection of unusual animals and birds that had been imported from abroad.[14]

However, the person to whom both Rajendra Mallick and Wajid Ali Shah were indebted for supplying to them a large collection of rare animals was the distinguished zoologist and an international animal trader, Edward Blyth (1810–73). Blyth joined the Asiatic Society of Calcutta in 1841 as a curator and remained at that post till 1863. He started his own business by exporting animals captured in Indian wilderness to various collectors and zoo gardens in Europe, but most of his specimens could not survive the long and arduous journey and often succumbed before they reached their destination. Furthermore, he was thwarted by his deceitful English agents. Edward Blyth had tried to involve his close contemporaries Charles Darwin and the famous English ornithologist John Gould to join his venture. Nevertheless, the market of living creatures was lucrative.[15]

With the annexation of Awadh, the fate of the royal menagerie hung in balance. Edward Blyth grabbed this opportunity to buy the entire collection of Wajid Ali Shah's at his own expense. He bought eighteen magnificent tigers, which were supposedly the 'finest cage specimen in the world,' all at the cost of twenty rupees a head only.[16] There were rumours that Blyth was sponsored by a notable German animal merchant Jamrach who was based in London. Overcoming some casualties that occurred in transit, Edward Blyth managed to bring sixteen tigers, one leopard, one bear, two cheetahs, three caracals, two rhinoceroses and one giraffe to Calcutta from Awadh. Blyth faced many constraints in sending his collection to England. In order to defray the substantial cost of maintaining such a large collection of animals, Blyth exhibited the tigers in a godown at Territibazar near Bowbazar in Calcutta on a daily show at the cost of one rupee per spectator. He promoted the show as: 'The Great Fighting Tigers of Lucknow'.[17]

Finally he was able to ship only one tiger to London in December 1858, which he sold at a cost of one hundred and forty pounds.[18] Blyth had still to dispose some of his Lucknow collection by the end of 1859. Meanwhile, Wajid Ali Shah had started his menagerie at Metiyaburj and had bought back some of his old specimens from Blyth. The deposed king paid a sum of three hundred pounds for three tigresses, which had once been on display in his menagerie at Lucknow. Charles Darwin (1809–82) was keeping a close eye on Wajid Ali Shah's animals as he had come to know about him from his friend Edward Blyth. Darwin was amused to learn from his friend in October 1855, that the King was looking for a trainer to train a pair of giraffes to draw his carriage.[19]

From Edward Blyth's correspondences with Darwin and Gould it is clear that the flow of animals was not one-way; instead, in the latter part of his stay in Calcutta, Blyth discovered a potential market of exotic fauna in India. Blyth was confident that both Darwin and Gould would be able to source exotic species for him from London. Blyth's valued customers were Raja Rajendra Mallick of Chorabagan in Calcutta, the Maharaja of Burdwan, the Nawab of Musrhidabad and last but not the least, the ex-king of Awadh. In a letter written to John Gould, Blyth expressed:

> *I have received unlimited orders from the ex-king of Oudh and from the Nawab of Marshidabad, both of enormous wealth, as you doubtless know, to procure for them any kind of animal I can for the menageries they are about to establish. Let us therefore be at once and first in the field, and moreover keep our own secret. I propose that we share the cost and share the profits equally.*[20]

Edward Blyth, in his later life in Calcutta, concentrated on importing animals from Latin America, Australia and Europe. He left India for good at the end of 1862, with a ship full of animals collected from Indian wilderness. Yet, his immense contribution to build a menagerie known for its finest collection of exotic creatures at Metiyaburj cannot be denied.

Wajid Ali's collection of animals at Metiyaburj also finds entry in Lady Dufferin's diary during her visit to the place in 1886, although the Marchioness viewed the King's hobby with a critical eye. The Lady witnessed a variety of birds, llamas and poisonous snakes as the last remnants but there was no mention of the King's tigers and cheetahs. The Lady's diary read:

> *We all went off in the afternoon to see the ex-King of Oude's gardens. He is an old gentleman, who is described to me as being utterly devoid of every moral sense. He never does any good to anybody, and he spends his monthly lac of rupees in*

> *keeping 25,000 pigeons, whose food costs him 400l a year; in buying sick creatures which the animal merchants sell him just before they reach their last gasp; in building houses for those of them that survive; and in the partial maintenance of several hundred ladies [sic].*[21]

A newspaper scoop from the *Calcutta Englishman* had drawn the attention of many amateur game hunters of Calcutta. On 6 January 1879, two full-grown Royal Bengal tigers escaped from the King's menagerie. While one was shot dead in the King's garden by a superintendent of police, the other swam across the Hooghly and sought refuge in the Botanical Garden on the opposite side of the river. The tiger caused serious menace to the visitors, picnic parties and the surrounding villagers for two days. Finally, allured by a bullock-bait, the brute was killed by one Mr Wace from Howrah.[22]

When the Calcutta Zoo was formally inaugurated on 1 January 1876 by the Prince of Wales, much of the lustre of Wajid Ali's menagerie had faded away. Responding to the keen interest shown by the British community in Calcutta to establish a menagerie as in other major cities in the world, the British Government finally evinced the idea to open the oldest government-managed zoo under the supervision of C.T. Buckland.

Premature senectitude had its unkind touch on the Badshah's physical health, but the sensibilities of his artistic mind and his interest in animals were alive and alert. Ram Brahma Sanyal, the first Superintendent of the Calcutta Zoo was an admirer of the King and recalled in his memoirs how the King, even with his disabling physical health would visit the garden on a decorated sedan chair drawn by eight bearers while Sanyal accompanied him on foot. The King felt ashamed and begged to be excused for not being able to walk beside Sanyal on the pathways of the garden because of his ill-health. After his death many of his zoo animals were transferred from Metiyaburj to the Calcutta Zoo. Ram Brahma Sanyal reported that an adult female Javan rhino living in the Calcutta Zoo since 1887 had 'also lived for about ten years in the menagerie of the Late King of Oudh.'

The interest in maintaining private menagerie was not new to the Bengali gentry. Even the British officers raised their collection of animals in captivity since 1801 at Barrackpore, which eventually became a centre for scientific endeavour. The exotic collection at Marble Palace in Calcutta, founded two years before the deposed king came to Calcutta, is worth mentioning. But few of them were passionate to know the biology and behaviour of the different species kept by them. Probably, the King was the first to bring about the noble idea to rear his animals in the open air and to watch them for hours.

Fourteen

The Epitaph

It was a brilliant dawn on the river and hues of ochre flickered on the water as the morning advanced. Subtle rays of the rising sun emblazoned the minarets of the Shahi Imambara. The Hooghly was reminiscent of melting ore. The Botanical Garden could be seen from the portico of the Sultan Khana if one's eyes were not bedazzled by the sunlight. Yet there was something eerie about the dawn, something dissonantly quiet. The naubat did not sound the time. A ghostlike silence prevailed over the mimic kingdom of Metiyaburj. Only a bemoaning sound of the ladies fell upon the ears of the onlookers. The wailing was reverberating from the Sultan Khana, where the banished king of Awadh was lying in his eternal sleep. The last crown of Burhan-ul-Mulk Saadat Ali Khan's dynasty had breathed his last in the fringes of Calcutta, the night before. There was nothing in his wretched death that could even remotely illustrate the past grandeur of the King. It was indeed, an ordinary death for a king.

No matter how ardent he had been to rule his state, Wajid Ali Shah was proud enough to send his crown to be displayed at the Crystal Palace Exhibition of London in 1851. To this Dalhousie had remarked, 'The wretch at Lucknow, who sent his crown to the Exhibition, would have done his people and us a good service if he had sent his head in it.'[1] The King lost his crown one day, but held his head high for thirty-one years in his kingdom of Metiyaburj even after Dalhousie, Sleeman and Outram had left the stage forever. Ali Naqi Khan also died in 1871. Yet, Wednesday, 21 September 1887 was a defining moment in the imperial history of India and the birth of a cultural legacy in Bengal, which continues even to this day.

A progressive decline of the King's health had been perceptible to his immediate attendants for a couple of years, but it was not till the month of April that the state of his health indicated any serious apprehensions. He was treated by his own physician Hakim Abdul Ali who had been summoned from Lucknow. Hakim Abdul Ali settled in Metiyaburj as the royal physician as Wajid Ali was reluctant to call an English physician or any other doctor. He was possessed by a fear of conspiracy and assassination. Though the King had been ailing for a long time, he appeared better on the fateful day. He had attended the morning Majlis-e-Husain in his Sibtainabad Imambara and appeared before the public without any distress. Yet, the King could not evade his destiny and he left for his heavenly abode at ten in the night, the same day.

His ministers broke the news of his death to the British Agent Lieut Col. W.F. Prideaux who lived in Metiyaburj. Prideaux managed to reach Sultan Khana within an hour and telegraphed the news to the Viceroy Lord Dufferin who was in Simla. Prideaux was quick to post sentinels as he apprehended lawlessness, which could arise out of conflicts over succession. A small British military force headed by Prideaux was stationed in Metiyaburj as a permanent guard to demonstrate the British authority over the King. The corps was to provide personal security to the King in exile but actually carried out spying in disguise. The Colonel worked as an 'Agent' for the Viceroy of India who lived in Belvedere at Alipore and relayed every detail of activity that occurred in the King's durbar. Prideaux regularly attended the durbar in Metiyaburj as an informer and became close to the King and his cohorts.[2]

A contemporary journalist documented the mourning event and noted that it was only at the break of day, at eight in the morning after the fateful night, that Khas Mahal was informed. It took ten hours for the news to reach the Begum who lived in her palace at Suroor Baugh a stone's throw away from the King's palace! The Begum was upset, yet she came out of her palace and joined the funeral with Mirza Jahan Qadr, the king's nephew.[3] As the day progressed, the mutá wives, the princes, the princesses and a throng of bewailing people started to gather inside Sultan Khana. The British sentinels were asked to move aside to make room for the King's relatives to pay their last homage. A decision was taken by the grieving members of King's family to inter the dead body inside Sibtainabad Imambara and preparations were started for the royal burial. At around 10 o'clock in the evening, the bier was taken out from Sultan Khana and the funeral journey began.[4] It was preceded by martial music and two platoons of soldiers. An impressive guard of honour was also given by the government. Messages of condolence were flooding the newspapers and long editorials extolling the ex-monarch's contributions could be read in several international literary media.

An article published on 31 October in *Indian Daily News* testifies that the stunning funeral cortege was virtually out of sync with the desolate and forlorn life that the King lived during his last days. The royal coffin was followed by a host of notables from Metiyaburj and Calcutta. The funeral was attended by

Nawab Abdul Latif, the distinguished educator of Bengal, Maulavi Sayid Amir Hussain, the Deputy Magistrate, Syed Amir Ali, a renowned Muslim scholar from Lucknow, Maulvi Muhammad Yusuf Khan Bahadur, the pleader of the Calcutta High Court, the great scholar Haji Noor Mohammad Zakaria, Prince Rahimuddin, the grandnephew of Tipu Sultan who lived in Calcutta, Prince Muhammad Farruk Shah, the great-grandson of Tipu Sultan and Prince Muhammad Anwar Shah, the grandson of Tipu Sultan[5] amongst hundreds of bemoaning followers. The dead body was interred in Sibtainabad Imambara at eleven thirty in the evening, with great pomp and show and military honour under aegis of the British Government.[6] Wajid Ali Shah was the only ruler of Awadh to build his own mausoleum during his lifetime.

Colonel Prideaux's apprehension was not unjustified. Wajid Ali Shah was survived by roughly seventy children and innumerable wives, and a struggle for succession was imminent. A contemporary government record of pension classified the living wives of the deceased king in Metiyaburj into eight classes—from A to H. There were thirty-three Mahals, (belonging to Classes A, B and C) and 217 Begums. There was one Dulari Begum who was expelled by the King, but was entitled to get a pension of fifteen rupees only. The total amount paid towards pension of his wives was 11,230 rupees at the time of his death.[7]

First, there was a disagreement amongst his heirs over the rights to perform 'Chehlum'—the ceremony to be performed on the fortieth day after the death to give solace to his unembodied soul. An article published on 3 November in *The Statesman* from Calcutta stated that finally Colonel Prideaux came forth and after debating the issue with the King's family members, declared that

Prince Qamar Qudr, the eldest amongst the King's sons living in Metiyaburj, would perform the rituals. The pronouncement was also ratified by Begum Khas Mahal. The government affirmed its concurrence in executing the rituals of Chehlum in the best possible manner to honour the deceased king but warned against needless profligacy and wastage of money. The King's kitchen was opened to the poor people in the neighbourhood. Sentinels were also relaxed for free movement of the family women in Sibtainabad Imambara.[8]

While in Lucknow the King had nominated his elder son Mirza Hamid Ali Bahadur, the son of Khas Mahal, as his heir-apparent. Mirza Hamid Ali went to England as a member of the futile Oudh Mission and returned to his father in 1859. He died during his father's lifetime in 1874 and was buried in Sibtainabad Imambara. Prince Mirza Sikandar Hasmat, Wajid Ali's only brother who went to England to plead for justice, died in London in 1858. Hazrat Mahal died in Nepal in 1879. After her death, her son who was also living in asylum in Nepal was granted clemency by Queen Victoria on the occasion of her golden jubilee of reign in 1888. With the death of the last king, the colonial rulers sought to grasp the estate of Metiyaburj and to annihilate the name of the Awadh royalty from the pages of history. A commission was constituted under Colonel Predaux to initiate the process of assimilation without delay. The drama that was enacted three decades ago was being repeated once again in 1887, only the place and the artists had changed.

On 1 November 1887, a notification was issued by Colonel Prideaux announcing the forceful retirement of the King's employees and servants against exiguous compensations. The employees who had been working for less than six months were to receive a gratuity of one month's pay; those who had worked for more than six months but less than three years were given an amount equivalent to two months' pay and for those whose services had exceeded three years a gratuity of three months was paid. However, special packages were announced for those who had worked for more than fifteen years. In the succession protocol of Awadh, the descendants of the King's son or brother who had died during the his's lifetime were barred from inheritance or from seeking any title. They were called Mahjoob-ol-irs.[9] The government took this opportunity to disqualify the descendants of Mirza Hamid Ali and Mirza Sikandar Hasmat.

The process of assimilation had started albeit subtly during the King's lifetime itself. A scornful editorial published in *The Statesman* elucidated that a substantial sum had been deducted from the King's receivable pension of one lakh rupees while he was still alive. The government constituted a commission with two British officers and Syed Amir Ali, a jurist from Awadh, to decide upon the distribution of a portion of the King's pension amongst his family members, which previously the King used to pay from his own. The commission allotted three thousand rupees per month to his eldest son, three hundred rupees per month to his second son and one hundred and fifty rupees per month to his other sons in Metiyaburj who were over the age of twelve. Some amount of money was also granted to his daughters and the Begums living in Metiyaburj. After meeting all obligations, the balance of seventy thousand rupees was handed over to the King per month. The editor expressed doubts as to whether the government would distribute a legitimate portion of his pension amongst his heirs after his death. Eventually, his apprehensions came true.

The government finally recognized Prince Qamar Qadr as the representative of the Awadh family in January 1888.

Meanwhile, the strife continued amongst the descendants as a consequence of the government's iniquitous policy in distributing pension. The charge of nepotism to favour some of the King's heirs, who had stealthily abetted the colonial rulers, was abounding. The government was waiting in the wings and immediately formed a syndicate to assimilate all movable and immovable properties in Metiyaburj and put them up for sale.[10] The fund was distributed amongst all eligible heirs although the process was not free of controversy. Before that, Colonel Prideaux opened the property of the late King of Awadh to the public. Visitors could come and see the incredible estate especially the zoo, but had to buy a ticket from a counter at the Asad Manzil gate. Often the Colonel was seen strolling in the park and recounting vibrant tales of the King's court-life in Metiyaburj to the enthralled visitors.[11]

The fauna of the King's favourite menagerie was put on sale and the responsibility for the same was bestowed upon Messrs Milton and Co. An article published in *The Statesman* in December 1888 describes the extravagance that surrounded the auction of the animals. The Calcutta Tramway Company extended a special service by running a horse-drawn tram up to Kidderpore for the convenience of the buyers. On the first day, the syndicate decided to clear off twenty thousand choice pigeons. The rest of the animals were sold subsequently. Another article published in the same newspaper on 20 December announced the sale of varieties of birds at lucrative prices. A subsequent article published in *The Statesman* on 23 December 1888 bears witness to the sale of his entire landed property in Metiyaburj comprising two hundred fifty seven bighas. Eventually, the dream of the ex-king of Awadh was wiped off within just a few years after his death and the money was distributed amongst his heirs. The

Sibtainabad Imambara, Quasrul Buka and few other religious places and the graveyard of the King's family remain as evidence of the King's lost glory.

Sharar laments:

The inevitable result was that Matiya Burj was destroyed to the last brick. Property which was worth thousands of rupees was sold for cowries and that place which in a short time had become an earthly paradise was now a veritable hell.[12]

Meanwhile, an incident took place for which the King's heirs and the British Agent were not prepared. Mirza Birjis Qadr arrived in Metiyaburj from Nepal in 1892 to claim his rights. Birjis was only eleven years old when his father was exiled and had not seen his father since then. Wajid Ali Shah had decided to leave behind his fourth son in Lucknow under the able guidance of his spirited wife Hazrat Mahal. The rest is history.

What prompted Birjis to come and stake his claim five years after his father's death is not known. Mirza Birjis Qadr declared himself as the legal heir of the King to succeed his deceased father. He put forth the legitimate reasoning that as the eldest surviving son of Wajid Ali Shah and the titular 'King' of Awadh, he was the claimant to his father's pension. The King's eldest son Mirza Muhammad Ali Hyder was deaf and mute, and had died during his father's lifetime. His second son Mirza Muhammad Javid Ali Khan had died of smallpox in 1849. The Badshah's third son Mirza Hamid Ali Bahadur was the heir-apparent and had passed away in 1874. Mirza Birjis was his fourth son. His first three sons were by his first wife Khas Mahal. Mirza Qamar Qadr was his eighth son and was born of his wife Fakhr-i-Mahal. He was the eldest of his living sons in Metiyaburj.

Mirza Birjis Qadr referred to Article V of the proposed Treaty of 1856 and put forward his claim of twelve lakh rupees per annum. He asserted that he was the most exalted and qualified amongst the sons of his father and was capable of looking after the members of the family as well as their twenty thousand protégés.[13] While he was preparing to pursue his case before the British Empress and was arranging to leave for England, he was invited with his family by one of his relatives to dinner. On return to his Atabaugh Palace, he fell ill from food poisoning and died. On that single night of 14 August 1893, his elder son Prince Khurshid Qadr, and a daughter along with three companions succumbed to the treachery. Mirza Birjis Qadr was buried in Sibtainabd Imambara. The death of Mirza Birjis Qadr removed the last impediment in Prince Qamar Qadr's path. Incidentally, his pension was increased from three thousand rupees to four thousand by the government. The taleteller whispered around the alleyways of Metiyaburj, of the invisible hand and role of Qamar Qadr behind the tragedy.

Although the life of Begum Mahtab Ara Akhtar (1859–1929) wife of Mirza Birjis Qadr, was spared, her only son and heir Prince Khurshid Qadr met with a tragic end. Begum Mahtab Ara Akhtar, who was pregnant and did not attend the fatal dinner, gave birth to a posthumous child on 24 December 1893. Prince Maher Qadr, as he was named, was debarred from his claim after his father's death by the application of Muslim law (Mahjoob-ol-irs). He was a man of subtle sensibilities like his grandfather and was a poet himself. Prince Maher Qadr relinquished his claims after the country's independence and died on 12 March 1961 in independent India.

Even the death of Wajid Ali Shah is not free from controversy. Wajid Ali was ill for sometime but the palace gossip alleged that the death had been due to poison. Prince Anjum Quder, the son of Prince Maher Qadr, had reasons to believe that like his grandfather, his great-grand father too had met with an unnatural death. The finger of suspicion was pointed towards Badshah's vazir, Munsarim-ud-Daulla who was a puppet in the hands of Colonel Predaux. Mirza Ali Azhar, a retired judge of Jaipur, who did extensive research in 1943 on Wajid Ali Shah, referred to an article[14] published in an unidentified newspaper. The article alleges that Munsarim-ud-Daulla added poison to a medicine prepared by the Royal Hakim and made his master consume the concoction. This is how he met his end. At the solemn moment of his death, the King had asked for a piece of paper and a pen to scribble his dying declaration. The vazir deceptively evaded his request, saying that the Huzur should take rest and avoid strain!

Colonel W. F. Prideaux prepared detailed reports that were forwarded to his authority on the method of distribution of life pension amongst the family members and employees of the deceased King. Paragraph four of his memo No. 351 in Calcutta dated 31 March 1888 addressed to the Secretary of the Government of India, Foreign Department, has merits that are relevant to the present context. Prideaux spent an entire paragraph to eulogize Munsarim-ud-Daulla's faithfulness to the British Crown and recommended a pension equivalent to the amount granted to nineteen sons of the deceased King. Perhaps Prideaux was obliged. A few lines from his memo could be a noteworthy testimony of the assassination plan hatched by the colonial rulers.

When the illness of His Majesty developed serious symptoms, I asked him (Munsarim-ud-Daula) to furnish me with

> *a complete list of all the persons who in any shape were dependant on the king together with the rates of pay which they received. During the progress of the administration of the king's Estate, he has acted under me as Superintendent of Affairs at Garden Reach, and I cannot speak too highly of the zeal and activity with which he has executed my orders. I would venture to recommend that in consideration of his long and faithful services and the assistance which in very eminent degree he has rendered since the death of His Majesty, a pension, amounting to two thirds of his former emoluments, or five hundred rupees per mensem, be granted to him for the remainder of his life.*[15]

The motive of assassination is not obscure. The King died at the age of sixty-five and could have lived for another ten years considering that his ancestors had lived much longer lives. Moreover, advanced medical help was available in Calcutta at that time. Yet the British granted a pension of one lakh rupees per month hoping that it would not be for long. However, there was no likelihood for him to die and the Agent had no other alternative. The suspicion in the minds of the King's descendents may have some merit, but there is lack of evidence to support the argument. Thus, there is no point in raising accusing fingers against the British Agent purely on the basis of subjective hunches and conjectures.

Professor Meerza Kaukub believes that Wajid Ali Shah died a natural death at Metiyaburj and he was not poisoned. During his younger days in Lucknow, he had suffered a heart attack.

It is unkind to say that even in good health it would have been an excruciating experience for the King to continue witnessing the crumbling of his haven. At the end of his life there were perceptible signs of financial irregularities. His pension had been curtailed by thirty per cent on the grounds of meeting certain obligations decided unilaterally by the government. The jewels in his treasury, which he had been able to bring from Awadh at the time of his departure, were gradually being depleted. Often the King was seen stealthily moving out of the palace in his own carriage without his attendants. The carriage would take him through the roads of Khidderpore and Dharmatolla before coming to a halt in front of an edifice in Burrabazar where an eminent jewel merchant lived. After an exchange of mutual courtesies, the King would furtively hand over a fistful of jewels tied in a silk handkerchief in exchange of a bunch of paper notes![16]

The death of the deposed King of Awadh pulled down the curtain on the utopian kingdom of Metiyaburj. It had taken several years for the King to convert a piece of desolated riverbank into a paradise on earth, and it took the British only a couple of years to raze it into oblivion. The rich Awadhi family was reduced to penury and members dispersed to other places when the royalty had disintegrated. Some of them returned to Lucknow. Sir Evan Cotton, an Indian born barrister-turned-historian and a member of the British Parliament recounts:

> *Their departure has been the signal for the erection of Jute Mills and the construction of the enormous Tidal Docks and their connected wharves and works with the result that a complete transformation has taken place in the aspect of Kidderpur and the upper end of Garden Reach, and the memories of the past have been altogether obliterated.*[17]

Professor Meerza Kaukub, the grandson of Mirza Birjis Qadr and a living descendent of the royal family in Calcutta, narrates his childhood days when he would play in the compound of Sultan Khana behind the Shahi Masjid. Professor Kaukub informs that bulk of the property of the deceased king was purchased at an auction by Meerza Jahan Qudr, son-in-law and nephew of the Badshah. Another source reveals that bulk of the asset was bought by a Bengali millionaire of the nineteenth century.[18]

The King's property was fractioned and sold in bits by his descendants to bear the cost of ongoing litigations and to maintain their extravagant lifestyle. Nevertheless, the picturesque skyline of the King's earthly paradise had morphed into gigantic factory sheds, massive machineries, soot-filled chimneys, dockyards, and wharves jostling with each other for space. Today, only the Sibtainabad Imambara, Baitul Naajat and the Quasrul Buka have escaped the axe of time. Quasrul Buka was the first imambara to be built in Metiyaburj. The entrance is wedged between the remains of a dilapidated wall and a factory that occupies its sacred ground. The Atabaugh Palace where Mirza Birjis breathed his last is used as a godown today. The pillars even in their ruined state are reminiscent of its regal days.

History had never been kind to the King. It is difficult to decipher the real man from all that has been written about him. The prying of a superior power forced him to relinquish his crown and prudence urged him to accept his destiny. Yet, his heart refused to settle down in a dull life of blankness. In the misery of banishment, the King tried to paint subtle impressions of life in the style he had nurtured all through his life. It was with his keenness that the archetypical mannerism of Lucknowi sensibilities was implanted in the hearts of the Bengali intelligentsia. A new style of dance, drama, poetry, cuisine, etiquette, music and melody was impregnated into Calcutta and continues to exist even today, deeply entrenched into the city's culture. The long chronicles of pathos and romance that could be heard from his mausoleum can fill endless volumes. Notwithstanding the British conspiracy to obliterate all traces of Awadh royalty from Calcutta and to annihilate the last chance of insurrection against the colonial power, Wajid Ali Shah successfully left his indelible footprint on the sands of time.

Today, Wajid Ali Shah's Metiyaburj is lost in the dingy alleyways, stinking sewerage, dump yards, hyacinth-choked ponds and feculent riverbanks. It is sad to note that very few Calcuttans today are aware that Wajid Ali Shah lived almost half of his life in the city. His final days in this colonial capital remain unknown even to the people of his native town. Only the inconspicuous Sibtainabad Imambara with seventeen odd graves of the royal family and few dilapidated holy places in Metiyaburj can dredge up the memories of the deposed king in Calcutta. Yet unknowingly, the mesmerizing spell and enthral of the Badshah's momentous labour of love remains entwined even today in every skein of the Bengalis' cultural life.

Only the propounder remains an unknown entity.

Notes

Chapter 1

1. Nagendra Kumar Singh, *Encyclopaedia of Muslim Biography: S–Z– Volume 5 of Encyclopaedia of Muslim Biography: India, Pakistan, Bangladesh*, A.P.H. Pub. Corp., 2001, page 415.
2. Sir James Outram became the Chief Commissioner of Awadh following his resignation as Resident from 1 February 1856.
3. Mirza Ali Azhar, *King Wajid Ali Shah of Awadh*, Royal Book Company, 1982, Vol. 1, page 491.
4. S.Kamal-ud-Deen Haidar, *Qaisar-ul-Tawarikh*, Vol II page 159; Mirza Ali Azhar, *King Wajid Ali Shah of Awadh*, Royal Book Company, 1982, page 488.
5. Mirza Ali Azhar, *King Wajid Ali Shah of Awadh*, Royal Book Company, 1982, Vol. 1, page 490.
6. Sreepanth, *Metia Burjer Nawab*, Ananda Publisher, 1990, page 40.
7. Rosie Llewellyn Jones, *Engaging Scoundrels: True Tales of Old Lucknow*, Oxford University Press, 2000, page 130.
8. Rosie Llewellyn Jones, *Engaging Scoundrels: True Tales of Old Lucknow*, Oxford University Press, 2000, page 81.
9. Susheela Misra, *Musical Heritage of Lucknow*, Harman Pub. House, 1991, page 82.
10. Sir John William Kaye, *A History of the Sepoy War in India 1857–1858*, W.H. Allen & Co, 1864, Page 401. Another source says Ali Naqi Khan was released from Lucknow in the month of July and started his journey towards Calcutta on 15 July 1856. His caravan reached Allahabad from where he boarded a steamer and embarked at

Calcutta on 29 July 1856.
11. Abdul Halim Sharar, *Lucknow: The Last Phase of an Oriental Culture*, Oxford University Press, 1994 edn, page 69.
12. Wm. H. Allen & Co's *Allen's Indian Mail, and Register of Intelligence for British and Foreign India, China, and All Parts of the East*, Oxford University Press, 1856, page 254.
13. Sir John Lawrence was the younger brother of Sir Henry Laurence who became the Chief Commissioner of Awadh on 21 March 1857.
14. Indian soldiers in British Army.
15. John Bruce Norton (ed.), *Topics for Indian Statesmen*, Oxford University Press, 1858, page 50.
16. Mirza Ali Azhar, *King Wajid Ali Shah of Awadh*, Royal Book Company, 1982, Vol. 1, page 492; Hyder Qurratulain's, *River of Fire*, Oxford University Press, 1999, page 152.
17. Sreepanth, *Metia Burjer Nawab*, Ananda Publisher, 1990, page 42.
18. Mirza Ali Azhar, *King Wajid Ali Shah of Awadh*, Royal Book Company, 1982, Vol. 1, Vol. 2, page 97.
19. Indigenous vessels with rows.
20. Prof. Meerza Kaukub's personal communication.
21. Mirza Ali Azhar, *King Wajid Ali Shah of Awadh*, Royal Book Company, 1982, Vol. 1, page 98.
22. Mirza Ali Azhar, *King Wajid Ali Shah of Awadh*, Royal Book Company, 1982, Vol. 1, page 491, 'Letter from the Chief Secretary addressed to Wajid Ali Shah'.
23. Sir Lawrence Peel retired as the Chief Justice of the Supreme Court in Calcutta in November 1855.
24. Prof. Meerza Kaukub—Personal communication. Prof. Meerza Kaukub believes that arrangement of renting the house was made by his people before the retinue reached Calcutta.
25. John Matheson, *England to Delhi. A Narrative of Indian Travel*, Longmans, Green, 1870, page 450.
26. Mirza Ali Azhar, *King Wajid Ali Shah of Awadh*, Royal Book Company, 1982, Vol. 1, page 491.

27. Reginald Heber, *Narrative of a Journey Through the Upper Provinces of India: From Calcutta to Bombay, 1824–1825*, John Murray, 1856, Vol.1, page 28.
28. Wm. H. Allen & Co's *Allen's Indian Mail, and Register of Intelligence for British and Foreign India, China, and All Parts of the East*, Oxford University Press, 1856, page 313.
29. Wm. H. Allen & Co's *Allen's Indian Mail, and Register of Intelligence for British and Foreign India, China, and All Parts of the East*, Oxford University Press, 1856, page 313.
30. Wm. H. Allen & Co's *Allen's Indian Mail, and Register of Intelligence for British and Foreign India, China, and All Parts of the East*, Oxford University Press, 1856, page 313.
31. Graham MacPhee and Prem Poddar, *Empire and After: Englishness in Post Colonial Perspective*, Berghahn Books, 2007, page 80.
32. Wm. H. Allen & Co's *Allen's Indian Mail, and Register of Intelligence for British and Foreign India, China, and All Parts of the East*, Oxford University Press, 1856, page 447.

Chapter 2

1. Sir Edwin Arnold, *The Marquis of Dalhousie's Administration of British India* Saunders, Otley, and Co., 1865, Vol. 2, page 329.
2. Mirza Ali Azhar, *King Wajid Ali Shah of Awadh*, Royal Book Company, 1982, Vol. 1, page 196.
3. Mirza Ali Azhar, *King Wajid Ali Shah of Awadh*, Royal Book Company, 1982, Vol. 1, page 201.
4. Wajid Ali Shah, *Reply to the Oude Blue Book*, page 24–25; Mirza Ali Azhar, *King Wajid Ali Shah of Awadh*, Royal Book Company, 1982, Vol. 1, page 198–9.
5. Mirza Ali Azhar, *King Wajid Ali Shah of Awadh*, Royal Book Company, 1982, Vol. 1, page 206.
6. G.S. Chabbra, *Advanced Study in the History of Modern India*, Lotus Press, 2005, page 215.
7. John William Kaye, *A History of the Sepoy War in India, 1857-1858*;

W. H. Allen, 1875, page 143.
8. Samuel Lucas, *Dacoitee in Excelsis; or, The Spoliation of Oude*, J.R. Taylor, 1857, page 153.
9. J.G.A. Baird, *Private Letters of the Marquess of Dalhousie*, William Blackwood and Sons, 1910, page 33.
10. P.C. Mukherjee, *The Pictorial Lucknow*, Asian Educational Services, 2003, page 37.
11. Mirza Ali Azhar, *King Wajid Ali Shah of Awadh*, Royal Book Company, 1982, Vol. 1, page 242.
12. Ranbir Singh, '*Wajid Ali Shah—The Tragic King*, Publication Scheme, 2002, page 48.
13. Samuel Lucas, *Dacoitee in Excelsis; or, The Spoliation of Oude*, J.R. Taylor, 1857, page 109.
14. Sir William Sleeman, *A Journey Through the Kingdom of Oude*, R. Bentley, 1858, page 310.
15. Dalhousie's letter to Colonel Sleeman from Government House Calcutta, dated 16 September 1848.
16. Sleeman's letter to Dalhousie from Jhansee dated 24 September 1848; Sir William Sleeman, *A Journey Through the Kingdom of Oude*, R. Bentley, 1858, Vol. 2, page xliii.
17. Ranbir Singh, *Wajid Ali Shah: The Tragic King*, Publication Scheme, 2002, page 49.
18. Sleeman's letter to Mr H.M. Elliot from Lucknow dated 20 March 1849. Sir William Sleeman, *A Journey Through the Kingdom of Oude*, R. Bentley, 1858, Vol. 2 page li.
19. The sixth Nawab of Awadh, Saadat Ali Khan, ascended the throne taking the help of the British after deposing his nephew Nawab Wajir Ali Khan and became a puppet in the hands of the British. During his time in 1801 a treaty was signed by which Saadat Ali ceded half of his kingdom to the East India Company and also agreed to disband his army in favour of a hugely expensive British troop, which he was coerced to engage at his own cost.
20. Translated by Prof. Meerza Kaukub.
21. William Knighton, *Elihu Jaan's story: or, The Private Life of an Eastern*

Queen, Longman, Green, Longman, Roberts & Green, 1865, page 30.

22. Sleeman's letter to Sir H.M. Elliot dated 23 September 1849, from Lucknow; Sir William Sleeman, *A Journey Through the Kingdom of Oude*, R. Bentley, 1858, Vol. 2, page lxxiii.
23. Sleeman's letter to Lord Dalhousie dated 18 March 1852, from Lucknow; Sir William Sleeman, *A Journey Through the Kingdom of Oude'*, R. Bentley, 1858, Vol. 2, page 355.
24. Sleeman's letter to Sir H.M. Elliot dated 11 October 1849, from Lucknow; Sir William Sleeman, *A Journey Through the Kingdom of Oude*, R. Bentley, 1858, Vol. 2, page lxxix.
25. Sir William Sleeman, *A Journey Through the Kingdom of Oude*, R. Bentley, 1858, Vol. 2, page 378.
26. Edward Thompson, Geoffrey Theodore Garratt, *History of British Rule in India*, Atlantic Publishers & Distributors, 1999, Vol. 2, page 408.
27. Sir William Sleeman, *A Journey Through the Kingdom of Oude*, R. Bentley, 1858, Vol. 2, page xxi.
28. Sleeman's letter to Sir James Weir Hogg dated 12 January 1853, from Lucknow; Sir William Sleeman, *A Journey Through the Kingdom of Oude*, R. Bentley, 1858, Vol. 2, page 392.
29. Sleeman's letter to Col. Low dated 5 march 1854, from Lucknow; Sir William Sleeman, *A Journey Through the Kingdom of Oude*, R. Bentley, 1858, Vol. 2, page 418.
30. Sleeman's letter to Col. Low dated 1 June 1854, from Lucknow; Sir William Sleeman, *A Journey Through the Kingdom of Oude*, R. Bentley, 1858, Vol. 2, page 421.
31. Sleeman's letter to Lord Dalhousie, dated September 1852, from Lucknow; Sir William Sleeman, *A Journey Through the Kingdom of Oude*, R. Bentley, 1858, Vol. 2, page 371.
32. John William Kaye, *A History of the Sepoy War in India, 1857–1858*, W. H. Allen, 1875, page 137.
33. Sleeman's letter to Lord Dalhousie, dated 11 September 1854, from Lucknow. Sir William Sleeman, *A Journey Through the Kingdom of*

Oude, R. Bentley, 1858, Vol. 2, page 423.
34. Lionel James Trotter, *The Bayard of India: A Life of General Sir James Outram*, Blackwood, 1903, page 320.
35. Sir Joseph Fayrer, later became a professor of surgery at the Medical College of Calcutta from 1859–1872, and became a fellow of the Royal Society in 1877. He was President of the Asiatic Society of Bengal in 1867. He would be remembered especially for his studies on the poisonous snakes of India and on the physiological effects produced by their venom.
36. Lionel James Trotter, *The Bayard of India: A Life of General Sir James Outram*, Blackwood, 1903, page 132.
37. J.G.A Baird, *Private Letters of the Marquess of Dalhousie*, William Blackwood and Sons, 1910, page 344.
38. In 1837, the Governor-General Lord Auckland forced on Oudh a treaty by which it asserted its right to take over what remained of Oudh if the Company felt that the country was being mismanaged. The treaty also imposed on Oudh an annual payment of 16,00,000 Rupees. This last clause was in violation of treaty of 1801 by which the Company had agreed to defend Oudh in return for cession of half of its territory. Even the Board of Directors of the EEIC viewed this treaty as unjust and unfair and declared it null and void. The Governor-General, however, never informed the King of Oudh that the treaty was entirely annulled; Ikram ul-Majeed Sehgal, *Defence Journal* 1999, Vol. 3.
39. Greg Barton, *Empire Forestry and the Origin of Environmentalism*, University of Cambridge Press, 2002, page 54.
40. John William Kaye, *A History of the Sepoy War in India, 1857–1858*; W. H. Allen, 1875, page 143; Mirza Ali Azhar, *King Wajid Ali Shah of Awadh*, Royal Book Company, 1982, Vol. 1, page 390.
41. Leslie Stephen and Sidney Lee, *Dictionary of National Biography*, Adamant Media Corporation, 2001, page 254.
42. J.G.A Baird, *Private Letters of the Marquess of Dalhousie*, William Blackwood and Sons, 1910, page 344, letter dated 12 May 1855.
43. Sir William Lee-Warner, *The Life of the Marquis of Dalhousie, K.T.*,

The Macmillan Co., Vol. 2, page 332.
44. Evans Bell, *Retrospects and Prospects of Indian Policy*, Trübner, 1868, page 52.
45. Baird, *Private Letters of the Marquess of Dalhousie*, William Blackwood and Sons,1910, page 367, letter dated 6 January 1856. Dalhousie received the despatch on a Wednesday (2 January), midnight. He called a council on Friday and started mobilizing the troops on Saturday.
46. J.G.A. Baird, *Private Letters of the Marquess of Dalhousie*, William Blackwood and Sons, 1910, page 344, letter dated 2 May 1855, Ootacumund.
47. J.G.A. Baird, *Private Letters of the Marquess of Dalhousie*, William Blackwood and Sons, 1910, page 367, letter dated 6 January 1856.
48. J.G.A. Baird, *Private Letters of the Marquess of Dalhousie*, William Blackwood and Sons, 1910, page 365, letter dated 20 January 1856.
49. J.G.A. Baird, *Private Letters of the Marquess of Dalhousie*, William Blackwood and Sons, 1910, page 365, letter dated 20 January 1856.
50. John Malcolm Ludlow, *British India, Its Races and Its History Considered with Reference to the Mutinies of 1857: A Series of Lectures Addressed to the Students of the Working Men's College*, Macmillan, 1858, Vol. 2, page 210.
51. William Knighton, *Elihu Jaan's Story: Or, the Private Life of an Eastern Queen* (Large Print Edition) BiblioBazaar, LLC, 2008, page 61.
52. Note from a conference with the Queen Mother, *Accounts and Papers of the House of Commons, Great Britain. Parliament. House of Commons*, 1856, page 284.
53. Curtain-traditional arrangement for the women who were debarred from being visible to the public.
54. Inclosure 11 in No. 4, Note of an interview which took place between the King of Oude and Major-General Outram, at the Zurd Kothee Palace, on the morning of the 4 February 1856: *Accounts and Papers of the House of Commons, Great Britain. Parliament. House of Commons*, 1856 (ordered to be printed), page 287.
55. Kamal-ud-din Haidar, *Qaisar-ul-Tawarikh* Vol. 2, page 130–33.

56. Landed gentries.

Chapter 3

1. Sreepanth, *Metia Burjer Nawab*, Ananda Publisher, 1990, page 57.
2. King Wajid Ali Shah, *Huzn-e-Akhtari*, 1922 edition, page 41.
3. Kaye and Malleson, *History of Indian Mutiny 1857–8*, Longmans, Green and Co., 1914, page 295.
4. Lawyer.
5. William Knighton, *Elihu Jaan's Story: Or, The Private Life of an Eastern Queen*; Longmans, Green and Co. 1865, page 12.
6. Kaye's and Malleson, *History of Indian Mutiny 1857–8*, Longmans, Green and Co., 1914, page 295.
7. Another source says S.S. Ripon. Mirza Ali Azhar, *King Wajid Ali Shah of Awadh*, Royal Book Company, 1982, Vol. 2, page 99.
8. Kaye and Malleson, *History of Indian Mutiny 1857–8*, Longmans, Green and Co. 1914, page 296.
9. Suez canal was excavated in 1969 and the wayfarers had to follow the land tract in Egypt to reach the Mediterranean.
10. Mirza Ali Azhar, *King Wajid Ali Shah of Awadh*, Royal Book Company, 1982, Vol. 2, page 102.
11. Legal representative.
12. H. Michael Fisher, *Counterflows to Colonialism*, Permanent Black, 2008, page 412.
13. *The Times* dated 22 August 1856.
14. *The Times* dated 28 August 1856.
15. *The Times* dated 27 August 1856 and 28 August 1856 citing *The Globe*.
16. Female court held by an Indian lady.
17. *The Times* dated 1 September 1856.
18. *The Times* dated 2 September 1856.
19. Officer or secretary.
20. Mirza Ali Azhar, *King Wajid Ali Shah of Awash*, Royal Book Company, 1982, Vol. 2, page 108.

21. House of Commons Debate, 22 February 1856; Mirza Ali Azhar, *King Wajid Ali Shah of Awadh*, Royal Book Company, 1982, Vol. 2, page 112–13.
22. J.G.A. Baird, *Private Letters of the Marquess of Dalhousie*, William Blackwood and Sons, 1910, page 369; Dalhousie's letter dated 8 February 1856.
23. This description of the Oudh Blue Book was given by one British official who had been involved in the operation described the parliamentary blue book (or paper) on Oudh. William Dalrymple, *The Last Mughal: The Fall of a Dynasty*, Alfred A. Knopf, 2007, page 534.
24. Mr Jones' speech in the Court of Proprietors of the East India Company on 24 September 1856: 'History of the Indian Mutiny', page 151.
25. Speeches in the Quarterly Meeting of the Court of Proprietors, held on 24 September 1856.
26. Michael H. Fisher, *Counterflows to Colonialism*, Permanent Black, 2008, page 417; Letters of Mussehood-Deen.
27. Farman means king's orders.
28. Mirza Ali Azhar, *King Wajid Ali Shah of Awadh*, Royal Book Company, 1982, Vol. 2, page 128.
29. Tenancy.
30. A court comprising women.
31. Queen Victoria's diary—preserved at Windsor caste, Berkshire.
32. Hannsard's Parliamentary Debates: Vol. CXLVII, 27 July 1857, pages 481–490.
33. *The Times* dated 8 August 1857.
34. *The Times* dated 8 August 1857.
35. Court Minute 25 November 1857 and again on 2 December 1857; Michael H. Fisher, *Counterflows to Colonialism'*, Permanent Black, 2008, page 419.
36. *The Times* dated 18 November 1857
37. *The Times* dated 21 April 1858.
38. Graham MacPhee and Prem Poddar, *Empire and After: Englishness*

in Post Colonial Perspective, Berghahn Books, 2007 page 79.
39. Harper's Magazine, Issue: 20 February 1858, page 118.
40. Ameer Ali S. Khan, *Wazirnamah*, 1875 edition, page 248–49; Mirza Ali Azhar, *King Wajid Ali Shah of Awadh*, Royal Book Company, 1982, Vol. 2, page 150.
41. Harper's Magazine, Issue: 27 March 1858, page 205–06.
42. H. Fisher, *Counterflows to Colonialism*, Permanent Black, 2008, page 417; Mirza Ali Azhar, *King Wajid Ali Shah of Awadh*, Royal Book Company, 1982, Vol. 2, page 150.
43. William Knighton, *The Private Life of an Eastern King: Together with Elihu Jaan's Story; Or, The Private Life of an Eastern Queen*, H. Milford, Oxford University Press, 1921, page 345.
44. H. Fisher, *Counterflows to Colonialism*, Permanent Black, 2008, page 421–22.
45. William Knighton, *Elihu Jaan's Story: Or, The Private Life of an Eastern Queen*; Longman, Green, Longman, Roberts, & Green, 1865, page 65.

Chapter 4

1. Feudal lords of Awadh.
2. Mirza Ali Azhar, *King Wajid Ali Shah of Awadh*, Royal Book Company, 1982, Vol. 2, page 150.
3. Dr Bhargava and Dr Rizvi, *Freedom Struggle in U.P.*, Oxford University Press, 1957, Vol. 1, page 274–75.
4. Darbar means court.
5. Surya Narain Singh, *The Kindom of Awadh*, Mittal Publications, 2003, page 62–66.
6. R.C. Majumdar, *History and Culture of The Indian People, British Paramountcy and Indian Renaissance*, The Vidya Bhavan, 2002, Vol. 9, page 536.
7. Rudrangshu Mukherjee, *Awadh in a Revolt, 1857–1858: A Study of Popular Resistance*, Orient Blackswan, 2002, page 37–36.
8. R.C. Majumdar, *History and Culture of The Indian People, British*

Paramountcy and Indian Renaissance, The Vidya Bhavan, 2002, Vol. 9, page 536.
9. Hari Narayan and Amit Verma, *Decisive Battles of India Through the Ages*, GIP Books, 1998, Vol. 2, page 204.
10. Rudrangshu Mukherjee, *Awadh in a Revolt, 1857–1858: A Study of Popular Resistance*, Orient Blackswan, 2002, page 94.
11. Qureshi, *Qaisar-ut-Tawarikh of Kamal-ud-din Haidar 1867 Classics*, New Royal Book Company, 2008, page 25–28.
12. Feud chief.
13. Rudrangshu Mukherjee, *Awadh in a Revolt, 1857–1858: A Study of Popular Resistance*, Orient Blackswan, 2002, page 135.
14. Once a begum gave birth to a child, her prefix 'begum' would be replaced by the suffix 'mahal'.
15. George Bruce Malleson, *The Indian Mutiny of 1857*, Seeley & Co. Ltd, 1896, page 205–06.
16. William Brock, *A Biographical Sketch of Sir Henry Havelock*, Oxford University Press, 1858, page 223.
17. George Bruce Malleson, *The Indian Mutiny of 1857*, Seeley & Co. Ltd, 1896, page 238.
18. George Bruce Malleson, *The Indian Mutiny of 1857*, Seeley & Co. Ltd ,1896, page 245.
19. George Bruce Malleson, *The Indian Mutiny of 1857*, Seeley & Co. Ltd ,1896, page 245.
20. Carnegy's intelligence for Dept., Secret Branch, 26 February 1858, news of 4 October 1857; Rudrangshu Mukherjee, *Awadh in a Revolt, 1857–1858: A Study of Popular Resistance*, Orient Blackswan, 2002, page 91.
21. Outram's telegram to Canning dated 17 September 1857; Rudrangshu Mukherjee, *Awadh in a Revolt, 1857–1858: A Study of Popular Resistance*, Orient Blackswan, 2002, page 90.
22. Khuda (God); Carnegy's intelligence for Dept., Secret Branch, 26 February 1858, news of 15 October 1857; Rudrangshu Mukherjee, *Awadh in a Revolt, 1857–1858: A Study of Popular Resistance*, Orient Blackswan, 2002, page 91.

23. Rudrangshu Mukherjee, *Awadh in a Revolt, 1857–1858: A Study of Popular Resistance*, Orient Blackswan, 2002, page 94.
24. George Bruce Malleson, *The Indian Mutiny of 1857*, Seeley & Co. Ltd ,1896, page 318.
25. George Bruce Malleson, *The Indian Mutiny of 1857*, Seeley & Co. Ltd ,1896, page 330.
26. George Bruce Malleson, *The Indian Mutiny of 1857*, Seeley & Co. Ltd ,1896, page 332–33.
27. Sir John William Kaye and George Bruce Malleson, *Kaye's and Malleson's History of the Indian Mutiny of 1857–8*, W.H. Allen & Co., 1889, page 228.
28. Digby Roy Thomas, *Outram in Indian: The Morality of Empire*, Author House, 2007, page 237; Bruce Watson, *The Great Indian Mutiny: Colin Campbell and the Campaign at Lucknow*, Praeger, 1991, page 89.
29. Qureshi, *Qaisar-ut-Tawarikh of Kamal-ud-din Haidar 1867 Classics*, New Royal Book Company, 2008, page 115.
30. Chaulakhi Kothi—A palace in Lucknow closely associated with the name of the Hazrat Mahal, who is said to have taken many vital decisions regarding the independence of Awadh in this kothi; P.J.O. Taylor, *A Companion to the 'Indian Mutiny' of 1857*, Oxford University Press, 1996, page 82.
31. Rosie Llewellyn Jones, *Fatal Friendship: The Nawabs, the British, and the City of Lucknow*, Oxford University Press, 1985, page 194.
32. Baundi is located at Bahraich district; Hashia, M. Haseena, *Muslim Women in India Since Independence: Feminine Perspectives*, Institute of Objective Studies, 1998, page 42.
33. Rudrangshu Mukherjee, *Awadh in a Revolt, 1857–1858: A Study of Popular Resistance*, Orient Blackswan, 2002, page 125.
34. Archibald Forbes, *Colin Campbell, Lord Clyde*, BiblioBazaar, LLC, 2008, page 198.
35. Sushila Tyagi, *Indo-Nepalese Relation*, Concept Publishing Company, page 82.
36. Sushila Tyagi, *Indo-Nepalese Relation*, Concept Publishing Company,

page 86.

37. Christopher Hibbert, *The Great Mutiny: India, 1857*, Penguin Books, 1980, page 374.
38. Sushila Tyagi, *Indo-Nepalese Relation*, Concept Publishing Company, page 83.
39. Kadambi Srinivasa Santha, *Begum of Awadh*, Bharati Prakashan, 1980, page 261.
40. M.G. Agarwal, *Freedom Fighters of India*, Gyan Publishing House, 2008, Vol. 4, page 199.
41. William Howard Russell (28 March 1820–11 February 1907) was an Irish reporter with *The Times*, and is considered to have been one of the first modern war correspondents. He was sent to India where he witnessed the final re-capture of Lucknow in 1858.
42. M.G. Chitkara, *Women and Social Transformation*, APH Publishing, 2001, page 403.
43. Simmi Jain, *Encyclopaedia of Indian Women Through the Ages: Period of Freedom Struggle*, Gyan Publishing House, 2003, page 21.
44. Kadambi Srinivasa Santha, *Begum of Awadh*, Bharati Prakashan, 1980, page 261.
45. Simmi Jain, *Encyclopaedia of Indian Women Through the Ages: Period of Freedom Struggle*, Gyan Publishing House, 2003, page 20.
46. Simmi Jain, *Encyclopaedia of Indian Women Through the Ages: Period of Freedom Struggle*, Gyan Publishing House, 2003, page 20.
47. John Pemble, *The Raj, the Indian Mutiny, and the Kingdom of Oudh, 1801–1859*, Fairleigh Dickinson University Press, 1977, page 247.
48. P.J.O. Taylor, *A Companion to the 'Indian Mutiny' of 1857*, Oxford University Press, 1996, page 208.
49. Simmi Jain, *Encyclopaedia of Indian Women Through the Ages: Period of Freedom Struggle*, Gyan Publishing House, 2003, page 20–21.

Chapter 5

1. Maude and Sherer *Memories of the Mutiny*, Adegi Graphics LLC, 1894, Vol. 2, page 513.

2. George Bruce Malleson, *The Mutiny of the Bengal Army: An Historical Narrative*, Part 2, Adegi Graphics LLC, 2005 (reprint), page 105.
3. Sir William Cavenagh, *Reminiscences of an Indian Official*, A.H. Allen & Co., 1884, page 217.
4. Sidney Laman Blanchard, *The Ganges and the Seine: Scenes on the Banks of Both*, Chapman and Hall, 1862, page 34.
5. Kaye and Malleson, *History of the Indian Mutiny*, A.H. Allen & Co., 1889, Vol. 3, page 1.
6. Kaye and Malleson, *History of the Indian Mutiny*, A.H. Allen & Co., 1889, Vol. 3, page 9.
7. Minute by Lord Canning, The Governor-General of India. IOL/PS/5/230, dated 18 June 1857.
8. Sir William Cavenagh, *Reminiscences of an Indian Official*, A.H. Allen & Co., 1884, page 213.
9. The count is four hundred according to Sir William Cavenagh.
10. Destiny.
11. Sir Colin Campbell, *Narrative of the Indian Revolt from Its Outbreak to the Capture of Lucknow*, George Vickers, 1858, page 70.
12. The source is *Masnavi Huzn-e-Akhtari*. Other researchers mention different names.
13. Extracts from—Khan Sahib Abdul-Wali's *Sorrows of Akhtar: An Autobiographical Account of the Deposition and Imprisonment of Sultan-i-Ālam Wājid Alī Shah, the Last King of Oudh*; translation of Wajid Ali's *Masnavi Huzn-e-Akhtari*,1925.
14. Sir William Cavenagh, *Reminiscences of an Indian Official*, A.H. Allen & Co., 1884, page 213–22.
15. Sir William Cavenagh, *Reminiscences of an Indian Official*, A.H. Allen & Co. London, 1884, page 230.
16. Throne.
17. Edmund Bruke, *The Annual Register*—Extract from a Letter to His Excellency Sir Alured Clarke, Vice-Resident, Benares, City Court, 15 Jan 1799, Vol. 60, page 576.
18. Ahad Ali page 23, End note of no. 143, page 245 of the translation of E.S. Harcourt and Kakir Hussain of Abdul Sharar's—*Lucknow:*

The Last Phase of an Oriental Culture, Oxford University Press, 1975 edition, page 245.
19. Landlords.
20. Summary translation of the Bengali version.
21. Bengali intellectuals.
22. Swati Chattopadhyay, *Representing Calcutta: Modernity, Nationalism, and the Colonial Uncanny*, Routledge, 2005, page 163.
23. M.L. Augustine, *Fort William: Calcutta's Crowning Glory*, Prabhat Prakashan, 1999, page 159; G.B. Malleson, The Mutiny of the Bengal Army, By One Who Has Served Under Sir Charles Napier, Oxford Press, 1857, page 106.
24. G.B. Malleson, The Mutiny of the Bengal Army, By One Who Has Served Under Sir Charles Napier, Oxford Press, 1857, page 17.
25. Letter from Col. Sleeman to The Marquis of Dalhousie, dated 11 November 1853; Sir W.H. Sleeman, *A Journey Through the Kingdom of Oude, in 1849–1850*, with private correspondence related to the annexation of the kingdom of Oudh to British India, Vol. 2, page 468.
26. Rosie Llewellyn Jones, *Engaging Scoundrels: True Tales of Old Lucknow*, Oxford University Press, 2000, page 150.
27. Wajid Ali Shah came to Calcutta with only three of his wives. It appears that his other wives came to Calcutta on a later date.
28. Paan means betel leaf.
29. Wajid Ali Shah's knack of painting portrait has never been documented.
30. Great Britain Parliament papers 'Accounts and papers of the House of Commons'—from the letter issued by Cecil Beadon, Secretary to the Government of India to Major C. Herbert dated 26 September 1859.
31. *The Caledonian Mercury and Daily Express*, Tuesday, 6 September 1859; issue 21824.
32. Abdul Halim Sharar, *Lucknow: The Last Phase of an Oriental Culture*, Oxford University Press, 1994 edition, page 70.
33. *A Collection of Treaties, Engagements, and Sanads relating to India and*

Neighbouring Countries, Cutter for Foreign and Political Department of India, 1863, Vol. 2, page 75.

Chapter 6

1. Great Britain Parliament papers, Accounts and Papers of the House of Commons, The Secretary of State for India to the Governor-General of Indian in council, dated 8 February 1860, Oxford University Press, page 41.
2. But probably this is not correct. Sultan Khana was built later by the King. The King first sojourned in the riverside mansion of Sir Laurence Peel; Abdul Halim Sharar, *Lucknow: The Last Phase of an Oriental Culture*, Oxford University Press, 1994 edition, page 71.
3. Translated by Prof. Meerza Kaukub.
4. Translated by Prof. Meerza Kaukub.
5. Poem.
6. Abdul Halim Sharar, *Lucknow: The Last Phase of an Oriental Culture*, Oxford University Press, 1994 edition, page 151.
7. Abdul Halim Sharar, *Lucknow: The Last Phase of an Oriental Culture*, Oxford University Press, 1994 edition, pages 152–53.
8. Sir Charles Wentworth Dilke, *Greater Britain: A Record of Travel in English-speaking Countries, during 1866–1867*, Macmillan & Co., 1868, page 403,
9. *London Times*, 27 October and 30 October 1874.
10. Prof. Kamal Sheel's paper 'Some Observations on Chinese Disclosures on India' read at Indian History Congress 66th Session, 28–30 January 2006, sectional president's address for the section on countries other than India.
11. Abdul Halim Sharar, *Lucknow: The Last Phase of an Oriental Culture*, Oxford University Press, 1994 edition, page 74.
12. Mahals were wives who bore children.
13. *The New York Times*, 11 November 1874, article captioned 'A Retired King: The Ex-King of Oude at Calcutta'.
14. Ranbir Singh, *Wajid Ali Shah—The Tragic King*, Publication Scheme,

page 4.
15. Abdul Halim Sharar, *Lucknow: The Last Phase of an Oriental Culture*, Oxford University Press, 1994 edition, page 74.
16. Frederick F. Wyman, *From Calcutta to the Snowy Range: Being the Narrative of a Trip Through the Upper Provinces of India to the Himalayas*, Tinsley bros., 1866, page 188.
17. Frederick F. Wyman, *From Calcutta to the Snowy Range: Being the Narrative of a Trip Through the Upper Provinces of India to the Himalayas*, Tinsley Bros., 1866, page 140.
18. Frederick F. Wyman, *From Calcutta to the Snowy Range: Being the Narrative of a Trip Through the Upper Provinces of India to the Himalayas*, Tinsley bros., 1866, page 142.
19. Mirza Ali Azhar, *King Wajid Ali Shah of Awadh*, Royal Book Company, 1982, Vol. 2, page 175.
20. Mirza Ali Azhar, *King Wajid Ali Shah of Awadh*, Royal Book Company, 1982, Vol. 2, page 176.
21. Maqalat-e-Garcin de Tassy (Lecturs) 1943 edition, Vol. 2, page 215.
22. Mirza Ali Azhar, *King Wajid Ali Shah of Awadh*, Royal Book Company, 1982, Vol. 2, page 177.
23. Mirza Ali Azhar, *King Wajid Ali Shah of Awadh*, Royal Book Company, 1982, Vol. 2, page 177.
24. Abdul Halim Sharar, *Lucknow: The Last Phase of an Oriental Culture*, Oxford University Press, 1994 edition, page 74.
25. Abdul Halim Sharar, *Lucknow: The Last Phase of an Oriental Culture*, Oxford University Press, 1994 edition, page 74–75.
26. A Mujtahid is an educated Muslim who makes up his own ruling on the permissibility of an Islamic law. Wajid Ali Shah came across four mujtahids during his stay in Calcutta. They were Tajul-Ulema Mufti Meer Md Abbas, Qaimat uddin Mirza Mohammad Ali, Mair-ul-Ulemma Mirza Mohammad Taqi and Ikleel-ul-ulema Mirza Mohammad Ali.
27. Article 'The Uncrowned King of Matiaburj—Another Side of the Picture', *Muslim Institute Review*, July–September issue in 1905.
28. Women's quarters. Article 'The Uncrowned King of Matiaburj—

Another Side of the Picture', *Muslim Institute Review*, July–September issue in 1905.
29. Rosie Llewellyn-Jones, 'Engaging Scoundrels: True Tales of Old Lucknow', Oxford University Press, 2000, page 44.
30. Abdul Halim Sharar, *Lucknow: The Last Phase of an Oriental Culture*, Oxford University Press, 1994 edition, page 122.
31. Abdul Halim Sharar, *Lucknow: The Last Phase of an Oriental Culture*, Oxford University Press, 1994 edition, page 131.
32. Abdul Halim Sharar, Preface of *Huzn-e-Akhtari*, 122nd edition, page 9.

Chapter 7

1. Abdul Halim Sharar, Preface of *Huzn-e-Akhtari*, 122nd edition, page 10; Mirza Ali Azhar, *King Wajid Ali Shah of Awadh*, Royal Book Company, 1982, Vol. 2, page 73.
2. Abdul Halim Sharar, Preface of *Huzn-e-Akhtari*, 122nd edition, page 63.
3. Permanent marriage.
4. Mirza Ali Azhar, *King Wajid Ali Shah of Awadh*, Royal Book Company, 1982, Vol. 2, page 157.
5. Abdul Halim Sharar, Preface of *Huzn-e-Akhtari*, 122nd edition, page 36–37.
6. Abdul Halim Sharar, Preface of *Huzn-e-Akhtari*, 122nd edition, page 36–37.
7. Abdul Halim Sharar, *Lucknow: The Last Phase of an Oriental Culture*, Oxford University Press, 1994 edition, page 63.
8. Michael Edward, *Red Year: The Indian Rebellion of 1857*, Hamilton, 1973, page 104.
9. Shiek Tasadduq Hussain, *Begum-e-Awadh* 1956 edition, page 202; Mirza Ali Azhar, *King Wajid Ali Shah of Awadh*, Royal Book Company, 1982, Vol. 2, page 167.
10. Oudh pension record in personal possession of Prof. Meerza Kaukub.

Chapter 8

1. Prof. Meerza Kaukub—Personal communication.
2. M. Aslam Qureshi, *Wajid Ali Shah's Theatrical Genius*, Vanguard, 1987, page 8.
3. S. Masud Hasan Rizvi, *Urdu Drama and Stage*, Part 1, 1957 edition, page 123.
4. 'Mudra' means movement of fingers and 'bhav' is the expression of face.
5. Madhu Trivedi, *The Making of the Awadh Culture*, Primus Books, 2010, page 115–17.
6. Madhu Trivedi, *The Making of the Awadh Culture*, Primus Books, 2010, page 116.
7. Susheela Misra, *Musical Heritage of Lucknow*, Harman Pub. House, 1991, page 103.
8. Sreepanth, *Metia Burjer Nawab*, Ananda Publishers, 1990, page 83; Madu Trivedi,*The Making of the Awadh Culture*, Primus Books, 2010, page 133.
9. S. Masud Hasan Rizvi, *Urdu Drama and Stage*, Part 1, 1957 edition, page 213.
10. Adib Masud Hassan Rizvi (1893–1975) was an Indian author and a scholar of Urdu literature, who was born in 1893 in Lucknow.
11. M. Aslam Qureshi *Wajid Ali Shah's Theatrical Genius*, Vanguard, 1987, page 36.
12. A female yogi.
13. Susheela Misra, *Musical Heritage of Lucknow*, Harman Pub. House, 1991, page 103.
14. Manohar Laxman Varadpande, *History of Indian Theatre*, Abhinav Publications, 1992, Vol. 2, page 144; Ranbir Singh, *Wajid Ali Shah—The Tragic King*, Publication Scheme, page 94.
15. Abida Samiuddin, *Encyclopaedic Dictionary of Urdu Literature*, Global Vision Publishing House, 2007, page 288.
16. Abdul Halim Sharar, *Lucknow: The Last Phase of an Oriental Culture*, Oxford University Press, 1994 edition, page 146.

17. Abdul Halim Sharar, *Lucknow: The Last Phase of an Oriental Culture*, Oxford University Press, 1994 edition, page 146.

Chapter 9

1. Emma Roberts, *Scenes and Characteristics of Hindostan: With Sketches of Anglo-Indian Society*, W. H. Allen and Co., 1837, page 192; Sumanta Banerjee, 'Under the Raj: Prostitution in Colonial Bengal', Part 2, *Monthly Review Press*, 1998, page 13.
2. Shovana Narayan, *Indian Theatre and Dance Traditions*, Harman Publishing House, 2004, page 65.
3. Projesh Banerjee, *Kathak Dance Through Ages*, Cosmo Publications, 1982, page 62–65.
4. Projesh Banerjee, *Kathak Dance Through Ages*, Cosmo Publications, 1982, page 64, 131.
5. Projesh Banerjee, *Kathak Dance Through Ages*, Cosmo Publications, 1982, page 129; Madhu Trivedi, *The Making of the Awadh Culture*, Primus Books, 2010, page 133.
6. 'Gats' are fixed compositions usually played in single and double compositions.
7. Projesh Banerjee, *Kathak Dance Through Ages*, Cosmo Publications, 1982, page 126.
8. Mansion.
9. Sreepanth, *Metia Burjer Nawab*, Ananda Publisher, 1990, page 101.
10. Abdul Halim Sharar, *Lucknow: The Last Phase of an Oriental Culture*, Oxford University Press, 1994 edition, page 138.
11. Abdul Halim Sharar, *Ja-e-Alam*, 1951, page 68; Mirza Ali Azhar, *King Wajid Ali Shah of Awadh*, Royal Book Company, 1982, Vol. 2, page 169.
12. Sumanta Banerjee, The *Parlour and the Streets: Elite and Popular Culture in Nineteenth Century Calcutta*, Seagull Books, 1989, page 96.
13. Sumanta Banerjee, *The Parlour and the Streets: Elite and Popular Culture in Nineteenth Century Calcutta*, Seagull Books, 1989, page 105.

14. Sumanta Banerjee, *The Parlour and the Streets: Elite and Popular Culture in Nineteenth Century Calcutta*, Seagull Books, 1989, page 123.
15. *Calcutta Review*—47, 1868, page 142.
16. Abdul Halim Sharar, Preface of *Huzn-e-Akhtari*, 122nd edition, page 145.

Chapter 10

1. Susheela Misra, *Great Masters of Hindustani Music*, Hem Publishers, 1981, page 47.
2. Patrick Colm Hogan and Lalita Pandit, *Rabindranath Tagore: Universality and Tradition*, Fairleigh Dickinson University Press, 2003, page 68; *Journal of the Indian Musicological Society*, 1980, Vol. 11–12, page 12.
3. Dilip Mukhopadhyay, *Ajodhyar Nabab Wajid Ali Shah* (Bengali), Sankha Prakashan, 1984, pages 165–66.
4. Dilip Kumar Mukherjee, *Bangaleer Rang Sangit Carcha* (Bengali), Firma KLM Private Limited, 1976, page 293–94.
5. *Classical and Folk Dances of India*, Marg Publications, 1963, page 42.
6. Peter Manuel, *Thumri in Historical and Stylistic Perspective*, Motilal Benarasidass, 1989, page 37.
7. Nivedita Singh, *Tradition of Hindustani Music: A Sociological Approach*, Kanishka Publishers & Distributors, 2004, page 64.
8. Amir Hasan, *Vanishing Culture of Lucknow*, B.R. Pub. Corp., 1990, page 113.
9. K.C. Kanda, *Urdu Ghazals: An Anthology, from 16th to 20th Century*, Sterling Publishers Pvt. Ltd, 1995, page 140.
10. Prabhat Kumar Saha, *Some Aspects of Malla Rule in Bishnupur, 1590–1806 A.D.*, Ratnabali, 1995, pages 314–21.
11. Vinayak Purohit, *Arts of Transitional India Twentieth Century*, Popular Prakashan, Vol. 1, 1986, page 863.
12. Abdul Halim Sharar, *Lucknow: The Last Phase of an Oriental Culture*, Oxford University Press, 1994 edition, page 138.

13. Ashok Damodar Ranade, *Music Contexts: A Concise Dictionary of Hindustani Music*, Bibliophile South Asia, 2006, page 131.
14. Tappa-Kheyal is a new style which is an amalgamation of Tappa and some features of Kheyal. Tappa became so popular in Wajid Ali Shah's court, that often Kheyal was sung in Tappa style, giving rise to this new style of semi-classical music.
15. Dilip Mukhopadhyay, *Ajodhyar Nabab Wajid Ali Shah* (Bengali), Sankha Prakashan, 1984, page 171.
16. Abdul Halim Sharar, *Jan-e-Alam*, 1951, page 68.
17. Ali Baksh settled in Benaras after annexation of Awadh.
18. Dilip Mukhopadhyay, *Ajodhyar Nabab Wajid Ali Shah* (Bengali), Sankha Prakashan, 1984, pages 167–68.
19. Swami Abhedānanda and Swami Prajnanananda, *The Bases of Indian Culture: Commemoration Volume of Swami Abhedananda*, Ramakrishna Vedanta Math, 1971, page 545.
20. Sarod player.
21. Here there is a confusion. 'Kadar Piya' was the pseudonym of Wajid Ali Shah's court musician Mirza Bala Qadar. But Sharar has quoted Kaukab, where Kadar Piya is mentioned as pseudonym of Wajid Ali Shah. It was said that Wajid Ali composed thumris in his pseudonym–Kadar Piya.
22. Abdul Halim Sharar, *Lucknow: The Last Phase of an Oriental Culture*, Oxford University Press, 1994 edition, page 137–38.

Chapter 11

1. Bin—a form of North Indian veena, rabab—a string instrument, sursringar—a string instrument like sarod, pukhwaj—a barrel shaped two-headed drum.
2. Peter Manuel, *Thumri in Historical and Stylistic Perspective*, Motilal Banarasidass, 1989, page 161.
3. Brahspati, 1976: 241–2, 1974: 14,79.
4. Allyn Miner, *Sitar and Sarod in the 18th and 19th Centuries*, Motilal Banarsidass, 1997, page 23.

5. Dilip Kumar Mukherjee, *Bangaleer Rang Sangit Carcha* (Bengali), Firma KLM Private Limited, 1976, page 24.
6. Allyn Miner, *Sitar and Sarod in the 18th and 19th Centuries*, Motilal Banarsidass, 1997, page 112.
7. Dharis are musicians associated with dancers and accompanists who figured low in the musico-social hierarchy.
8. Sir Henry William Sleeman, *A Journey Through the Kingdom of Oude in 1849–1850: with private correspondence relative to the annexation of Oude to British India*, R. Bentley, 1858, Vol. 1, page 22.
9. Allyn Miner, *Sitar and Sarod in the 18th and 19th Centuries*, Motilal Banarsidass, 1997, page 71.
10. Allyn Miner, *Sitar and Sarod in the 18th and 19th Centuries*, Motilal Banarsidass, 1997, page 145.
11. Bonnie C. Wade, *Performing Arts in India: Essays on Music, Dance, and Drama*, Center for South and Southeast Asia Studies, University of California, 1983, page 163.
12. Allyn Miner, *Sitar and Sarod in the 18th and 19th Centuries*, Motilal Banarsidass, 1997, page 150.
13. Dilip Kumar Mukherjee, *Bangaleer Rang Sangit Carcha* (Bengali), Firma KLM Private Limited, 1976, page 339.
14. Allyn Miner, *Sitar and Sarod in the 18th and 19th Centuries*, Motilal Banarsidass, 1997, page 117.
15. Dilip Mukhopadhyay, *Ajodhyar Nabab Wajid Ali Shah* (Bengali), Sankha Prakashan, 1984, pages 165–66.
16. Dilip Kumar Mukherjee, *Bangaleer Rang Sangit Carcha* (Bengali), Firma KLM Private Limited, 1976, page 379.
17. Yoshikata Terada, *Music and Society in South Asia: Perspectives from Japan*, National Museum of Ethnology, 2008, page 197; Ustad Amzad Ali's interview published in *Sangeet Natak*, Issues 27–30, page 18.
18. Adrian McNeil, *Inventing the Sarod: A Cultural History*, Seagull, 2004, page 56.
19. Masakazu Tamori, 'The Transformation of Sarod Gharana: Transmitting Musical property in Hindustani Music', article

published in *Music and Society in South Asia: Perspectives from Japan*, 2008, page 188.
20. Allyn Miner, *Sitar and Sarod in the 18th and 19th Centuries*, Motilal Banarsidass, 1997, page 68.
21. Personal communication with Ustad Irfan Md. Khan. Irfan Muhammad Khan is a contemporary sarodiya representing Lucknow-Shahjahanpur gharana and a descendant of Enayat Ali Khan family (great-great-grandson of Enayat Ali Khan); Adrian McNeil, *Inventing the Sarod: A Cultural History*, Seagull, 2004, page 89.
22. Masakazu Tamori, 'The Transformation of Sarod Gharana: Transmitting Musical property in Hindustani Music', article published in *Music and Society in South Asia: Perspectives from Japan*, 2008, page 188.
23. Dilip Mukhopadhyay, *Bharatiya Sangeetey Gharanar Itihas*, A. Mukherjee & Co., 1977, page 49.
24. Personal communication with Ustad Irfan Md. Khan, who is a contemporary sarodiya representing Lucknow-Shahjahanpur Gharana and a descendant of Enayat Ali Khan's family.
25. Adrian McNeil, *Inventing the Sarod:, A Cultural History*, Seagull, 2004, page 117.
26. Dilip Mukhopadhyay, *Bharatiya Sangeetey Gharanar Itihas*, A. Mukherjee & Co., 1977, page 112.
27. Dilip Mukhopadhyay, *Ajodhyar Nabab Wajid Ali Shah* (Bengali), Sankha Prakashan, 1984, page 171.
28. Robert S. Gottlieb, *The Major Traditions of North Indian Tabla Drumming: A Survey Presentation Based on Performances by India's Leading Artists*, Musikverlag E. Katzbichler, 1977, page xii; James Kippen, *The Tabla Gharana of Lucknow*, Manohar, 2005, page 77.
29. Dilip Mukhopadhyay, *Ajodhyar Nabab Wajid Ali Shah* (Bengali), Sankha Prakashan, 1984, page 169; Durgadas Lahiri, (edited) 'Bangalir Gaan' (Bengali), published by Natabar Chakraborty 1905, page 1002.
30. Amala Dāśaśarmā, *Musicians of India: Past and Present Gharanas of*

Hindustani Music and Genealogies, Naya Prokash, 1993, page 284; Dilip Mukhopadhyay, *Ajodhyar Nabab Wajid Ali Shah* (Bengali), Sankha Prakashan, 1984, pages 169–72.

31. Jame Kippen, *The Tabla Gharana of Lucknow*, Manohar, 2005, page 74.
32. Robert S. Gottlieb, *Solo Tabla Drumming of North India: Text & Commentary*, Motilal Banarsidass, 1998, Vol. 1, page 12; Robert S. Gottlieb, *The Major Traditions of North Indian Tabla Drumming: A Survey Presentation Based on Performances by India's Leading Artists*, Musikverlag E. Katzbichler, 1977, page 10; Sumanta Banerjee, *The Parlour and the Streets: Elite and Popular Culture in Nineteenth Century Calcutta*, Seagull Books, 1989, page 196.
33. Dilip Mukhopadhyay, *Ajodhyar Nabab Wajid Ali Shah* (Bengali), Sankha Prakashan, 1984, page 170.
34. Swami Prajnanananda, Historical Development of Indian Music, Firma K.L.M. Private Limited, 1973, page 468.

Chapter 12

1. Abdul Halim Sharar, *Lucknow: The Last Phase of an Oriental Culture*, Oxford University Press, 1994 edition, page 101.
2. Lecture on Hindustani literature at Imperial School; Ranbir Singh, *Wajid Ali Shah: The Tragic King*, Publication Scheme, 2002, page 138.
3. S. Masud Hasan Rizvi, *Sultani-i-Wajid Ali Shah* (in Urdu), 1897, page 184; Kaukub Meerza's thesis, *The Literary and Cultural Contributions of Wajid Ali Shah*.
4. Annemarie Schimmel, *A History of Indian Literature*, Otto Harrassowitz Verlag, 1975, Vol. 8, page 189.
5. Prof.Meerza Kaukub—Personal communication.
6. Ram Babu Saksena, *A History of Urdu Literature*, Ram Narain Lal Publisher and Bookseller, 1940, page 118.
7. Ranbir Singh, *Wajid Ali Shah: The Tragic King*, Publication Scheme, 2002, page 142.

8. Mirza Ali Azhar, *King Wajid Ali Shah of Awadh*, Royal Book Company, 1982, Vol. 2, page 166.
9. Mirza Ali Azhar, *King Wajid Ali Shah of Awadh*, Royal Book Company, 1982, Vol. 2, page 156.
10. Ranjeswar Mitra, *Mughal Bharater Sangeet Chinta* (Bengali), 1985.
11. Gosai is the typical term used to denote a devotee of Vaishnavism cult.
12. Dilip Mukhopadhyay, *Ajodhyar Nabab Wajid Ali Shah* (Bengali), Sankha Prakashan, 1984, page 170.
13. Translation of Tareekh-e-Parikhana, *Ajodhyar Nabab Wajid Ali Shah* (Bengali), Sankha Prakashan, 1984, page 21.
14. Dilip Mukhopadhyay, *Ajodhyar Nabab Wajid Ali Shah* (Bengali), Sankha Prakashan, 1984, page 112.
15. Translation of Tareekh-e-Parikhana, *Ajodhyar Nabab Wajid Ali Shah* (Bengali), Sankha Prakashan, 1984, page 23.
16. Abdul Halim Sharar, *Lucknow: The Last Phase of an Oriental Culture*, Oxford University Press, 1994 edition, page 62.
17. Raja Durga Prasad, *Bostan-e-Awadh*, Sandila, 1888.
18. Ram Babu Saksena, *A History of Urdu Literature*, Ram Narain Lal Publisher and Bookseller, 1940, page 119.
19. Mirza Ali Azhar, *King Wajid Ali Shah of Awadh*, Royal Book Company, 1982, Vol. 2, page 348.
20. Abida Samiuddin, *Encyclopaedic Dictionary of Urdu Literature*, Global Vision Publishing, 2007, page 473.
21. Ram Babu Saksena, *A History of Urdu Literature*, Ram Narain Lal Publisher and Bookseller, 1940, page 106.
22. Ram Babu Saksena, *A History of Urdu Literature*, Ram Narain Lal Publisher and Bookseller, 1940, page 172; Ranbir Singh, Wajid Ali Shah: The Tragic King, Publication Scheme, 2002, page 144.
23. Prof. Meerza Kaukub—Personal communication.
24. Mildred Archer, *Company Drawings*, H.M. Stationery Off., 1972, page 157.
25. Toby Falk, India Office Library, Mildred Archer, *Indian Miniatures in the India Office Library*, Sotheby Parke Bernet, 1981, page 150.

26. From the art catalogue of the British Museum.
27. The painting was in the possession of a shopkeeper of Metiyaburj and had been looted during the post Babri tumult.
28. Royal chefs.
29. Fried vegetables.
30. The narration was taken from an article titled 'The Uncrowned King of Matiaburj: Another Side of the Picture'—the signature of which is illegible. Probably the article was written by Syed Mohammad or Nawabzada A.F.M. Abdul Ali, Secretary of the Historical Records Commission, Calcutta. The article provides a vivid description of the Nawab's day-to-day life at Metiyaburj.
31. Abdul Halim Sharar *Lucknow: The Last Phase of an Oriental Culture*, Oxford University Press, 1994 edition, page 166.
32. Abdul Halim Sharar *Lucknow: The Last Phase of an Oriental Culture*, Oxford University Press, 1994 edition, page 157.
33. Dilip Mukhopadhyay, *Ajodhyar Nabab Wajid Ali Shah* (Bengali), Sankha Prakashan, 1984, page 191.
34. Refer to Note 30. The author addressed the Nawab as Jan-e-Alam; Mirza Ali Azhar, *King Wajid Ali Shah of Awadh*, Royal Book Company, 1982, Vol. 2, page 182.
35. William Knighton, *Elihu Jaan's Story: Or, The Private Life of an Eastern Queen'*, Longman, Green, Longman, Roberts, & Green, 1865, page 263.
36. William Knighton, *Elihu Jaan's Story: Or, The Private Life of an Eastern Queen*, Longman, Green, Longman, Roberts, & Green, 1865, page 270.
37. Binayendra Dasgupta, *Atulaprasada: Atulaprasada Sena Prasage*, Bagartha, 1971, page 11; Dilip Mukhopadhyay, *Ajodhyar Nabab Wajid Ali Shah* (Bengali), Sankha Prakashan, 1984, page 187.
38. Binayendra Dasgupta, *Atulaprasada: Atulaprasada Sena Prasage*, Bagartha, 1971, page 11; Dilip Mukhopadhyay, *Ajodhyar Nabab Wajid Ali Shah* (Bengali), Sankha Prakashan, 1984, page 188.

Chapter 13

1. Sachchidanan Sahai, *India in 1872, as Seen by the Siamese*, B.R. Pub. Corp., 2002, page 195.
2. Garcin's Lecture, 1874–1877, Vol. 2, page 54–55.
3. Abdul Halim Sharar, *Lucknow: The Last Phase of an Oriental Culture*, Oxford University Press, 1994 edition, page 72.
4. James Routledge, *English Rule and Native Opinion in India: From Notes Taken 1870–74*, elibron.com, 1878, page 124.
5. Frank Vincent, *Through and Through the Tropics: 30,000 Miles of Travel in Polynesia, Australasia, and India*, Harper & Bros., 1882, page 135.
6. Abdul Halim Sharar, *Lucknow: The Last Phase of an Oriental Culture*, Oxford University Press, 1994 edition, page 73.
7. Ursula Low,, *Fifty Years with John Company: From the Letters of General Sir John Low of Clatto, Fife, 1822–1858*, John Murray, 1936, page 355.
8. Abdul Halim Sharar, *Lucknow: The Last Phase of an Oriental Culture*, Oxford University Press, 1994 edition, page 73.
9. Article, 'The Uncrowned King of Matiaburj—Another Side of the Picture'—the signature of which is illegible. Probably the article was written by Syed Mohammad or Nawabzada A.F.M. Abdul Ali, Secretary of the Historical Records Commission, Calcutta.
10. Abdul Halim Sharar, *Lucknow: The Last Phase of an Oriental Culture*, Oxford University Press, 1994 edition, page 73.
11. Abdul Halim Sharar, *Lucknow: The Last Phase of an Oriental Culture*, Oxford University Press, 1994 edition, page 73.
12. James Routledge, *English Rule and Native Opinion in India: From Notes Taken 1870–74*, elibron.com, 1878, page 124.
13. William Knighton, *The Private Life of an Eastern King*, Hope & Co., 1855, page 3.
14. Edward Blyth, 'Report on the Collection of Australian Vertebrates, Contained in the Museum of the Asiatic Society, Calcutta', The Asiatic Society of Bengal, 1848, page 3.

15. Harriet Ritvo, *The Animal Estate: The English and Other Creatures in the Victorian Age*, Harvard University Press, 1987, pages 206–10.
16. Arthur Grote's biography of late Edward Blyth which was used as forward note to Edward Blyth's article 'Catalogue of Mammals and Birds of Burma', which was published posthumously in the *Journal of Asiatic Society of Bengal* in 1875.
17. *Bengal Hurkaru* and *India Gazette*, 3 July 1856.
18. Arthur Grote's biography of late Edward Blyth which was used as forward note to Edward Blyth's article 'Catalogue of Mammals and Birds of Burma', which was published posthumously in the *Journal of Asiatic Society of Bengal* in 1875; Blyth's article published in 'Annals and Magazine of Natural History'.
19. Blyth to Darwin, October 1–8, 1855, CCD, VI, 463.
20. Blyth to Gould, 21 December 1859, Gould Correspondence; Christine Brandon-Jones, 'Edward Blyth, Charles Darwin, and the Animal Trade in Nineteenth-Century India and Britain', *Journal of the History of Biology 30*, 1997, 145–178.
21. Marchioness Of Dufferin and Ava's, *Our Viceregal Life In India: Selections From My Journal, 1884-1888*. John Murray, 1889, Vol. 1, page 282.
22. *Daily Evening Mercury* 13 March 1879.

Chapter 14

1. J.G.A. Baird (ed.), *Private Letters of the Marques of Dalhousie*, William Blackwood and Sons, 1910, page 169. The letter was written by Lord Dalhousie on 11 August 1951, from Shimla.
2. Article of Anjum Quder, Chairman, Wajid Ali Shah Trust Dated 22 September 1996.
3. The son of Sikandar Hashmat.
4. Mirza Ali Azhar, *King Wajid Ali Shah of Awadh*, Royal Book Company, 1982, Vol. 2, pages 190–91.
5. Son of Prince Munir-ud-Din (1795–1837) who was the son of Tipu Sultan.

6. Mirza Ali Azhar, *King Wajid Ali Shah of Awadh*, Royal Book Company, 1982, Vol. 2, pages 190–91; Prince Anjum Quder's, article as the Chairman of the Trustee of Sibtainabad Imambara—Metiyaburj.
7. Source of the Government Pension Record—Prof. Meerza Kaukub.
8. *The Statesman* dated 3 November 1887.
9. Sir W.H. Sleeman, *A Journey Through the Kingdom of Oude, in 1849–1850* Echo Library, 2006, page 301.
10. Sir Evan Cotton, *Calcutta, Old and New: A Historical & Descriptive Handbook to the City* W. Newman, 1907, page 278.
11. *The Statesman* dated 3 November 1887.
12. Abdul Halim Sharar, *Lucknow: The Last Phase of an Oriental Culture*, Oxford University Press, 1994 edition, page 76; Cowrie was the shell currency in ancient times. By 1887 cowries were abolished, here Sharar used the term to indicate meagre amount of money.
13. Link, Issues 26–51, United India Periodicals, 1962, Vol. 4, page 15.
14. Mirza Ali Azhar, *King Wajid Ali Shah of Awadh*, Royal Book Company, 1982, Vol. 2, pages 188–90.
15. Para 4 of Colonel W. F. Prideaux's memo No. 351 in Calcutta dated 31 March 1888, addressed to the Secretary of the Government of India, Foreign Department, Oudh Pension Papers, page 19.
16. Dilip Kumar Mukherjee, *Bangaleer Rang Sangit Carcha* (Bengali), Firma KLM Private Limited, 1976, page 192.
17. Sir Evan Cotton, *Calcutta, Old and New: A Historical and Descriptive Handbook to the City*, W. Newman, 1907, page 278.
18. Dilip Kumar Mukherjee, *Bangaleer Rang Sangit Carcha* (Bengali), Firma KLM Private Limited, 1976, page 194.

Royal Family Tree of Awadh

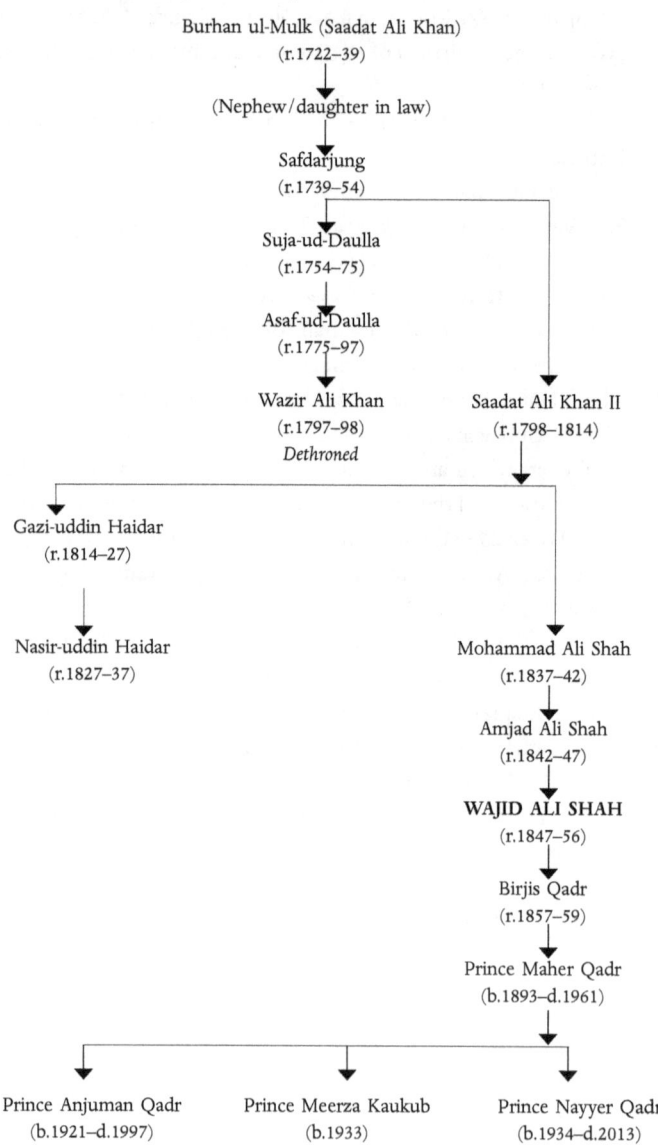

List of the buildings built by Wajid Ali Shah in Metiyaburj:

Sultan Khana
Radha Manzil
Adalat Manzil
Murassa Manzil
Hassan Manzil
Fateh Manzil
Hussain Manzil
Sikander Manzil
Rahas Manzil
Meher Manzil
Shah Manzil
Asmani Manzil
Badami Manzil
Jhauwali Manzil
Murassawali Manzil
Singare Manzil
Shahinshah Manzil
Delhiwali Manzil
Asad Manzil
Atabaugh Palace
Qasr ul Baiza
Gosha-e-Sultani
Nur Manjil
Tafrih Baksh
Tahaniyat Manzil
Had-e-Sultani
Sad-e-Sultani

Bibliography

Abdul Halim Sharar, *Lucknow: The Last Phase of an Oriental Culture*, Oxford University Press, 1994.

Abdul Shahar, *Lucknow: The Last Phase of an Oriental Culture*, Oxford University Press, 1975.

Abida Samiuddin, *Encyclopedia Dictionary of Urdu Literature*, Global Vision Publishing House, 2007.

Adrian Mcneil, *Inventing the Sarod: A Cultural History*, Seagull, 2004.

Adrian McNeil, *Making Modernity Audible: Sarodiyas and the Early Recording Industry*, Thema, 2007.

Ajitakumāra Ghosha, *Dino Bandhu*, Sahitya Akademi, 1999.

Alfred Spencer (ed.), William Hickey, *Memoirs of William Hickey*, Hurst & Blackett Ltd., 1782.

Allamah Tabatabai and Seyyed Hossain Nasr, *Shi'ite Islam*, Malaysia, Islamic Book Trust, 2010.

Allen, *Indian*, Maul, Allen & Co., 1857.

Allyn Miner, *Sitar and Sarod in the 18th and 19th Centuries*, Motilal Banarsidass Publ., 1997.

Amala Dāśaśrmā, *Musicians of India: Past and Present Gharanas of Hindustani Music and Genealogies*, Naya Prokash, 1993.

Ameer Ali S. Khan (ed.), *Wazeernama*, 1875.

Amir Hassan, *Palace Culture of Lucknow*, BR Publishing Corporation, 1983.

Amir Hasan, *Vanishing Culture of Lucknow*, BR Publishing Corporation, 1990.

Amlan Dasgupta, *Music and Modernity: North Indian Classical Music in an Age of Mechanical Reproduction*, Thema, 2007.

Ananda Krishna Bose, *A Short Account of the Residents of Calcutta in the*

Year 1822, Calcutta, 1928.

Annemarie Schimmel, *A History of Indian Literature*, Otto Harrassowitz Verlag, Vol. 8, 1975.

Archibald Forbes, *Colin Campbell, Lord Clyde*, Biblio Bazaar, LLC, 2008.

Ashok Damodar Ranade, *Music Contexts: A Concise Dictionary of Hindustani Music*, Bibliophile South Asia, 2006.

Ava, Marchioness of Dufferin, *Our Viceregal Life In India Selections from My Journal, 1884–1888*, John Murray, Vol. 1, 1889.

Baman Das Basu, *Rise of the Christian Power in India*, R. Chatterjee, 1923.

Baptist Wriothesley Noel, *England and India: An Essay on the Duty of Englishmen Towards the Hindoos*, James Nisbet, 1859.

Bigamudre Chaitanya Deva, *An Introduction to Indian Music*, Publications Division, Ministry of Information and Broadcasting, Government of India, 1981.

Bonnie C. Wade, *Khyāl: Creativity Within North India's Classical Music Tradition*, CUP Archive, 1984.

Bruce Watson, *The Great Indian Mutiny: Colin Campbell and the Campaign at Lucknow*, Praeger, 1991.

Caroline Fox, *Memories of Old Friends: Being Extracts From the Journals and Letters of Caroline Fox, of Penjerrick, Cornwall, from 1835 to 1871*, J. B. Lippincott & Co., 1882.

Charles MacFarlane, *A History of British India*, Routledge, 1853.

Christine Brandon-Jones, 'Edward Blyth, Charles Darwin, and the Animal Trade in Nineteenth-Century India and Britain', *Journal of the History of Biology*, 1997.

Christopher Hibbert, *The Great Mutiny: India, 1857*, Penguin Books, 1980.

Dalit Singh, *Invitation to Indian Music*, Classical Music Circle, 1978.

David Arnold, *Science, Technology, and Medicine in Colonial India*, Cambridge University Press, 2000.

Digby Roy Thomas, *Outram in Indian: The Morality of Empire*, Author House, 2007.

Dilip Mukhopadhyay, *Ajodhyar Nabab Wajid Ali Shah* (Bengali), Sankha Prakashan, 1984.

Dr Bhargava and Dr Rizvi, *Freedom Struggle in U.P.*, Vol. 1, 1957.

Dr Rizvi and Dr Bhargava, *Freedom Struggle in U.P.*, 1957.

Edward Blyth, 'Catalogue of Mammals and Birds of Burma,' *Journal of Asiatic Society*, 1875.

Edward Thompson and Geoffrey Theodore Garratt, *History of British Rule in India*, Atlantic Publishers & Distributors, Vol. 1 & 2, 1999.

Emma Roberts, *Scenes and Characteristics of Hindostan: With Sketches of Anglo-Indian Society*, W. H. Allen and Co., 1837.

Evans Bell, *Retrospects and Prospects of Indian Policy*, Trübner, 1868.

Fanny Parks, *Wanderings of a Pilgrim, in Search of the Picturesque, During Four-and-twenty years in the East*, Richardson, 1850.

Frank Vincent, *Through and Through the Tropics: 30,000 Miles of Travel in Polynesia, Australasia, and India*, Harper & Bros., 1882.

Frederick F. Wyman, *From Calcutta to the Snowy Range: Being the Narrative of a Trip Through the Upper Provinces of India to the Himalayas*, Tinsley Bros., 1866.

G.B. Malleson, *The Mutiny of the Bengal Army, By One Who Has Served Under Sir Charles Napier*, Oxford Press, 1857.

G.D. Bhatnagar, *Awadh Under Wajid Ali Shah*, Bharatiya Vidya Prakashan, 1968.

G.S. Chabbra, *Advanced Study in the History of Modern India*, Lotus Press, 2005.

George Bruce Malleson, *The Mutiny of the Bengal Army: An Historical Narrative*, Adegi Graphics LLC, 2005.

George Vickers, *Narrative of the Indian revolt from its outbreak to the capture of Lucknow*, 1858.

Graham MacPhee and Prem Poddar, *Empire and After: Englishness in Post Colonial Perspective*, Berghahn Books, 2007.

Greg Barton, *Empire Forestry and the Origin of Environmentalism*, University of Cambridge Press, 2002.

H. Michael Fisher, *Counterflows to Colonialism*, Permanent Black, 2008.

Hari Narayan and Amit Verma, *Decisive Battles of India Through the Ages*, GIP Books, 1998.

Harriet Ritvo, *The Animal Estate: The English and Other Creatures in the*

Victorian Age, Harvard University Press, 1987.

Ikramuddin Qidwai, research thesis, *The Court Life Under The Nawabs of Awadh*.

J.G.A. Baird, *Private Letters of the Marques of Dalhousie*, William Blackwood and Sons, 1910.

J.G.A. Baird, *Private Letters of the Marquess of Dalhousie*, William Blackwood and Sons, 1910.

Jame Kippen, *The Tabla Gharana of Lucknow*, Delhi, Manohar, 2005.

James Hope Grant, *Incidents in the Sepoy War, 1857–58*, Adegi Graphics LLC, 2002.

James Routledge, *English Rule and Native Opinion in India: From Notes Taken 1870–74*, elibron.com.

James Sadler Hamilton, *Sitar Music in Calcutta*, Motilal Banarsidass Publishers, 1994.

John Brook and Lewis Namier, *The House of Commons, 1754–1790*, Boydell & Brewer, Vol. 1, 1985.

John Clark Marshman, *Memoirs of Major-General Sir Henry Havelock*, Oxford University Press, 1860.

John Malcolm Ludlow, *British India, Its Races and Its History Considered with Reference to the Mutinies of 1857: A Series of Lectures Addressed to the Students of the Working Men - College'*, Macmillan, Vol. 1 & 2, 1858.

John Matheson, *England to Delhi: A Narrative of Indian Travel*, Longmans, Green, 1870.

John Pemble, *The Raj, the Indian Mutiny, and the Kingdom of Oudh, 1801–1859*, Fairleigh Dickinson University Press, 1977.

John William Kaye, *A History of the Sepoy War in India, 1857–1858*, W. H. Allen, 1875.

Joseph Thomas and Baldwin Joseph, *Lippincott's Pronouncing Gazetteer: A Complete Pronouncing Gazetteer, Or Geographical Dictionary of the World* J.B. Lippincott, 1856.

K.C. Kanda, *Masterpieces of Urdu Ghazal: From the 17th to the 20th Century*, Sterling Publishers Pvt. Ltd, 1992.

K.C. Kanda, *Mirza Ghalib: Selected Lyrics and Letters*, Sterling Publishers Pvt. Ltd, 2005.

K.C. Kanda, *Urdu Ghazals: An Anthology, from 16th to 20th century*, Sterling Publishers Pvt. Ltd, 1995.

Kaliprasanna Sinha, *The Observant Owl Hootum: Vignettes of Nineteenth Century Calcutta*, translated from the original Bengali by Swarup Roy Permanent Black, 2008.

Kamal-ud-din Haidar, *Qaisar-ut-Tawareekh*, Vol. 2.

Kathleen Blechynden, *Calcutta, Past and Present*, Calcutta, Thacker, Spink & Co., 1905.

Kaye and Malleson, *History of the Indian Mutiny*, W.H. Allen & Co., 1889.

Khan Sahib Abdul-Wali, *Sorrows of Akhtar: An Autobiographical Account of the Deposition and Imprisonment of Sultan-i-Ālam Wājid Alī Shah, the Last King of Oudh*, 1925.

King Wajid Ali Shah, *Reply to the Oude Blue Book*, India Office Library.

Lalit Ramkrishna, *Musical Heritage of India*, Shubhi Publication, 2003.

Lionel James Trotter, *The Bayard of India: A Life of General Sir James Outram*, Blackwood, 1903.

Lokhnath Ghose, *The Modern History of the Indian Chiefs, Rajas, Zamindars: The Native Aristocracy and Gentry*, 1981.

M. Aslam Qureshi, *Wajid Ali Shah's Theatrical Genius*, Vanguard, 1987.

M. Haseena Hashia, *Muslim Women in India Since Independence: Feminine Perspectives*, Institute of Objective Studies, 1998.

M.G Chitkara, *Women and Social Transformation*, APH Publishing, 2001.

M.G. Agarwal, *Freedom Fighters of India*, Gyan Publishing House, 2008.

M.L. Augustine, *Fort William: Calcutta Crowning Glory*, Prabhat Prakashan, 1999.

Madhu Trivedi, *The Making of the Awadh Culture*, Primus Books, 2010.

Major Agha Humayun Amin, *Sir Colin Campbell's Final Relief and Evacuation of Lucknow Residency Garrison—November 1857*, Defense Journal, Pakistan.

Malik Ram, *Mirza Ghalib*, National Book Trust of India, 1968.

Manohar Laxman Varadpande, *History of Indian Theatre*, Abhinav Publications, Vol. 1 & 2, 1992.

Masud Hassain Rizvi, *Sultan-e-Alam Wajid Ali Shah*, 1977.

Maude and Sherer, *Memories of the Mutiny*, Adegi Graphics LLC Vol. 1 & 2, 1894.

Michael Edwardes, *Red Year: The Indian Rebellion of 1857*, Hamilton, 1973.

Mildred Archer, *Company Drawings*, H.M. Stationery Off., 1972.

Mirza Ali Azhar, *King Wajid Ali Shah of Awadh*, Royal Book Company, Vol. 1 & 2, 1982.

Mirza Asadullah Khan Ghalib, *Ghalib: Life and Work*, Ministry of Information and Broadcasting, Govt. of India, 1969.

Mirza Ghalib and Daud Rahbar, *Urdu Letters of Mirza Asadullah Khan Ghalib*, Suny Press, 1987.

Nagendra Kumar Singh, *Encyclopedia of Muslim Biography: India, Pakistan, Bangladesh*, A.P.H. Pub. Corp., 2001.

Nagendranath Gupta, *Reflections and Reminiscences*, Hind Kitabs Limited, 1947.

Nivedita Singh, *Tradition of Hindustani Music: A Sociological Approach*, Kanishka Publishers, Distributors, 2004.

P.J.O. Taylor, *A Companion to the Indian Mutiny of 1857*, Oxford University Press, 1996.

Patrick Colm Hogan and Lalita Pandit, *Rabindranath Tagore: Universality and Tradition*, Fairleigh Dickinson Univ Press, 2003.

Peter Manuel, *Thumri in Historical and Stylistic Perspective*, Motilal Banarasidass, Delhi, 1989.

Poonam Trivedi and Dennis Bartholomeusz, *India's Shakespeare: Translation, Interpretation, and Performance*, Pearson Education India, 2006.

Prabhat Kumar Saha, *Some Aspects of Malla rule in Bishnupur, 1590–1806 A.D.*, Ratnabali, 1995.

Projesh Banerjee, *Kathak Dance Through Ages*, Cosmo Publications, 1982.

R.B. Sanyal, *A Handbook of the Management of Animals in Captivity in Lower Bengal*, 1892.

R.C. Majumdar, *History and Culture of the Indian People, British Paramountcy and Indian Renaissance*, The Vidya Bhavan, Vol. 9, 2002.

R.M. Maitra, *Ustad Mohammad Amir Khan Sahib, the Great Sarode Newaj of Shahjahanpur*, Calcutta, 1976.

Raja Durga Prasad, *Bostan-e-Awadh*, Sandila, 1888.

Ram Avtar, *History of Indian Music and Musicians*, Pankaj Publications, 1987.

Ram Babu Saksena, *A History of Urdu Literature*, Ram Narain Lal Publisher and Bookseller, 1940.

Ranbir Singh, *Wajid Ali Shah: The Tragic King*, Publication Scheme, Jaipur.

Ranjeswar Mitra, *Mughal Bharater Sangeet Chinta*, Bengali edition, 1985.

Reginald Heber, *Narrative of a Journey Through the Upper Provinces of India: From Calcutta to Bombay, 1824–1825*, John Murray, 1856.

Rev W.K. Ferminger, *Thacker's Guide to Calcutta*, Thacker, Spink & Co., 1906.

Robert S. Gottlieb, *Solo Tabla Drumming of North India: Text & Commentary* Motilal Banarsidass Publishers, 1998.

Robert S. Gottlieb, *The Major Traditions of North Indian Tabla Drumming: A Survey Presentation Based on Performances by India's Leading Artists*, Musikverlag E. Katzbichler, 1977.

Rosie Llewellyn Jones, *Engaging Scoundrels: True Tales of Old Lucknow*, Oxford University Press, 2000.

Rosie Llewellyn Jones, *Fatal Friendship: the Nawabs, the British, and the City of Lucknow*, Oxford University Press, 1985.

Rosie Llewellyn Jones, *Reflections from Lucknow on the Great Uprising of 1857*, United Service Institution of India, 2005.

Rudrangshu Mukherjee, *Awadh in a Revolt, 1857–1858: A Study of Popular Resistance*, Permanent, 2002.

S. Masud Hasan Rizvi, *Urdu Drama and Stage*, 1957.

S.N. Das (ed.), *Religion and Bengali Culture*, Genesis Publishing Pvt. Ltd, 2002.

Sachchidanan Sahai, *India in 1872, As Seen by the Siamese*, B.R. Pub. Corp., 2002.

Samaren Roy, *Calcutta: Society and Change, 1690–1990*, Universe, 2005.

Samuel Lucas, *Dacoitee in Excelsis; or, The Spoliation of Oude*, J.R. Taylor, 1857.

Sharmistha Ghosh, *String Instruments (plucked variety) of North India*, Eastern Book Linkers, Vol. 2, 1988.

Shovana Narayan, *Indian Theatre and Dance Traditions*, Harman Pub. House, 2004.

Sidney Laman Blanchard, *The Ganges and the Seine: Scenes on the Banks of Both* Chapman and Hall, 1862.

Sidney Lee and Leslie Stephen, *Dictionary of National Biography*, Adamant Media Corporation, 2001.

Simmi Jain, *Encyclopaedia of Indian Women Through the Ages: Period of Freedom Struggle*, Gyan Publishing House, 2003.

Sir Charles Wentworth Dilke, *Greater Britain: A Record of Travel in English-speaking Countries, During 1866–1867*, Macmillan & Co. 1868.

Sir Edwin Arnold, *The Marquis of Dalhousie: Administration of British India* Saunders, Otley, and Co., Vol. 1 & 2, 1865.

Sir Evan Cotton, *Calcutta, Old and New: A Historical and Descriptive Handbook to the City*, W. Newman, 1907.

Sir William Cavenagh, *Reminiscences of an Indian Official*, A.H. Allen & Co. London, 1884.

Sir William Lee-Warner, *The Life of the Marquis of Dalhousie, K. T.*, The Macmillan Co., Vol. 2.

Sir William Sleeman, *A Journey Through the Kingdom of Oude*, R. Bentley, Vol. 1& 2, 1858.

Sivaprasad Sammadar (ed.), *Calcutta in Other Tongues*, Sahitya Samsad, 1995.

Sreepanth, *Metia Burjer Nawab*, Anand Publisher, 1990.

Subodh Kapoor, *The Indian Encylopedia*, Genesis Publishing Pvt Ltd, Vol. 1, 2002.

Sumanta Banerjee, 'Under the Raj: Prostitution in Colonial Bengal', *Monthly Review Press*, 1998.

Sumanta Banerjee, *The Parlour and the Streets: Elite and Popular Culture in Nineteenth Century Calcutta*, Seagull Books, 1989.

Suneeta Dhar, *Senia Gharana: Its Contribution to Indian Classical Music*,

Reliance Pub. House, 1989.

Susheela Misra, *Musical Heritage of Lucknow*, Harman Pub. House, 1991.

Sushila Tyagi, *Indo-Nepalese Relation*, Concept Publishing Company.

Swami Abhedananda and Swamu Prajnanananda, *The Bases of Indian Culture: Commemoration Volume of Swami Abhedananda*, Ramakrishna Vedanta Math, 1971.

Swami Prajnanananda, *Historical Development of Indian Music*, Firma K.L.M. Limited, 1973.

Swati Chattopadhyay, *Representing Calcutta: Modernity, Nationalism, and the Colonial Uncanny*, Routledge, 2005.

Terence R. Blackburn, *A Miscellany of Mutinies and Massacres in India*, APH Publishing, 2007.

Theodore Solis, *The Sarod: Its Gats-Tora Tradition, with Examples by Amir Khan and Three of His Students*, University of Hawai.

Toby Falk and Mildred Archer, *Indian Miniatures in the India Office Library*, Sotheby Parke Bernet, 1981.

Ursula Low, *Fifty Years with John company: From the Letters of General Sir John Low of Clatto, Fife, 1822–1858*, John Murray, 1936.

Vinayak Purohit, *Arts of Transitional India Twentieth Century*, Popular Prakashan, 1986.

William Brock, *A Biographical Sketch of Sir Henry Havelock*, Oxford University, 1858.

William Forbes-Mitchell, *Reminiscences of the Great Mutiny 1857–59*, 1910.

William Knighton, *The Private Life of An Eastern King: Together with Elihu Jaan's Story; or, The Private Life of an Eastern Queen*, Oxford University Press, 1921.

William Ward, *A View of the History, Literature, and Religion of the Hindoos: Including a Minute Description of Their Manners and Customs, and Translations from their Principal Works*, Mission Press, Vol. 1 & 2, 1815.

Wm. H. Allen & Co., *Allen's Indian Mail, and Register of Intelligence for British and Foreign India, China, and All Parts of the East*, Oxford University, 1856.

Additional Readings

Article of Anjum Quder, Chairman, Wajid Ali Shah Trust Dated 22 September 1996.

Cultural News from India, Indian Council for Public Relations, 1976.

Great Britain Parliament papers, 'Accounts and Papers of the House of Commons', 1856.

Journal of the Indian Musicological Society, Indian Musicological Society, Vol. 11–12, 1980.

The Music of Bengal: Essays in Contemporary Perspective, Indian Musicological Society, 1988.

The Uncrowned King of Matiaburj—Another Side of the Picture, *Muslim Institute Review*, July–September issue in 1905.

www.ingramcontent.com/pod-product-compliance
Lightning Source LLC
Chambersburg PA
CBHW031310150426
43191CB00005B/168